First World War
and Army of Occupation
War Diary
France, Belgium and Germany

61 DIVISION
Divisional Troops
Machine Gun Corps
61 Battalion
7 June 1916 - 26 September 1919

WO95/3049/2

The Naval & Military Press Ltd
www.nmarchive.com
Published in association with The National Archives

Published by

The Naval & Military Press Ltd

Unit 10 Ridgewood Industrial Park,

Uckfield, East Sussex,

TN22 5QE England

Tel: +44 (0) 1825 749494

www.naval-military-press.com

www.nmarchive.com

This diary has been reprinted in facsimile from the original. Any imperfections are inevitably reproduced and the quality may fall short of modern type and cartographic standards.

© Crown Copyright
Images reproduced by permission of The National Archives, London, England, 2015.

Contents

Document type	Place/Title	Date From	Date To
War Diary	St Venant	07/06/1916	12/06/1916
War Diary	La Gorgue	13/06/1916	30/06/1916
Heading	War Diary For July 1916 61st Divnl Signal Co Vol 3		
War Diary	La Gorgue	01/07/1916	30/09/1916
Miscellaneous	Q Branch 61st Division	10/11/1916	10/11/1916
Heading	War Diary of 61st Divl. Signal Coy. R.E. For The Month Of October 1916 Volume 6		
War Diary	La Gorgue	01/10/1916	28/10/1916
War Diary	St Venant	29/10/1916	31/10/1916
Heading	61st Divl. Signal Co. R.E. November 1916 Vol 7		
War Diary	St Venant	01/11/1916	02/11/1916
War Diary	Chelers	03/11/1916	04/11/1916
War Diary	Rollecourt	05/11/1916	06/11/1916
War Diary	Frohen Le-Grand	07/11/1916	15/11/1916
War Diary	Bernaville	16/11/1916	16/11/1916
War Diary	Canaples	17/11/1916	17/11/1916
War Diary	Contay	18/11/1916	21/11/1916
War Diary	Bouzincourt	22/11/1916	30/11/1916
Miscellaneous	Officer i/c A.G's Office Base		
Heading	War Diary Dec 16 61st Signal Coy Vol 8		
War Diary	Bouzincourt	01/12/1916	31/12/1916
Diagram etc	Straight Line Diagram		
Map	61st Divisional Signal Communications		
Heading	War Diary of 61st Divnl Signal Coy January 1917 Vol 9		
War Diary	Bouzincourt	01/01/1917	18/01/1917
War Diary	Bernaville & Brailly	19/01/1917	31/01/1917
Heading	War Diary of 61st Divnl Signal Coy Feb. 1917 Vol 10		
War Diary	Brailly	01/02/1917	04/02/1917
War Diary	Long	05/02/1917	13/02/1917
War Diary	Guillaucourt	14/02/1917	17/02/1917
War Diary	Harbonnieres	18/02/1917	28/02/1917
Miscellaneous	61st Div.	24/02/1917	24/02/1917
Heading	War Diary of 61st Divl. Signal Company R.E. 1st To 31st March 1917 Volume 10		
War Diary	Harbonnieres	01/03/1917	19/03/1917
War Diary	Albert	19/03/1917	27/03/1917
War Diary	Guizancourt	28/03/1917	31/03/1917
Heading	War Diary of 61st Div. Signal Coy. For The Month Of April 1917 Volume 12		
War Diary	Guizancourt	01/04/1917	10/04/1917
War Diary	Voyennes	12/04/1917	22/04/1917
War Diary	Auroir	23/04/1917	30/04/1917
Heading	War Diary of 61st Div. Signal Coy For The Month Of May 1917 Vol. 13		
War Diary	Auroir (66D-E22C)	01/05/1917	14/05/1917
War Diary	Auroir	15/05/1917	16/05/1917
War Diary	Vignacourt	16/05/1917	20/05/1917
War Diary	Doullens	21/05/1917	22/05/1917
War Diary	Le Cauroy	23/05/1917	23/05/1917

War Diary	Le Cauroy Warlus	24/05/1917	31/05/1917
Heading	War Diary of 61st Div. Signal Coy RE For The Month Of June 1917 Vol 14		
War Diary	Warlus 51.C.K.36.d	01/06/1917	01/06/1917
War Diary	Arras	02/06/1917	11/06/1917
War Diary	Warlus	12/06/1917	22/06/1917
War Diary	Willeman	23/06/1917	30/06/1917
Heading	War Diary of the 61st Divl. Signal Coy. R.E. For The Month Of July 1917		
War Diary	Willeman	01/07/1917	25/07/1917
War Diary	Zeggers Cappel	26/07/1917	31/07/1917
Heading	War Diary of 61st Divl Signal Co. For The Month Of September 1917 Vol 17		
War Diary	Mersey Camp Brandhoek	01/09/1917	14/09/1917
War Diary	Watou	15/09/1917	18/09/1917
War Diary	Duisans	18/09/1917	24/09/1917
War Diary	St. Nicholas	25/09/1917	30/09/1917
Miscellaneous	Communications in the Fampoux Area Telephone Communication.		
Heading	War Diary of the 61st Divl Signal Co. For August 1917 Volume 16		
War Diary	Zeggers Cappel	01/08/1917	15/08/1917
War Diary	Poperinghe	16/08/1917	18/08/1917
War Diary	Mersey Camp H.1.a Sheet 38	19/08/1917	22/08/1917
War Diary	Mersey Camp	23/08/1917	31/08/1917
Miscellaneous	Signal Instructions Telephonic Communication for Ward of Wieltje	19/08/1917	19/08/1917
Miscellaneous	Report On Communications During The Attack By The 184th Inf. Bde.	22/08/1917	22/08/1917
Heading	War Diary of 61st Divl. Signal Coy. For The Month Of October 1917 Vol 18		
War Diary	St. Nicholas Camp	01/10/1917	31/10/1917
Heading	War Diary of 61st Div. Signal Coy. For The Month Of November 1917 Vol 19		
War Diary	Arras	01/11/1917	01/12/1917
Diagram etc	Grevillers		
Heading	War Diary of 61st Div. Signal Coy. RE For The Month Of December 1917 Vol. 20		
War Diary		01/12/1917	30/12/1917
War Diary	Harbonnieres	31/12/1917	31/12/1917
Heading	War Diary of 61st Divl. Signal Coy. R.E. For The Month Of January 1918		
War Diary		01/01/1918	31/01/1918
Heading	War Diary of 61st Div. Signal Coy. R.E. For The Month Of February 1918		
War Diary	Auroir	01/02/1918	22/03/1918
War Diary	Matigny	22/03/1918	22/03/1918
War Diary	Rethonvillers	23/03/1918	24/03/1918
War Diary	Parvillers	24/03/1918	25/03/1918
War Diary	Beaucourt	25/03/1918	27/03/1918
War Diary	Villers-Bretonneux	28/03/1918	28/03/1918
War Diary	Boves	28/03/1918	31/03/1918
Heading	61st Divisional Engineers 61st Divisional Signal Company R.E. April 1918		
Heading	61st Divl. Signal Coy. R.E. War Diary April 1918 Volume 24		

War Diary	Boves		01/04/1918	01/04/1918
War Diary	Longeau		02/04/1918	02/04/1918
War Diary	Pissy		03/04/1918	11/04/1918
War Diary	Aire P. ID		12/04/1918	12/04/1918
War Diary	Aire Molinghem		13/04/1918	30/04/1918
Heading	War Diary of 61st Divl. Signal Coy. R.E. May 1918 Volume 25			
War Diary	Molinghem Aire		01/05/1918	17/05/1918
War Diary	Molinghem Lambres		18/05/1918	30/06/1918
War Diary	Molinghem		01/07/1918	13/07/1918
War Diary	Norrent Fontes		14/07/1918	21/07/1918
War Diary	Wardrecques		22/07/1918	31/08/1918
War Diary	Croix Marraisse		01/09/1918	08/09/1918
War Diary	Rill Works Croix Maraisse		09/09/1918	30/09/1918
Map	Map			
Heading	War Diary of 61st Div Signal Coy. For The Month Of October 1918			
War Diary	Rill Works Croix Maraisse		01/10/1918	03/10/1918
War Diary	La Lacque Croix Maraisse		04/10/1918	07/10/1918
War Diary	Doullens		08/10/1918	08/10/1918
War Diary	Lagnicourt		09/10/1918	12/10/1918
War Diary	Noyelles		13/10/1918	22/10/1918
War Diary	St Aubert Rieux		23/10/1918	24/10/1918
War Diary	Montrecourt St Aubert		24/10/1918	25/10/1918
War Diary	Vendegies St Aubert		25/10/1918	28/10/1918
War Diary	Vendegies		29/10/1918	31/10/1918
Heading	War Diary of 61st Divl. Signal Coy. R.E. For November 1918 Volume 31			
Heading	War Diary of 61st Divl. Signal Coy. For The Month Of March 1918 Vol 23			
War Diary	Vendegies		01/11/1918	02/11/1918
War Diary	St Aubert		03/11/1918	07/11/1918
War Diary	Vendegies		08/11/1918	13/11/1918
War Diary	Rieux		14/11/1918	14/11/1918
War Diary	Cambrai		15/11/1918	30/11/1918
Miscellaneous	Headquarters 61st Division		14/02/1919	14/02/1919
Miscellaneous	D.A.G. G.H.Q. 3rd Echelon		18/02/1919	18/02/1919
War Diary	Bernaville		01/12/1918	01/12/1918
War Diary	St. Riquier		08/12/1918	00/02/1919
War Diary	Le Treport		00/04/1919	00/06/1919
Heading	WO95/3049/2 61 Battalion Machine Gun Corps			
Heading	61st Division 61 Bn Machine Gun Corps Jan 1918-Sep 1919			
Heading	War Diary of 267th Machine Gun Company From 13 January To 31 January 1918			
War Diary	Southampton		13/01/1918	13/01/1918
War Diary	Havre		14/01/1918	16/01/1918
War Diary	Villers St Christophe		17/01/1918	17/01/1918
War Diary	Foreste		18/01/1918	31/01/1918
Miscellaneous	267th Machine Gun Company		31/01/1918	31/01/1918
Heading	War Diary of 267th Machine Gun Company From 1 February To 28 February 1918 2			
War Diary	Foreste		01/02/1918	28/02/1918
Miscellaneous	267 Machine Gun Company		01/03/1918	01/03/1918
War Diary	Vaux		01/03/1918	22/03/1918
War Diary	Rethonvillers		23/03/1918	24/03/1918

War Diary	Bouchoir	25/03/1918	25/03/1918
War Diary	Villers-Aux-Erables	26/03/1918	27/03/1918
War Diary	Cachy	28/03/1918	28/03/1918
War Diary	Line Just W of Marcelcave	29/03/1918	30/03/1918
War Diary	Gentelles	31/03/1918	31/03/1918
Map	Identification Trace For Use With Artillery Maps		
Miscellaneous	A Form Messages And Signals		
Miscellaneous	Messages And Signals		
Miscellaneous	A Form Messages And Signals		
Miscellaneous	A. 1, B. 1, C. 3, D. 2		
Miscellaneous	A Form Messages And Signals		
Miscellaneous	List of Messing Offers to Q.M.		
Miscellaneous	61st Division Locations of Units	27/03/1918	27/03/1918
Miscellaneous	61st Division No.Q. 1186/13/54	27/03/1918	27/03/1918
Heading	61st Divisional Troops 61st Battalion Machine Gun Corps April 1918		
War Diary	Gentelles	01/04/1918	02/04/1918
War Diary	Boutillerie	03/04/1918	03/04/1918
War Diary	Guignemicourt	04/04/1918	10/04/1918
War Diary	Guarbecque	11/04/1918	11/04/1918
War Diary	St Venant	12/04/1918	30/04/1918
Map	Map		
Miscellaneous	Headquarters, 61st Division (G)	03/06/1918	03/06/1918
Heading	War Diary 61st Bn. M.G.C. May 1918 Vol 4		
War Diary	St. Venant	01/05/1918	31/05/1918
Map	Identification Trace For Use With Artillery Maps		
Map	Appendix 2		
Map	Orre		
Heading	War Diary June 1918 61 Bn. Mg Corps Vol 5		
War Diary	St. Venant	01/06/1918	30/06/1918
Map	Map		
Operation(al) Order(s)	61st Battalion Machine Gun Corps Operation Order No.29	04/08/1918	04/08/1918
Heading	War Diary Volume No.V Month Of July 1918 61 Bn. M.G.C.		
War Diary	St. Venant	01/07/1918	13/07/1918
War Diary	Rombly	14/07/1918	22/07/1918
War Diary	Blaringhem	23/07/1918	31/07/1918
Heading	War Diary Month Of August 1918 Volume No.6 61 Bn. M.G. Corps		
War Diary	Witternesse	01/08/1918	04/08/1918
War Diary	Pecquer	05/08/1918	21/08/1918
War Diary	Haverskerque	22/08/1918	31/08/1918
Operation(al) Order(s)	61st Battalion Machine Gun Corps Operation Order No.30	05/08/1918	05/08/1918
Miscellaneous	Movement Table To Accompany 61st Bn. M.G.C. Operation Order No.30	05/08/1918	05/08/1918
Operation(al) Order(s)	61st Battalion Machine Gun Corps Operation Order No.31	07/08/1918	07/08/1918
Operation(al) Order(s)	61st Battalion Machine Gun Corps Operation Order No.32	11/08/1918	11/08/1918
Operation(al) Order(s)	61st Battalion Machine Gun Corps Operation Order No.36	20/08/1918	20/08/1918
Operation(al) Order(s)	61st Battalion Machine Gun Corps Operation Order No.37	21/08/1918	21/08/1918

Operation(al) Order(s)	61st Battalion Machine Gun Corps Operation Order No.38	26/08/1918	26/08/1918
Operation(al) Order(s)	61st Battalion Machine Gun Corps Operation Order No.39	31/08/1918	31/08/1918
Heading	War Diary for the month of September Volume No.VII		
Miscellaneous	Cover For Documents. Nature Of Enclosures.		
War Diary	Haverskerque	01/09/1918	05/09/1918
War Diary	La Gorgue	05/09/1918	30/09/1918
Operation(al) Order(s)	61st Battalion Machine Gun Corps Operation Order No.40	02/09/1918	02/09/1918
Operation(al) Order(s)	61st Battalion Machine Gun Corps Operation Order No.41	04/09/1918	04/09/1918
Operation(al) Order(s)	61st Battalion Machine Gun Corps Operation Order No.42		
Miscellaneous	Addendum To 61st Battalion Operation Order No.42	03/09/1918	03/09/1918
Operation(al) Order(s)	61st Battalion Machine Gun Corps Operation Order No.45	14/09/1918	14/09/1918
Miscellaneous	Amendment No.1 To Operation No.43	14/09/1918	14/09/1918
Operation(al) Order(s)	61st Battalion Machine Gun Corps Operation Order No.44	14/09/1918	14/09/1918
Operation(al) Order(s)	61st Battalion Machine Gun Corps Operation Order No.45	25/09/1918	25/09/1918
Operation(al) Order(s)	61st Battalion Machine Gun Corps Operation Order No.47	29/09/1918	29/09/1918
Heading	War Diary for the month of October 1918 61 M.G. Bn. Vol 9		
Miscellaneous	Cover For Documents. Nature Of Enclosures.		
War Diary	La Gorgue	01/10/1918	04/10/1918
War Diary	Manqueville	05/10/1918	06/10/1918
War Diary	Terramesnil	07/10/1918	09/10/1918
War Diary	Moeuvres	10/10/1918	10/10/1918
War Diary	Graincourt	11/10/1918	16/10/1918
War Diary	Rieux	17/10/1918	23/10/1918
War Diary	St. Aubert	24/10/1918	24/10/1918
War Diary	Vendegies	25/10/1918	31/10/1918
Miscellaneous	Warning Order M.G.106	01/10/1919	01/10/1919
Map	Map		
Operation(al) Order(s)	61st Battalion Machine Gun Corps Operation Order No.49	02/10/1918	02/10/1918
Miscellaneous	Addendum To Operation Order No.49	02/10/1918	02/10/1918
Miscellaneous	March Table To Accompany 61st Battalion Machine Gun Corps Operation Order No.49		
Miscellaneous	61st Battalion Machine Gun Corps Administrative Instructions for move by Rail	06/10/1918	06/10/1918
Miscellaneous	61st Battalion Machine Gun Corps Order for Move by Rail	09/10/1918	09/10/1918
Miscellaneous	Entraining Table		
Operation(al) Order(s)	61st Battalion Machine Gun Corps Operation Order No.51	17/10/1918	17/10/1918
Miscellaneous	March Table Issued in Connection With Operation Order No. 51	17/10/1918	17/10/1918
Miscellaneous	Amendment No.1 To 61st Battalion Machine Gun Corps Operation Order No.52	19/10/1918	19/10/1918
Operation(al) Order(s)	61st Battalion Machine Gun Corps Operation Order No.52	19/10/1918	19/10/1918

Operation(al) Order(s)	61st Battalion Machine Gun Corps Operation Order No.53	22/10/1918	22/10/1918
Miscellaneous	March Table to Accompany Operation Order No.53	22/10/1918	22/10/1918
Operation(al) Order(s)	61st Battalion Machine Gun Corps Operation Order No.54	23/10/1918	23/10/1918
Operation(al) Order(s)	61st Battalion Machine Gun Corps Operation Order No.55	27/10/1918	27/10/1918
Operation(al) Order(s)	61st Battalion Machine Gun Corps Operation Order No.56	29/10/1918	29/10/1918
Heading	War Diary for the month of November 1918 61 Bn M.G. Corps Vol 10		
Miscellaneous	Cover For Documents. Nature Of Enclosures.		
War Diary	Vendegies-Sur-Ecaillon	01/11/1918	02/11/1918
War Diary	Avesnes Lez Aubert	03/11/1918	08/11/1918
War Diary	St. Martin	09/11/1918	13/11/1918
War Diary	St. Aubert	14/11/1918	14/11/1918
War Diary	Cambrai	15/11/1918	23/11/1918
War Diary	Berneuil	24/11/1918	30/11/1918
Operation(al) Order(s)	61st Battalion Machine Gun Corps Operation Order No.60	02/11/1918	02/11/1918
Miscellaneous	March Table		
Operation(al) Order(s)	61st Battalion Machine Gun Corps Operation Order No.61	03/11/1918	03/11/1918
Operation(al) Order(s)	61st Battalion Machine Gun Corps Operation Order No.63	08/11/1918	08/11/1918
Miscellaneous	March Table To Accompany 61st Batt. M.G.C. Operation Order No.63	08/11/1918	08/11/1918
Operation(al) Order(s)	61st Battalion Machine Gun Corps Operation Order No.66	15/11/1918	15/11/1918
Operation(al) Order(s)	61st Battalion Machine Gun Corps Operation Order No.67	14/11/1918	14/11/1918
Operation(al) Order(s)	61st Battalion Machine Gun Corps Operation Order No.68	22/11/1918	22/11/1918
Miscellaneous	In Continuation of G.O 66	22/11/1918	22/11/1918
Miscellaneous	Administrative Instructions Issued In Connection With 61st Bn. Machine Gun Corps Operation Order No.66	22/11/1918	22/11/1918
Miscellaneous	Table "A" Entraining Table Issued In Connections With Administrative Instructions	23/11/1918	23/11/1918
Miscellaneous	Table "B"	23/11/1918	23/11/1918
Heading	War Diary For Month December 1918 Volume No. X 61 Bn. M.G. Corp.		
Miscellaneous	Cover For Documents. Nature Of Enclosures.		
Miscellaneous			
War Diary	Berneuil	01/12/1918	07/12/1918
War Diary	Bernaville	08/12/1918	31/12/1918
Miscellaneous	Appendix "A"	06/12/1918	06/12/1918
Heading	61st Battalion Machine Gun Corps War Diary 1st January 1918 To 31st January 1919 (Volume No.11)		
Miscellaneous	Cover For Documents. Nature Of Enclosures.		
War Diary	Bernaville	01/01/1919	21/01/1919
Miscellaneous	D.A.G. 3rd Echelon	01/03/1919	01/03/1919
War Diary	Bernaville	22/01/1919	31/01/1919
Heading	War Diary 61st Battalion Machine Gun Corps 1st February 1919 To 28th February 1919 (Volume No.12)		
Miscellaneous	Cover For Documents. Nature Of Enclosures.		
War Diary	Bernaville	01/02/1919	09/02/1919

War Diary	Drucat	10/02/1919	28/02/1919
Heading	War Diary 1st March 1919 To 31st March 1919 (Volume No.13) 61st Battalion Machine Gun Corps		
Miscellaneous	Cover For Documents. Nature Of Enclosures.		
War Diary	Drucat	01/03/1919	31/03/1919
Miscellaneous	Headquarters 61st Division	01/05/1919	01/05/1919
Heading	61st Battalion Machine Gun Corps War Diary 1st April 1919 To 30th April 1919 (Volume No.14)		
Miscellaneous	Cover For Documents. Nature Of Enclosures.		
War Diary	Drucat	01/04/1919	17/04/1919
War Diary	Abbeville	18/04/1919	30/04/1919
Heading	61st Battalion Machine Gun Corps War Diary 1st May 1919 To 31st May 1919 (Volume No.15)		
Miscellaneous	Cover For Documents. Nature Of Enclosures.		
War Diary	Abbeville	01/05/1919	31/05/1919
Miscellaneous	PA 1098/1	30/06/1919	30/06/1919
Heading	61st. Battalion Machine Gun Corps War Diary 1st June 1919 To 30th June 1919 (Volume No.17)		
Miscellaneous	Cover For Documents. Nature Of Enclosures.		
War Diary	Abbeville	01/06/1919	03/06/1919
War Diary	Rouen	04/06/1919	30/06/1919
Miscellaneous	61st Battalion Machine Gun Corps Administrative Instructions No.1	30/05/1919	30/05/1919
Miscellaneous	61st Battalion Machine Gun Corps	30/05/1919	30/05/1919
Miscellaneous	61st Battalion Machine Gun Corps Administrative Instructions No.2	01/06/1919	01/06/1919
Miscellaneous	61st Battalion Machine Gun Corps Entraining Table "A" Issued with Administrative Instructions No.2	01/06/1919	01/06/1919
Miscellaneous	61st Battalion Machine Gun Corps Composition of Trains- Move of Battalion to Rouen-Table "B"	01/06/1919	01/06/1919
Miscellaneous	61st Bn. M.G.C.No.GR.24/187	06/06/1919	06/06/1919
Miscellaneous	Guards to be Taken Over by 61st Battalion Machine Gun Corps	06/06/1919	06/06/1919
Miscellaneous	61st Bn.M.G.C. BA/149/892	07/06/1919	07/06/1919
War Diary	Rouen	01/07/1919	31/07/1919
Heading	61st Battalion Machine Gun Corps War Diary 1st August 1919 To 31st August 1919 (Volume No.18)		
Miscellaneous	Cover For Documents. Nature Of Enclosures.		
War Diary	Rouen	01/08/1919	31/08/1919
Heading	61st Battalion Machine Gun Corps War Diary 1st September 1919 To 30th September 1919 (Volume No.19)		
Miscellaneous	Cover For Documents. Nature Of Enclosures.		
War Diary	Rouen	01/09/1919	26/09/1919
Miscellaneous	61st Bn. M.G. Corps TM/126/1	24/09/1919	24/09/1919

WAR DIARY
or
INTELLIGENCE SUMMARY

Army Form C. 2118.

6(1st) Div. Signal Coy.

Place	Date	Hour	Summary of Events and Information	Remarks and references to Appendices
STUENANT	June 7th		Day fine. Ordinary Company Parades today. Nothing to report.	
"	8th		Day fine. C.R.E. presented medals to Company Football Team for winning S.M.R.E. Football League.	
"	9th		Q.M.S. Lent to Corps Hdqrs. for few days instruction. Day fine. Ordinary Company Parades. Drill and Riding. Drill. Day passed quietly.	
"	10th		Day fine. 183rd and 184th Bdes now in LAVENTIE. Took them some smoke helmets and steel helmets. LT BENNETT attached to 35th Div. Sigs.	
"	11th		Day fine. Church Parade 9.30 a.m. at Drill Hdqrs. Sent advanced party of 12 linemen and some stores over to LA GORGUE in motor lorry this morning. Sent Capt. Clark and a relief of Operators to LA GORGUE this afternoon.	
"	12th		Day melted to rain. Moved to LA GORGUE today. G.O.C. took over everything G.O.C. 38th Div. at 12 noon. Took over lines etc. from 38th Div.	

WAR DIARY
or
INTELLIGENCE SUMMARY

(Erase heading not required.)

Army Form C. 2118.

61st Div. Signal Coy.

Place	Date 1916	Hour	Summary of Events and Information	Remarks and references to Appendices
LA GORGUE	June 13th		Heavy rain during night and this morning. Had to move our pickets line to a drier position.	
"	14th		Day fine. Very busy getting things settled down in new position. Laying new lines for new R.F.A. Battery positions.	
"	15th		Memorial service to Kitchener at 11 a.m. attended by party from Signal Company. Day finer. Visited left sector of trenches this morning with three Officers at Signal Coy.	
"	16th		Day fine. Company parade in gas helmets at 9 a.m. Baths at 1 p.m. Day passed quietly.	
"	17th		Day fine. Equipment and rifle inspection at 9 a.m. Day passed quietly.	
"	18th		Day fine. Church Parade 10 a.m. Visited 183 and 184 Brigades this morning.	
"	19th		Day fine. Visited Major Dobbs A.D.S. 1st Corps, Exchange at 61st Div. Supply Coln at Merville for I.T.	

WAR DIARY 61st Div. Signal Coy.
or
INTELLIGENCE SUMMARY

Place	Date 1916	Hour	Summary of Events and Information	Remarks and references to Appendices
LA GORGUE	June 20		Day fine. Went round night section with two of the Brigade Section Officers.	
"	21st		Day fine. Lines round Div. Hdqrs. sorted out and re-labelled. Rode over to visit Australian Div. Hdqrs. this afternoon on our left.	
"	22nd		183 Bde. relieved by 182 Bde. in night Section today. Day fine. Went to visit demonstration of Signalling to aeroplanes by 39th Divn. at FOSSE today. D.A.S. and Col. Clementi-Smith visited our Hdqrs today. Sent Lt. Spurr out to reconnoitre positions for buried cables.	
"	23rd		Day passed quietly. Nothing to report.	
"	24th		Day passed quietly. Nothing to report.	
"	25th		Day fine. Church parade this morning. Nothing to report.	
"	26th		Day inclined to rain. Part of Company went to Cable Demonstration at 4 P.m. this afternoon. Day passed uneventfully. Raid on German Trenches by 182 Brigade.	

WAR DIARY
or
INTELLIGENCE SUMMARY.
(Erase heading not required.)

Army Form C. 2118.

61st Signal Coy.

Instructions regarding War Diaries and Intelligence Summaries are contained in F. S. Regs., Part II. and the Staff Manual respectively. Title pages will be prepared in manuscript.

Place	Date	Hour	Summary of Events and Information	Remarks and references to Appendices
LAGORGUE	1916 June 27th		Day wet. Fine intervals. Visited 184 Bde. Hdqrs. and reconnoitred ground with reference to burying cable from Adv. Bde. to Batt. Hqrs. Nothing to report.	
"	28th		Day fine. Visited party burying cable this afternoon. Raid by 184 Brigade on German trenches failed to pass German wire. Some wires cut by enemy bombardment but party broken to mend. Day included to mend.	
"	29th		Held practice for aeroplane Signalling exercise with 183rd Bde. this afternoon. Visited flying corps to arrange for exercise tomorrow.	
"	30th		Attack by 39th Div. about 3 am. this morning with enemy's trenches but afterwards forced to retire. Heavy shelling all the morning. New line laid from left advanced Bore Hqrs. to "COCK SHY HOUSE" along ditches. Bad weather prevented aeroplane Signalling exercise.	

A.C.Mason Capt.
O.C. 61 Sig. Coy.

Vol III

War Diary for July 1916

61st Divnl Signal Co

Vol. 3

Confidential

61 Signal Coy.

WAR DIARY
or
INTELLIGENCE SUMMARY.
(Erase heading not required.)

Army Form C. 2118.

Place	Date	Hour	Summary of Events and Information	Remarks and references to Appendices
LA GORGUE	1916 July 1st	9.15 pm	Day fine. Aeroplane Exercise of Signalling between Infantry and aeroplanes carried out today by 183 Bde. (section). Not altogether successful. Heavy bombardment by the enemy of our front line trenches in the right sector held by 182 Bde. began about 9.15 p.m. this evening. Several casualties and all Company lines broken, but repaired before daylight.	
"	2nd		Day fine. Church parade at 10am. Visited Moated Grange O.P. Saw Signalling Officer of 2/5 Warwicks and discussed last night attack. A.S.C. Officer arrived to drive Signal Car.	
"	3rd		Day fine. German aeroplanes very active. Went up to Snowdon O.P. in the afternoon with Lt. Spink to reconnoitre buried routes for cable.	
"	4th		Fine morning, turned to rain in the afternoon. Day passed uneventfully.	
"	5th		Day fine. Reconnoitred exact route for burying cable to Snowdon O.P.	
"	6th		Day inclined to rain. Received information that the 61 Division was to take over more ground on the right. 184 Bde. to occupy the new position with Hdqrs. at LES 8 MAISONS. Went to 3rd Cam. Hdqrs. with Col. Wake to make arrangements about taking over lines. Had great difficulty in fixing up communication to Battys. but got it done during the night.	

Army Form C. 2118.

61 Signal Coy

WAR DIARY
or
INTELLIGENCE SUMMARY.
(Erase heading not required.)

Place	Date	Hour	Summary of Events and Information	Remarks and references to Appendices
LA GORGUE	1915 July 7th		Day wet. Spent day in sorting out lines from LES 8 MAISONS. Day passed quietly.	
"	8th		Day fine. Traced out several lines from 184th Bde at LES 8 MAISONS and reconnoitred position for Advanced Bde. Hqrs.	
"	9th		Very fine day. Church Parade 10 am. Visited Batln Hqrs. at RED and WHITE HOUSES to see the condition of their lines with G.S.O. 2. 5th Warwicks raided enemy's trenches but did not get in.	
"	10th		Day fine. Spent day making out scheme of communications for attack.	
"	11th		Day fine. Went out to arrange for new lines to be laid along ditch etc. and reconnoitred positions of new Battalion Battle Hqrs. Visited Bde. Hqrs. at LES 8 MAISONS.	
"	12th		Day fine. Arranged for new lines to be laid from COCKSHY HOUSE to Bennett scheduled 2/Lt Bader while latter was on course of Signalling to aeroplanes. Night passed quietly.	
"	13th		Day dull. Rained during night. 184 Bde. carried out an unsuccessful raid tonight. Some lines laid but communication not entirely broken.	

61 Signal Coy
WAR DIARY
INTELLIGENCE SUMMARY

Army Form C. 2118.

Place	Date 1916	Hour	Summary of Events and Information	Remarks and references to Appendices
LA GORGUE	July 14th		Day fine. Orders received to prepare for the attack by 61 Division AUBERS RIDGE in conjunction with 5th Australian Division on our left, 184 Bde. relieved tonight by 31st Division. Visited Australian Division this afternoon to see if any of their line wounded help us. Started off some working parties this afternoon.	
"	15th		Day fine. Cable Detachment out this morning laying 5 cables to left Bde. Hd.qrs. Two pairs and a Sounder line. Other parties out laying cable. Went out with G.S.O.3 to select new position for left Brigade Hd.qrs. Lieut. & F.S. Leader round Section he was to hold during the attack. Sent Lt. Bennet out to assist him.	
"	16th		Day fine. Parties out again to improve lines as far as possible. Lines much improved by the evening.	
"	17th		Day inclined to rain. Sent out party to check S.H.Y. under Capt. Clark at 6 a.m. Attack put off on account of weather & then postponed but today. Two wireless sets and a power buzzer arrived today and were fitted. Rode out to see the three Brigades this afternoon. A good deal of Artillery activity today.	
"	18th		Day muggy. Orders that Operations would take place tomorrow. Laid a line tonight to Adjt. of Heavy Artillery.	

WAR DIARY
INTELLIGENCE SUMMARY.

61 Signal Coy

Army Form C. 2118.

Place	Date	Hour	Summary of Events and Information	Remarks and references to Appendices
LA GORGUE	July 19	11 a.m.	Day overcast. Limit to Heavy Art. through by 8 am today. Correct time given out at 9 a.m. Nothing passed quietly. Artillery Bombardment commenced at 11 am	
		1.45 p.m.	181 Bde. Bdl. report all Company lines O.K. Information coming in well by runners. No lines cut up to 8h80. Relays at all Glory's farm afternoon. At 6 p.m. attack took place and reports came in that our Infantry were in the German trenches. Messages began to come through stating that the attack had failed, and that our troops had been compelled to withdraw. 5th Australians were overlying enemy front line trenches on our left, but had to withdraw at daylight rather stay during to front attacks and Heavy shelling.	
	20th		Day fine. Corps Commander decided this morning not to attempt a fresh attack. Communications held out well and two or three messages were received by Pigeon. Visited Brigade this morning.	
	21st		Day fine. Rode round to brigade Section Officers this morning and obtained reports about the attack. H. Bennett rocked up the line to Heavy Group this afternoon. Day given	

WAR DIARY or INTELLIGENCE SUMMARY.

Army Form C. 2118.

61 Signal Coy

Place	Date	Hour	Summary of Events and Information	Remarks and references to Appendices
LA GORGUE	July 1916 22nd		Day overcast. Orders issued for the Division to take over once more the line with two Brigades in LAVENTIE and one Brigade in Reserve in LA GORGUE. Starting relaying up cable round old trenches at ROUGE DE BOUT.	
"	23rd		Day fine. Church Parade at 10 a.m. Day passed quietly.	
"	24th		Day fine. Lt Bennett member of a Court Martial at LE DRUMEZ. Lt Bennett relieved Lt Leader at 184 Bde for a few days.	
"	25th		Day passed quietly. Day dull. Visited the trenches of 183rd Brigade this afternoon with Lt MORRIS. Speaking on Company phones not at all good. Telephone Lt 257 Tunnelling Coy R.E. put through at 6 p.m. today.	
"	26th		Day dull and muggy. Started working machine for twisting cable. Visited night section of trenches with Lt Bennett today. Saw IT who seemed satisfied with their position.	
"	27th		Day dull & fine later. Sent out party to put up "Label here" notices. Visited Reserve Brigade Signal Office at work this morning.	

61 Signal Coy

WAR DIARY
or
INTELLIGENCE SUMMARY.
(Erase heading not required.)

Army Form C. 2118.

Place	Date	Hour	Summary of Events and Information	Remarks and references to Appendices
LA GORGUE	1916 July 28		Day fine. Went out with RE Offrs to visit remaining Bns of Reserve Brigade at Visual Signalling. Day passed quietly.	
"	29		Day dull but turned out hot and sunny later. G.O.C. inspected the Signal Company on parade mounted today and expressed himself pleased with the turn out. Comp then went for Route March. 1st Ladder returned to 184th Bde. today.	
"	30th		Day dull. Very hot turn later. Church Parade 9 am. Horse Show held by 182nd Brigade. Day passed quietly.	
"	31st		Day fine and hot. Signalling Class started today. 24 Officers and N.C.O's from Infantry and Artillery. 4 Other ranks arrived from ABBEVILLE today	

R.C. Anson, Capt.
O.C. 61 Signal Coy

SECRET 1.   61

WAR DIARY
or
INTELLIGENCE SUMMARY.

Army Form C. 2118.

August 1916.   61 Divl. Signal Coy.

Vol 4

(Erase heading not required.)

Instructions regarding War Diaries and Intelligence Summaries are contained in F. S. Regs., Part II. and the Staff Manual respectively. Title pages will be prepared in manuscript.

Place	Date	Hour	Summary of Events and Information	Remarks and references to Appendices
	1916			
LA GORGUE	Aug 1st		Day fine and very hot. G.O.C. took over temporary command of 118th Corps during the absence of Genl. Hoking on leave. 182nd Bde. relieved 186th Bde. today at COCKSHY HQ. Visited the Brigades this afternoon.	
"	Aug 2nd		Day fine and very hot. Went out with Wireless Officer to COCKSHY HQ today. Went in to see A.D.A.S. 11th Corps this afternoon. Wireless Officer erected a Wireless Receiving Set at back of Bn. HQ. Day passed uneventfully.	
"	Aug 3rd		Day fine and hot sun. Visited the Brigades. Day passed quietly and nothing to report.	
"	Aug 4th		Day fine. Went out with C.R.E. this morning to examine IT dug-outs. Visited left sector of trenches and inspected buried cable.	
"	Aug 5th		Day fine. Commenced picking up spare lines in the Rubinol area today according to new system of labelling. Visited IT and Bath. 14 yrs. of right sector with Div. Gas Officer to inspect anti-gas arrangements.	
"	Aug 6th		Day fine. Telephone hut on to 61 Divn. Supply Column today. Went to Service at GRANDE PLACE BETHUNE today to commemorate outbreak of WAR. Quiet day	

SECRET

Army Form C. 2118.

WAR DIARY
or
INTELLIGENCE SUMMARY. 61 Div. Sig. Coy.
(Erase heading not required.)

Instructions regarding War Diaries and Intelligence Summaries are contained in F.S. Regs., Part II. and the Staff Manual respectively. Title pages will be prepared in manuscript.

Place	Date	Hour	Summary of Events and Information	Remarks and references to Appendices
LAGORGUE	1916 Aug 7th		A.D.A.S. 11th Corps visited us this morning and discussed burying cable. 184th Inf. Bde. had a Horse Show today. Signal Company entered a pair of mules won 2nd prize. Visited IT this afternoon and arranged with O.C. Right Group Artillery for working party for burying cable tonight. Went out tonight to start off working party digging TT TT	
near MOATED GRANGE	Aug 8th		Day fine. A.D.A.S. and another Officer came out and we went and visited buried cable route. Day passed quietly	
"	Aug 9th		Day fine. Went round right sector and visited new mine crater which was about 50 yards wide and 80 feet deep. Several improvements in trench lines to be carried out.	
"	Aug 10th		Day inclined to rain. Went round left Sector of trenches this morning. A good deal of shore cable to be picked up. Col. Twill, 1st Army Intelligence visited IT this afternoon. Quiet day.	
"	Aug 11th		Morning very foggy. Visited right sector of trenches	

Army Form C. 2118.

WAR DIARY
or
INTELLIGENCE SUMMARY.   6 / Div. Signal. Coy.
(Erase heading not required.)

S E C R E T

Instructions regarding War Diaries and Intelligence Summaries are contained in F.S. Regs., Part II. and the Staff Manual respectively. Title pages will be prepared in manuscript.

Place	Date 1915	Hour	Summary of Events and Information	Remarks and references to Appendices
LAGORGUE	Aug 12th		Day fine. Visited left Sector of trenches. Day passed quietly. Nothing to report.	
"	Aug 13th		Day fine. Company attended Church Parade this morning. Went to LESTREM and LES HUITS MAISONS this morning. Then visited 10th Squadron R.F.C. and arranged for a Signalling to Aircraft Scheme for 15th Apl.	
"	Aug 14th		Day fine. Visited the Signallers of 183rd Inf. Bde. out working today. (Brigade in Reserve) Day passed quietly.	
"	Aug 15th		Day fine. Went round NEUVE CHAPELLE Sector with two Officers of Signalling Class this morning. Enemy shelling near CHATEAU RED DOST with 5.9's.	
"	Aug 16th		183rd Brigade Horse Show today. Day passed uneventfully. Brig. fine. 183rd Bde. did signalling to Aeroplane exercise. Fairly successful show. Day passed quietly.	
"	Aug 17th		Day inclined to rain. IT dis. 200 Volt accumulator truck out. Buried cable progressing slowly with trunk trenches. Day passed quietly with trunk	

T2134. Wt. W708—776. 500000. 4/15. Sir J.C. & S.

WAR DIARY
or
INTELLIGENCE SUMMARY

Army Form C. 2118.

4   6/ Divit. Signal Coy.

Place	Date	Hour	Summary of Events and Information	Remarks and references to Appendices
LA GORGUE	1916 Aug 18		Thick fog this morning turned to heat later. LT BENNETT i/c Working Party burying cable last night. 183rd Bde. took over LES HUITS MAISONS sector today from 94th Brigade. Successful Raid by 184th Bde. tonight entered German trenches and killed a few. It rained tonight.	
"	Aug 19		Day fine. Inspected Company this morning. Digging progressing satisfactorily. Day fine.	
"	Aug 20		Day fine. Visited NEUVE CHAPELLE sector of trenches today. Saw progress of buried cable. Day passed quietly.	
"	Aug 21		Day fine. Went round Right Group Batteries tomorrow and found everything satisfactory. Nothing to report.	
"	Aug 22nd		Day fine. Visited O.C. No 6 Balloon Section to arrange for a practice signalling to Kite Balloon. Heavy thunderstorm and much rain last night prevented digging on trench for burying cable. Got digging done and cable started to be laid.	
"	Aug 23rd		Day fine. Visited front line trenches of Left Sector today. Enemy shelling SNOWDON O.P. Festurned Signalling Class 3 Km. Day passed quietly.	

WAR DIARY
INTELLIGENCE SUMMARY

61 Signal Coy.

Army Form C. 2118.

Place	Date	Hour	Summary of Events and Information	Remarks and references to Appendices
	1916			
LA GORGUE	Aug 24th		Day fine. Examination of Signalling Class starts today.	
"	Aug 25th		Day passed uneventfully. Nothing to report.	
"	Aug 26th		Day fine. Examination of Signalling Class continues today. Signal Office working smoothly and day passed quietly.	
"	Aug 27th		Day fine. 183rd Bde relieved at LES HUITS MAISONS by 4th Bde. 183rd Bde then relieved 182nd Bde at COCKSHY H.Q. and 182nd Bde then came into reserve in LA GORGUE. Day passed quietly.	
"	Aug 28th		Day fine. Visited party burying cable this morning and went to see Battalion Hdqrs of right sector. Signal Coy. played 61 Div. Supply Column at cricket today and we were beaten by 13 runs. Sent 4 men to Corps Hdqrs. for buzzerphone course.	
"	Aug 28th		Day fine. Proceeded to 10th Squadron R.F.C. and arranged for scheme Signalling between Infantry and Aircraft for 1st Sept. Called to the O.C. 10 Balloon Section.	
"	Aug 29th		Day fine. Went out with Bde Major and Signal Officer 182 Bde. & they arranged scheme for 1st September with O.C. 6th Warwicks. At 6 pm met half of jumper & buried cables up on some of the buried cables. Very heavy storm this evening and night.	

SECRET

Army Form C. 2118.

Instructions regarding War Diaries and Intelligence Summaries are contained in F. S. Regs., Part II. and the Staff Manual respectively. Title pages will be prepared in manuscript.

WAR DIARY
or
INTELLIGENCE SUMMARY.
(Erase heading not required.)

61 Divl. Signal Coy.

Place	Date	Hour	Summary of Events and Information	Remarks and references to Appendices
LA GORGUE	1916 Aug 31st		Day very wet. Went out to MOATED GRANGE this morning and collected up gunners to other end of Buried Cable. Visited M in O.P. Heavy rain came on about mid-day.	
"	Aug 31st		Day fine. Practised signalling to Kite Balloon with French pattern electric lamp today with success at about 6000 yds in bright sunlight. 1st & 2nd Infantry Officers taking part in Scheme tomorrow at 6 p.m. tonight & gave them full directions. Day passed quietly.	

R.C. Arnon, Capt.
O.C. 61 Signal Coy.

Page 1.

WAR DIARY September 1916
61st Divl. Signal Company
INTELLIGENCE SUMMARY.
Army Form C. 2118.

Vol 6

Place	Date 1916	Hour	Summary of Events and Information	Remarks and references to Appendices
LA GORGUE	Sept 1st		Day fine. Signalling between Infantry and Aircraft Scheme carried out today with 182nd Inf. Bde. went off successfully. Yellow flares were best for showing up position of infantry. R.A. held a Horse Show this afternoon.	
"	2nd		Day fine. Went round left Sector of trenches this morning with LTS ROGERS and LEADER. In afternoon went up in Observation Balloon to test Signalling with electric lamp from the ground. Test only partially successful. Best to have 2 Signallers up in the Balloon for good results.	
"	3rd		Day fine. Troops went to Church Parade service 9.30 am. Visited right Sector in afternoon. Saw N. TILLELOY burned cable trench. Not properly filled in yet.	
"	4th 5th		Officers & N.C.O.'s for new Signalling Class arrived today. Day fine. Visited left Sector of trenches. Nothing to report. Day inclined to rain. New Signalling Class commenced on Monday under LT BENNETT.	
"	6th		Day fine. Day passed quietly.	

Page 2.

WAR DIARY
INTELLIGENCE SUMMARY.
(Erase heading not required.)

Army Form C. 2118.

Place	Date 1916 Sept.	Hour	Summary of Events and Information	Remarks and references to Appendices
LA GORGUE	7th		Arranged to start new buried route from COTTAGE O.P. to RED HOUSE, and 100 men detailed to dig tomorrow night. Day fine. Nothing of importance happened	
"	8th		LT SPUR and self superintended digging of first portion of new trench tonight at 7.30pm. Smith Lam. Considerably wet in places.	
"	9th		Day fine and passed quietly. Capt. Clark & LT BROWNING superintended digging party tonight.	
"	10th		Day fine. Company went to Church Parade at 10 a.m. No working party tonight. Day passed quietly	
"	11th		Day fine. Capt CLARK and LT ROGERS superintended digging party deepening trench already dug. Raft passed quietly and nothing particular to report.	
"	12th		Day fine. Newcombed left Sectn. of trenches with LT Morris. Telephonic communication direct to No 10 Kite Balloon Section from Right Group Artillery established today; LT BROWNING superintended working party of 54 men tonight.	

WAR DIARY

Page 3.

Place	Date	Hour	Summary of Events and Information	Remarks and references to Appendices
LA GORGUE	Sept 1916 13th		Day inclined to rain. Went round Left Sector of trenches to locate exact positions of cement dug-outs for Company Telephone Offices. A.D.A.S. 11th Corps visited us this morning.	
"	14th		Day fine. Capt Clark & Lt Browning went to 11th Corps Hdqrs. in clew to get money for paying the Company. In afternoon went out with de Fath digging trench for burying cable. Lt Spur Superintending today. O5-Screening huzzers allotted to the Division went placed in position in the left Brigade Sector.	
"	15th		Day fine and bright. Rode out with Lt LEADER this morning. Visited N. TILLOY trench and Winchester Av. Major Statfold G.S.O.2 proceeded on leave today. 1130 yards of trench between COTTAGE O.P. and RED HO. completed today.	
"	16th		Day fine. Cable laid in the COTTAGE trench and working party finished filling in tonight.	

T2134. Wt. W708—776. 500000. 4/15. Sir J. C. & S.

Army Form C. 2118.

WAR DIARY

Page 4

~~INTELLIGENCE SUMMARY~~
(Erase heading not required.)

Place	Date 1916 Sept	Hour	Summary of Events and Information	Remarks and references to Appendices
LA GORGUE	17		Day fine. Church parade 10 am. Went round HOATE'D ORANGE Sector with Leader today. Had a look at new IT dug-out being made.	
"	18th		Pouring with rain today. Stayed in all day working out Artillery Communications for attack. Put men in bivouacs into Billets today. Signalling class lectured by Corps Wireless Officer today.	
"	19		Day fine. C.R.E. went on leave today. Day passed quietly and nothing to report.	
"	20th		CAPT. NIXON proceeded on leave today. CAPT. CLARK took over command of Signal Coy. temporarily. Nothing to report.	
"	21st		Day fine. Went over Battle HQ lines with Lt. Spur. Company worked on new line standings.	
"	22nd		Day fine. Went to Corps Hdqrs. and got more twisted cable for NEUVE CHAPELLE SEKTOR of trenches.	
"	23rd		Went down lines to see IT Dug-out. Forced out some bad gunner wires. Company worked on standings.	

Army Form C. 2118.

WAR DIARY
INTELLIGENCE SUMMARY.
(Erase heading not required.)

Page 5

Place	Date 1916	Hour	Summary of Events and Information	Remarks and references to Appendices
LA GARGUE	Sept. 24th		Sunday. Day fine. Notch on few Horse Standings and went round NEUVE CHAPELLE Sector. Arranged to send someone out to help clean up lines in this Sector.	
"	25th		Day inclined to rain. Walk hindered digging through RUE DETILLELOY near COTTAGE O.P. Well round left Sector of trenches.	
"	26th		Went into matter of cable required for new Artillery dispositions. Put in new leading in board in the office.	
"	27th		Cpl. Barton put in direct "in duct" for buried cable when it crossed ditch near LONE TREE, and started pumping water out of trench near Cottage. Day passed quietly.	
"	28th		Cpl. Barton finished burying near Cottage Sr. Bailey took party wiring in North Tilleloy.	
"	29th		Moved into new Company Office. Spur took working party and finished wiring in N. Tilleloy.	

Army Form C. 2118.

WAR DIARY
or
INTELLIGENCE SUMMARY.

Page 6.

(Erase heading not required.)

Instructions regarding War Diaries and Intelligence Summaries are contained in F. S. Regs., Part II. and the Staff Manual respectively. Title pages will be prepared in manuscript.

Place	Date	Hour	Summary of Events and Information	Remarks and references to Appendices
LA GORGUE	Sept. 30"		Day fine & bright. CAPT. NIXON returned from leave and resumed command of Company. Day passed quietly. Nothing to report. 2/10/16 R.C.Nixon, Capt. O.C. 61 Signal Coy.	

"Q" Branch,
    61st Division.

    Herewith War Diary for this Unit for the month of October 1916.
    I regret it is late, owing to the fact that the Division has been on the move for the last 10 days.

10.11.16.   R C Nixon
                        Capt.
          O.C. 61st Divl. Signal Coy. R.E.

A.G.
Base.

    Forwarded with reference to this office letter of 8th inst. covering War Diaries for other units of this Division.

                H C Singleton Lt Col
                      a.a. & qmg
D.H.Q.   for Major General
10.11.16   Commanding 61 Division

WAR DIARY

of

61st DIVL. SIGNAL COY. R.E.

for the Month of OCTOBER, 1916.

VOLUME 6.

WAR DIARY or INTELLIGENCE SUMMARY.

Army Form C. 2118.

61st Div. Signal Co. R.E.

Page 1.

(Erase heading not required.)

Instructions regarding War Diaries and Intelligence Summaries are contained in F. S. Regs., Part II. and the Staff Manual respectively. Title pages will be prepared in manuscript.

Place	Date 1916 Oct	Hour	Summary of Events and Information	Remarks and references to Appendices
LA GORGUE	1st		Day fine. Company attended Church Parade at 10 am. Visited Brigade Headquarters this morning. Watched Company Football match in afternoon. Played quite badly.	
"	2nd		Day dull. Russian Colonel named Irch was shown round Signal Company today and expressed himself pleased with what he saw. Visited LES HUITS MAISONS Brigade Hdqrs. 5th Signal Company now on our right at LESTREM. Visited Captain Lee Wright of 5th Signal Co. this afternoon. Concert by Signal Co. at Y.M.C.A. Hut tonight. Very wet evening.	
"	3rd		Day dull raining. Major Mitchell 15th Squadron R.F.C. turned up today to arrange scheme for signalling between Infantry and Aircraft. Visited 183rd Bde. Cleared up fine evening. Visited 184th Bde. area tonight.	
"	4th		Day fine and bright. Visited 182nd Bde. area today and saw that buried route was alright. Rode to BAILLY in afternoon.	

Army Form C. 2118.

Page 2

WAR DIARY
or
INTELLIGENCE SUMMARY.   61st Divnl. Signal Co. R.E.
(Erase heading not required.)

Place	Date	Hour	Summary of Events and Information	Remarks and references to Appendices
LA GORGUE	1916 Oct 5th		Day fine, strong wind. Went round FAUQUISSART section of trenches today and visited new Brick kiln station of company H.qrs. Inspected PICANTIN ground work of company H.qrs.	
"	6th		Day fine, very windy. G.O.C. visited H.Q. today. Day passed uneventfully.	
"	7th		Day fine. Company Kit Inspection today. Selected position for H.qrs. for Signalling to Aircraft Scheme.	
"	8th		Day fine. Cloudy. Church Parade 10 a.m.	
"	9th		FROMELLES - NEUVE CHAPELLE Sector this morning. Lines O.K. Capt. McLay & 2nd Div Sig Co. came to see me today. Day cloudy. Signalling to aeroplane scheme postponed. A.D.Signals 11th Corps came and visited the Picantin Buried Route today. Day passed uneventfully.	
"	10th		Day fine and bright. Chief wind. Signalling between infantry and Aircraft Scheme carried out successfully today. Visited new position for 1.T Sig. afternoon. Day passed quietly.	

Army Form C. 2118.

Page 3

WAR DIARY
or
INTELLIGENCE SUMMARY.   61st Divl. Signal Co R.E.
(Erase heading not required.)

Instructions regarding War Diaries and Intelligence Summaries are contained in F.S. Regs., Part II. and the Staff Manual respectively. Title pages will be prepared in manuscript.

Place	Date	Hour	Summary of Events and Information	Remarks and references to Appendices
LA GORGUE	1916 Oct 11		Day dull. Visited 184th Bde. Sector this morning. Capt went to HINGES to get money from Field Cashier.	
"	12		Day dull and gusty wind. Sent Company for a Route March today. Visited 34th Division HQ. Area. Inspected 34th Signals buried system.	
"	13		Day fine. Visited different working parties today. H.D. Signals came to visit me this afternoon.	
"	14		Day fine. Inspected Coys equipment etc. Went to HINGES in car this afternoon to get money. G.O.C. 5th Divn dined with G.O.C. tonight.	
"	15		Day dull. Successful raid carried out last night by 184 Inf. Bde. Several Germans killed. Company played Corps Signals at football today. Coys S.M. won 3–1.	
"	16		Day fine. Signalling between Infantry and Aircraft Scheme carried out successfully with 184 Inf. Bde. today. Visited I.T. with Corps Wireless Officer today.	

Army Form C. 2118.

Page 4.

WAR DIARY
or
INTELLIGENCE SUMMARY. (155th Divl. Signal Co. R.E.)
(Erase heading not required.)

Place	Date	Hour	Summary of Events and Information	Remarks and references to Appendices
L.A. GORGUF	17th Oct 1915		Day fine. Company went for Route March this morning. Visited trenches of VIEILLE CHAPELLE sector this afternoon. Went to tea tonight by Genl. Stephens and/or Divisn. in LAVENTIE at 5.30 tonight.	
"	18th		No any rain this evening and during night – Day dull - inclined to rain. Inspected Company on parade. Called in to see 183 Bde. Signal Section in afternoon. Visited Hdqrs. of 10th Squadron R.F.C. in afternoon to arrange for another Signalling to Aircraft Scheme.	
"	19th		Much rain during night and still raining this morning. Moved animals to new Horse Standings.	
"	20th		Day fine and cold. Sent Company for Route march this morning. Visited LAVENTIE in afternoon and inspected new lines laid along RUE TILLELOY by the Gunner O.P's.	
"	21st		Day fine. Visited 182nd Bde. and 183rd Bde. & 18th Bde. Hdqrs. Everything satisfactory.	
"	22nd		Day fine, bright and frosty. Went out to 183rd Bde. area to arrange for Signalling to Aircraft Scheme tomorrow Company. May 1st No 2 Divl N.S.C. of forthwith this afternoon (1-1)	

WAR DIARY
INTELLIGENCE SUMMARY.
(Erase heading not required.)

Army Form C. 2118.

Page 5

61st Div. Sig. Co. R.E

Place	Date 1916	Hour	Summary of Events and Information	Remarks and references to Appendices
LA GORGUE	Oct 23		Morning cold bright and frosty. Signalling to Aeroplane Scheme this morning went CROIX BARBÉS in conjunction with 183rd Inf. Bde. Went twenty off satisfactorily. Day passed uneventfully.	
"	24		Day fine. 1 Sergt. and 4 men of 168 Bde. Signal Section arrived tonight and proceeded to LES 8 MAISONS. LT PARKINSON of 56th Divn. Sigs. turned up today to see about taking over. He brings rain in afternoon.	
"	25		Day inclined to rain. Major Kennard 56th Signals came over today from LESTREM to see about taking over. Visited A.D. Signals 11 Corps with Major Kennard. Day fine. Party of 56th Signal Co. arrived this morning to take over along lines etc. 10th Major Kennard round the Brigades. Commenced changing over instruments and exchange tonight.	
"	26			
"	27		Day raining and cold. Capt. Clerk went on to ST VENANT today with Advance Party to see about billets etc. Day passed uneventfully.	

WAR DIARY
or
INTELLIGENCE SUMMARY. 61st Divl. Signal Co. R.E.
(Erase heading not required.)

Army Form C. 2118.
Page 6

Place	Date 1916	Hour	Summary of Events and Information	Remarks and references to Appendices
LA GORGUE	Oct 28		Day fine. Company paraded at 10.30 a.m. to march to ST VENANT. 5th Signal Co. arrived in Camp 10.45 a.m. 1st Cable Detl. behind with Lt SPUR for Gunners. Lorry left LA GORGUE about 2 p.m. with remainder of men and kites. Trouble with electric light lorry for being late — in getting lights running.	
ST VENANT	29		Day fine and bright. Rode round and visited Brigade Hdqrs. at MERVILLE, ROBECQ and BUSNES today. All communications working satisfactorily.	
"	30		Day fine. Capt Cleveland self visited ST POL, LILLERS and ROLLECOURT today to arrange for communications on the move.	
"	31		Day fine. Made out orders for communication by wire and DRLS during the move. Day passed uneventfully.	

R.C. Jersey Capt.
O.C. 61 Divl Sig Co. R.E.

Army Form C. 2118.

WAR DIARY

or

INTELLIGENCE SUMMARY.

(Erase heading not required.)

SECRET

Volume 7

61st Divl. Signal Co., R.E.

NOVEMBER, 1916.

Army Form C. 2118.

WAR DIARY November 1916

INTELLIGENCE SUMMARY. 61 Div. Signal Co. R.E.

(Erase heading not required.)

Instructions regarding War Diaries and Intelligence Summaries are contained in F.S. Regs., Part II. and the Staff Manual respectively. Title pages will be prepared in manuscript.

Place	Date 1916	Hour	Summary of Events and Information	Remarks and references to Appendices
ST VENANT	Nov 1st		Day inclined to rain. G.O.C. decided that Div. Hdqrs. would move to BAILLEUL tomorrow. Sent on Advanced Party under Capt. Clark this afternoon. BAILLEUL found to be too small to Div. Hdqrs. changed to CHELERS.	
"	2nd		Day raining. Div. H.Q. closed at ST VENANT at 7am. and opened up at CHELERS at same hour. Company paraded at 7.30 am, and marched via BUSNES and CHELERS. Communication established by phone to 183rd Bde at ORLENCOURT, 184 Bde at AUCHEL and 182 Bde at BUSNES.	
CHELERS	3rd		Day fine. 183rd Bde. move to BAILLEUL, 184th Bde moved to ORLENCOURT and 182nd Bde moved to AUCHEL. Communication established by wire to all Brigades by 5 pm.	
CHELERS	4th		Day fine. Rained in early morning. Company moved off at 8.30 am, to ROLLECOURT. 182 Bde. at ORLENCOURT, 183 Bde. at BAILLEUL and 184 Bde. at CHELERS. Through to all Brigades from Div. Hdqrs. at ROLLECOURT by wire using D3 telephones.	
ROLLECOURT	5th		Day fine. Church Parade 10 am. 182 Bde. moved to HOUVIN, 183 Bde. moved to MAISNIL-ST-POL. 184 Bde. moved to REBREUVE. Thro. to 182 telephone, Comm. with 184 via 3rd Army Sub-Office at FREVENT. 183 Bde. by D.R.	

T2134. Wt. W708-776. 500000. 4/15. Sir J. C. & S.

Army Form C. 2118.

Page 2. WAR DIARY or INTELLIGENCE SUMMARY. 61 Divl. Signal. Co. R.E.
(Erase heading not required.)

Place	Date 1916	Hour	Summary of Events and Information	Remarks and references to Appendices
ROLLECOURT	NOV. 5 (cont)	6.45	Sent Capt. Clark in charge of Advance Party to FROHEN-LE-GRAND.	
"	6		Day pouring with rain. Fine intervals. Company paraded at 8 a.m. and marched via ST POL and FREVENT to FROHEN-LE-GRAND. Laid line from VILLERS L'HOPITAL to FROHEN-LE-GRAND. (182 Bde) at VILLERS L'HOPITAL 183 Bde. at CANDAS BEAUVOIN and 184 Bde. at OCCOCHES. One try wire to 182 and 183 Bdes. D.R. to 184 Bde.	
FROHEN LE-GRAND	7		Day pouring with rain. Line laid by Cpl. Barton to OCCOCHES through rain. Cleared up in afternoon. Communication by wire to all 3 Brigades.	
"	8		Day unsettled and showery. Visited 182nd and 183rd Brigades today. Powered with 183 Brigades.	
"	9		Day fine. Visual Signalling Scheme worked satisfactorily with 182 Bde. and 183 Bdes. Communication between Div. H.Q. Country very suitable for visual.	
"	10		Day fine and sunny. Visual Signalling carried out. Officers of Signal Co. visited Battalion Signallers of half 3 Brigades today at work.	

Army Form C. 2118.

Page 3 WAR DIARY or INTELLIGENCE SUMMARY. 61 Signal Co. R.E.

Place	Date 1916	Hour	Summary of Events and Information	Remarks and references to Appendices
FROHEN LE-GRAND	NOV 10		Day fine and sunny. Visual Signalling Scheme, reflex, carried out in conjunction with Brigades. 61st Brigade Battalion Signallers visited by a Signal Officer at their work.	
"	11		Very misty day prevented any practice at visual. Bdy marked movement etc.	
"	12		Day fine but dull. Church Parade 10 a.m. I"Batt'd Camp & men's kitchens & saw all correct.	
"	13		Day inclined to be misty. Carried out visual Signalling work in morning and afternoon. Day fine and cold. Battalion Signallers of Division visited by Signal Officers today.	
"	14		Day fine and cold. Sent Capt. Clark on to BERNAVILLE with Advance Party this morning. 183rd Bde. moved to AUTHEUX and 182nd Bde. moved to FIENVILLERS. Div H.Q. at BERNAVILLE 184th Bde. remained at OCCOCHES. Communication by wire established to all three Brigades.	
"	15			

Army Form C. 2118.

WAR DIARY
or
INTELLIGENCE SUMMARY.

(Erase heading not required.)

Page 4

61st Div. Sig. Co. R.E.

Place	Date 1916	Hour	Summary of Events and Information	Remarks and references to Appendices
BERNAVILLE	Nov 16th		Day fine and cold. Divl. Hdqrs. moved from BERNAVILLE to CANAPLES. Communication established by wire between Divl. Hdqrs. and the 183rd Bde at ST. OUEN, the 182nd Bde at BERTEAUCOURT and 184th Bde at BONNEVILLE.	
CANAPLES	17th		Day fine. Very cold wind. Divl. Hdqrs. entered from CANAPLES to CONTAY. 2 Battns of 183rd Bde. and the 3 Field Coys taken on in motor lorries. Company marched at 8.45 a.m. Communication by wire to 182 Bde at RUBEMPRE 183 Bde at LAUICOGNE and 184 Bde at VADENCOURT.	
CONTAY	18th		Snow during night and very cold. Raining this morning. Went to see Maj. Davy, A.D.M.S, 2nd Corps, then went on to BOUZINCOURT and fixed up surrender for 183rd Bde. moving there today. 182nd Bde. moved to WARLOY and we laid a cable to them today.	
CONTAY	19th		Day fine. Went with Capt. Clark to 18th Divl. Hdqrs. at TARA HILL and saw 18th Divl. Sigs. Visited POZIERES in afternoon to see Advd. Divl. Exchange in dug-out	

Army Form C. 2118.

PAGE 5

WAR DIARY
—of—
INTELLIGENCE SUMMARY. 61st Divl. Sig. Co. R.E.
(Erase heading not required.)

Place	Date	Hour	Summary of Events and Information	Remarks and references to Appendices
CONTAY	1916 Nov. 20th 21st		Day fine. Went over to BOUZINCOURT this morning to look at proposed new position of Divl. Hdqrs and visited 18th Divn. again in afternoon. Day fine. Sent forward Advance Party to TARA HILL under Capt CLARK to take over Signal Office from 18th Divn. H. Browning and self went to BOUZINCOURT this evening to line up Instruments for taking over tomorrow. Lieut. Qr. Mr. Webber and a half there. 184th Bde. took over trenches tonight from Bde. of 18th Divn. 183rd Bde. moved to USNA and 182 Bde to MARTINSART.	
BOUZINCOURT	22nd		Day fine. Divl. Hdqrs. opened at BOUZINCOURT at 9am. Line from CONTAY to WARLOY sealed up by LT. B. BENNETT. Co. marched to BOUZINCOURT at 8.45 am Communication with 184 Bde. at MOUQUET FM via TARA HILL all right but speaking rather indistinct. Laid new line from NW to MOQUET FM this afternoon. Not good speaking. 3 men wounded during their latter days	

Page 6   61st Divnl Signal Co. R.E.

WAR DIARY
INTELLIGENCE SUMMARY.

Place	Date 1916	Hour	Summary of Events and Information	Remarks
BOUZINCOURT	Nov 23		Day fine. Ene to HOOPLET PM from NV on Ency informed and filed. 183 Bde moved from USNA to OVILLERS 182th remained at MARTINSART.	
"	24		Day fine. W and rain. Staff Captain of 184 Bde at CRUCIFIX CORNER connected up to Ene. Exchange enflused successfully. Lines informed. Hotel Daylight misty and rain. Day passed uneventfully. Lines via POZIERES out continually by shell-fire.	
"	25			
"	26		Day fine. Advanced Office at TARA HILL closed down. Capt. Clark and party came in to H.Q.R. 61 Divn Arty arrived and commenced taking over from " Div Art. Church Parade 10 am.	
"	27		Day fine. 182 Bde moved to HEDAUVILLE 183 Bde moved to MARTINSART. DADOS moved HEDAUVILLE line laid from TS en Bury to 308 Bde R.F.A.	
"	28		Day fine. CRE moved from TARA HILL to Camp at NW 94 b 3.9 between BOUZINCOURT and AVELUY.	

Army Form C. 2118.

WAR DIARY
or
INTELLIGENCE SUMMARY.

(Erase heading not required.)

Page 7

Instructions regarding War Diaries and Intelligence Summaries are contained in F.S. Regs., Part II. and the Staff Manual respectively. Title pages will be prepared in manuscript.

617 Divisional Signal Co. R.E.

Place	Date	Hour	Summary of Events and Information	Remarks and references to Appendices
Bertrancourt	Nov 1916 29		Day misty and cold. Day passed uneventfully.	
"	30		Day misty and raw. ST ANDREWS DAY. Cotton on leave. Orders from OLD TREE O.P. GHOQUETEH tonight. 183 Bde relieved 18th Bde in trenches tonight. 18th Div moved to MARTINSART. Commenced changing 4pm	

R. C. Mixon. Capt.
O.C. 617 Div. Sig. Co. R.E.

SECRET

Officer i/c
    A.G's Office,
        BASE.

        Herewith War Diary for Headquarters and No.1 Section, of the 61st Divl. Signal Coy., for the Month of May 1916.

                                  R. Chiscon Capt.
                                  O.C. 61st Div'l Sig. Coy.

War Diary Dec 16.
61st Signal Coy

Vol. 8

Army Form C. 2118.

WAR DIARY
or
INTELLIGENCE SUMMARY.
(Erase heading not required.)

Instructions regarding War Diaries and Intelligence Summaries are contained in F. S. Regs., Part II. and the Staff Manual respectively. Title pages will be prepared in manuscript.

Place	Date	Hour	Summary of Events and Information	Remarks and references to Appendices
BOUZINCOURT	DEC 1		2 Lt C.E. BENNETT appointed O/o "C" Signals 61st RFA vice 2 Lt R.J. Shyvr.	
	2		Regular Leave for R.E. Coy started	
	3		Sunday - Church parade	
	4		POZIERE exchange shelled and all lines cut.	
	5		A very quiet day.	
	6		MOUQUET farm heavily shelled. All lines cut. Had to resort to Visual within to report.	
	7			
	8		Nothing to report.	
	9		Nothing to report	
	10		163 Bde relieves 162 Bde. Heavy Shelling at 6.30 pm. Had to resort to Visual	
	11		POZIERE exchange shelled. Front difficult to keep up lines to Pys in line	
	12		MOUQUET FARM again heavily shelled. On lynx wen kept going. ZRD relieves ZRC (Supp) CAPT P.W. CLARK (RE) commencing the Coy vice CAPT R.C. NIXON. NW MOUQUET FARM line needs THIEPVAL ROAD	
	13		Relief of 2nd Lt CAPT C.D. TWYNAM joined R.E. Cy as 2 in command.	
	14		Trouble with lines from Test Pay Out to K. Test point. Otherwise nothing to report	
	15			

Army Form C. 2118.

WAR DIARY
or
INTELLIGENCE SUMMARY.
(Erase heading not required.)

Instructions regarding War Diaries and Intelligence Summaries are contained in F.S. Regs., Part II. and the Staff Manual respectively. Title pages will be prepared in manuscript.

Place	Date	Hour	Summary of Events and Information	Remarks and references to Appendices
BOEZINGHE	16		Work begun on new Bde HQs at Third St	
	17		Nothing to report.	
	18		Field Coy been relief	
	19		Nothing to report	
	20		ZRD took over from ZRB at Morquet Farm	
	21		Work finished at Third St Bde HQs	
	22		ZRD moved back to Third St Bde HQs at 2.0 PM. ZRC relieve ZRB at Martinsart	
	23		Very strong wind. All air lines gave a lot of trouble. Cot mains trouble blown down.	
	24		307 Bde Buzzet line beyond return. Canadian buzz lady damaged. Aircraft lines at 6.2.11 hrs	
	25		Christmas day. Very strong wind. Great trouble with air lines	
	26		All air lines were restored.	
	27		DD Sigs visited the area.	
	28		ZRC relieve ZRD in line.	
	29		Visual to Bde at Third St from Div HQs established	
	30		Work of clearing out old lines in area in full swing	
	31		Visual from Bde to Left Batt established also from Rt Batt to 2 Corps	

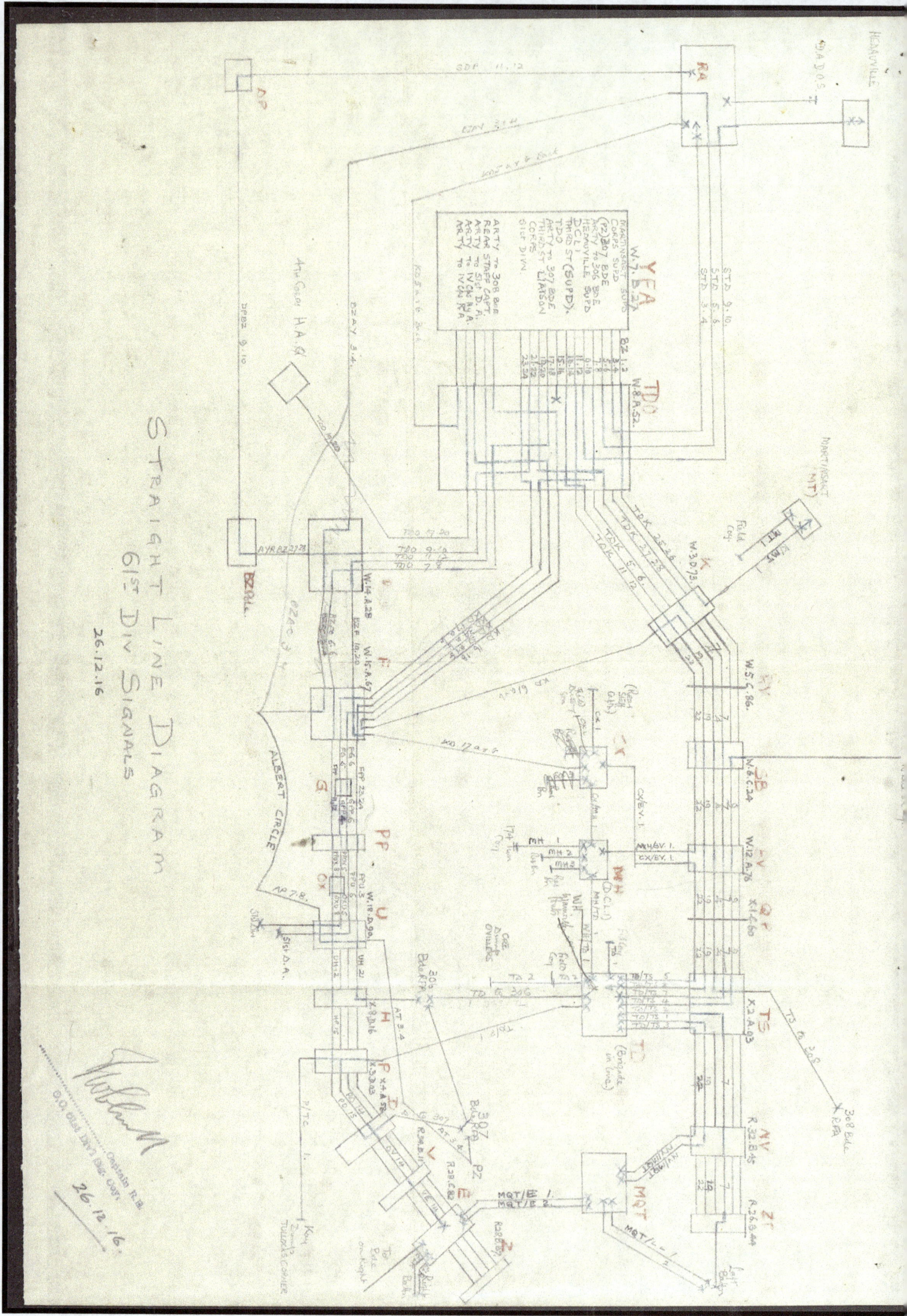

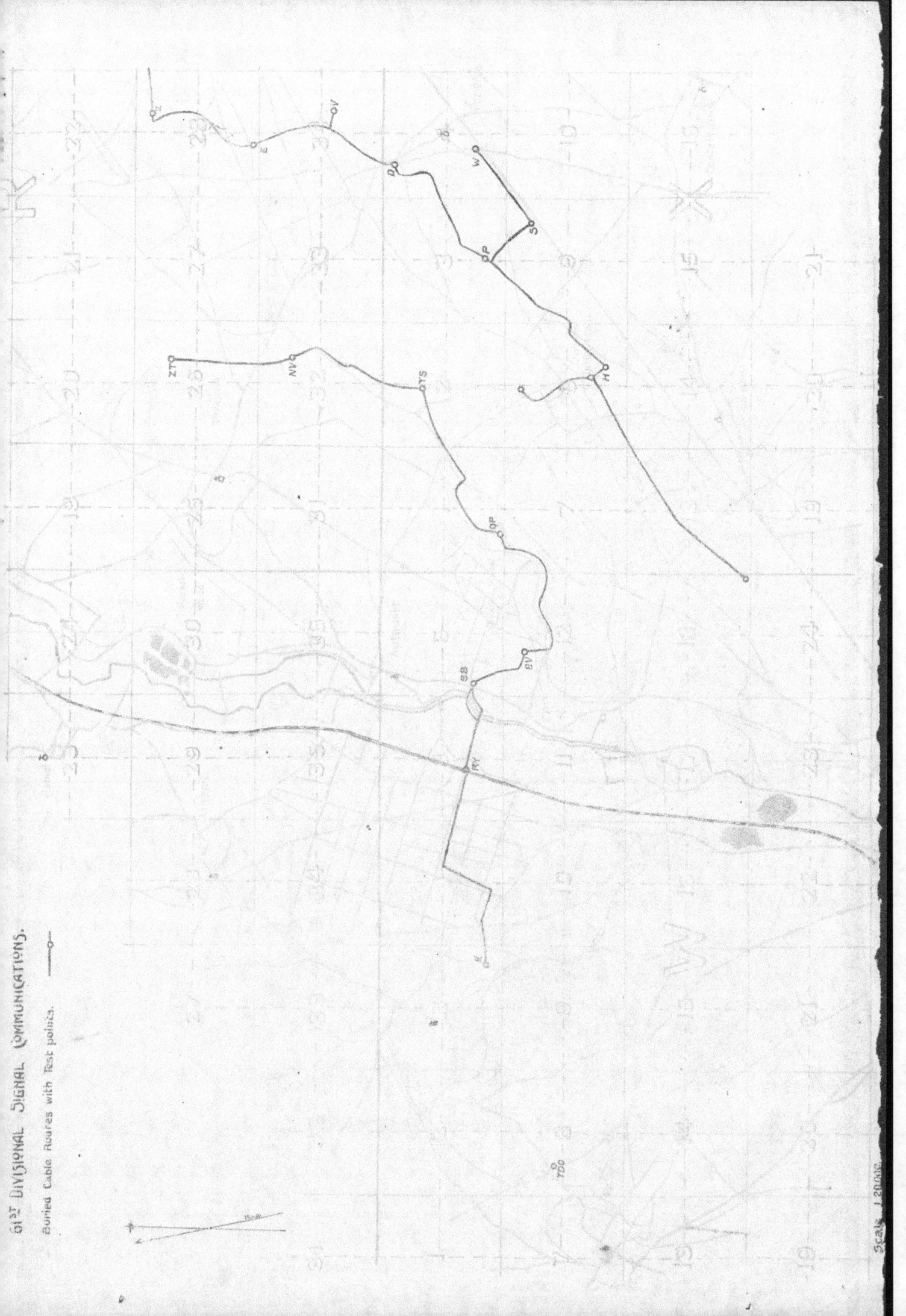

CONFIDENTIAL

WAR DIARY OF
61st DIVNL SIGNAL COY
JANUARY 1917.

VOL 9.

Vol 9

WAR DIARY
or
INTELLIGENCE SUMMARY.
(Erase heading not required.)

Army Form C. 2118.

Place	Date	Hour	Summary of Events and Information	Remarks and references to Appendices
BOUZINCOURT	JAN 1		ZRC in line at THIRD STREET: ZRB in support at MARTINSART; ZRD in reserve at HEDAUVILLE. Capt C D TWYNAM 2 in command of the Coy awarded the Military Cross (London Gazette JAN 1-17).	
	2		Communication lines out to ammunition motor ambulance out to the left of NAB ROAD as neg'd.	
	3, 4 & 5		Cleans up the forward areas of old cable.	
	6		ZRB relieved ZRC in line (ZRC in support at Martinsart)	
	7		Nothing to report	
	8		ZRD relieved ZRC in Support (ZRD returned into reserve at HEDAUVILLE)	
	9		O.C. 18th Div Signal Coy came over and went over the area with the O.C. 6th Sig Coy	
	10		Nothing to report	
	11		Changed over the Signal Office from R. 6th one into a large hut we had constructed for the purpose.	
	12		Nothing to report.	

Army Form C. 2118.

WAR DIARY
or
INTELLIGENCE SUMMARY.
(Erase heading not required.)

Instructions regarding War Diaries and Intelligence Summaries are contained in F. S. Regs., Part II. and the Staff Manual respectively. Title pages will be prepared in manuscript.

Place	Date	Hour	Summary of Events and Information	Remarks and references to Appendices
BOUZINCOURT	Jan 13		2nd Divn relieves the 51st Divn on our right	
	14		Nothing to report.	
	15		Our advance party left for MARIEUX to fix up our new HQs	
	16		YFA closed down at R.O.6m at BOUZINCOURT on being relieved by the 18th Divn. At R.H. same hour YFA opened up again at MARIEUX with ZRB, ZRD at ~~RAINCHEVAL~~ RUBEMPRE and ZRC at BEAUQUESNE	
	17		YFA closed down at 11.0 a.m. at MARIEUX and opened at same hour at BERNAVILLE with brigades at FIENVILLERS MON PLAISIR & GELAINCOURT. The weather was very bad and frost made marching very hard.	
	18		Divl HQs remained at Bernaville and Bdes halted. Every effort was made to lighten the wagons as our horses were in very poor condition and the march from MARIEUX had knocked them up. Bdes this night were at LE PLOUY (ZRB) PROUVILLE (ZRD) LONGVILLERS (ZRC).	

Army Form C. 2118.

WAR DIARY
or
INTELLIGENCE SUMMARY.
(Erase heading not required.)

Instructions regarding War Diaries and Intelligence Summaries are contained in F. S. Regs., Part II. and the Staff Manual respectively. Title pages will be prepared in manuscript.

Place	Date	Hour	Summary of Events and Information	Remarks and references to Appendices
BERNAVILLE & BRAILLY	19		YFA closed at Bernaville at 11·0 a.m. and reopened at BRAILLY. Same hour with ZRB at CANCHY ZRC at ARGENVILLERS & ZRD at MAISON PONTHIEU.	
	20		⎫	
	21		⎬ Refitting and overhauling equipment and stores.	
	22		⎭	
	23		O.C. granted leave to U.K. 23/1/17 to 2/2/17.	
	24		⎫	
	25		⎬	
	26		⎬ Refitting and Training. Hard frost lasts the whole	
	27		⎬ time.	
	28		⎬	
	29		⎬	
	30		⎭	
	31			

T2134. Wt. W708—776. 500000. 4/15. Sir J. C. & S.

Vol 10

CONFIDENTIAL

War Diary of 61st Divnl
Signal Coy.

Feb. 1917

Vol 10.

Army Form C. 2118.

WAR DIARY
or
INTELLIGENCE SUMMARY.
(Erase heading not required.)

Instructions regarding War Diaries and Intelligence Summaries are contained in F. S. Regs., Part II. and the Staff Manual respectively. Title pages will be prepared in manuscript.

Place	Date	Hour	Summary of Events and Information.	Remarks and references to Appendices
BRAILLY	Feb. 1		} Resting and training.	
	2			
	3			
	4		Advance party under Capt Turner left for LONG.	
LONG	5		YFA (lines) division at BRAILLY had returned at 11.0am at LONG. 182 Bde were at BELLANCOURT, 183 Bde at AILLY & 184 Bde at GORENFLOS. 2nd Lt R.J. SPURR returned from 5th Army Signal School.	
	6		} TRAINING.	
	7			
	8			
	9			
	10			
	11		Advance party left for HARBONNIERES. The OC & 2 2/D in command went out to the new Div Area with Sig Off of 154 Div	
	12		the transport of the Coy under 11 Lt R.J. SPURR began the march (3 days) to GUILLAUCOURT via ST SAUVEUR & FOUILLOY.	

WAR DIARY
or
INTELLIGENCE SUMMARY.
(Erase heading not required.)

Army Form C. 2118.

Place	Date	Hour	Summary of Events and Information	Remarks and references to Appendices
LONG	13		ZRD moved by Train to A Bner (Bois de Pierret nr WIENCOURT)	
GUILLAUCOURT	14		YFA closed down at 11.0 a.m. at Long and reopened at the same hour at GUILLAUCOURT. ZRC moved by train to DEMUM	
	15		ZRB moved by train to MARCELCAVE.	
	16		ZRD began to relieve the Hunneb left sector at 6.0 p.m. & completed the relief by 8.0 a.m. next morning.	
	17		ZRC began to relieve the Hunneb right sector at 6.0 a.m.	
HARBONNIERES	18		YFA closed down at GUILLAUCOURT and reopened at HARBONNIERES at 10.0 a.m. Communication was poor as the lines we took over were bad and the day fairly wet weather going wrong to wet. The lines to airforce R[?] Bg[?] Hd qrs were very bad. We were very hampered by having some of the Hunneb still in our area and it was found that our own telephones would not short the shutters of their exchanges.	
	19			
	20		If new main lines to R Bdes in the line and Place Blamche were laid.	

Army Form C. 2118.

WAR DIARY
or
INTELLIGENCE SUMMARY.
(Erase heading not required.)

Instructions regarding War Diaries and Intelligence Summaries are contained in F. S. Regs., Part II. and the Staff Manual respectively. Title pages will be prepared in manuscript.

Place	Date	Hour	Summary of Events and Information	Remarks and references to Appendices
HARBONNIERES	21		Work on lines was continued	
	22			
	23		The German Artillery heavily bombarded the line in the evening. Communication in Bath Bde areas was excellent. Both Bde section officers were congratulated on the efficient working of their systems. A copy of the report by the staff is attached.	
	24		} Nothing special to return	
	25			
	26			
	27			
	28		A raid on the left Bde was attempted by the Germans. He shelling was very heavy. Both main lines to the Bde from Divn HQs were cut. Communication with the Bde was never lost however and all divisional lines between infantry and gunners stayed. Sentries found of Batln HQs however were destroyed. On the whole communication was good.	

M.E.M. Capt R.E.

C O P Y.

61st Div.

With reference to the action of the German Artillery which continued for about ½-hour yesterday evening, during the relief of front line Battalions; I beg to say that the retaliation of our Artillery was very prompt and satisfactory.

No difficulty whatever was experienced in getting into telephonic communication with all concerned.

Information was sent at once from the front line through art. bn. liaison officers to the batteries; the infantry brigade was kept constantly informed; the O.C., R.A. Brigade was able to talk to me and to his liaison officer at any moment. Brigades on our right and left answered at once to our calls, and in short, in every direction communication was excellent, except in the case of one line to one of the front companies, which was broken by shell-fire.

The Signalling Section was ready to put the visual Scheme into operation had this been necessary.

(sd.) Robert White,
Brig. Gen.
184 Inf. Bde.

24th Feb. 1917.

O.C. Signal Coy.

The G.O.C. considers this report very satisfactory and creditable to the Divl. Signal Company.

Please let O.C. Sections with 184 & Divl. Arty. see it; also 183 Section, as they were very efficient also.

(sd). H. Wake,
Lt. Col.
G.S.

24/2/17.

C O N F I D E N T I A L.

WAR DIARY

61st Divl. Signal Company, R.E.

1st to 31st March 1917.

VOLUME - 10

Army Form C. 2118

WAR DIARY
INTELLIGENCE SUMMARY MARCH 1917
(Erase heading not required.)

Place	Date	Hour	Summary of Events and Information	Remarks and references to Appendices
HARBONNIERES	1 to 7		184 Bde at Demuin, Chateau, 182 Bde at 'ALBERT' Vermandovillers and 183 Bde in reserve at Guillaucourt.	
	8			
	9-17		183 Relieved 182 on the night at ALBERT Vermandovillers and 182 went into reserve at Guillaucourt. Mobilization stores were destroyed, wagons overhauled and everything possible done to be ready for a move in finer and cooler weather. In the meantime patrols and many rumours of the enemy's intention to retire obtained from enemy prisoners.	
	18		Advanced Div HQs moved up to ALBERT, ZRC moved at to "AMBERG" and ZRB to "VALET", ZRD remained at GUILLAUCOURT. 2 Cable Detachments were sent out to LIHONS under CAPT TWYNAM. They could not get over "No mans land" but cable and wires were taken over by a company party and the line from Advanced Div HQs to AMBERG was continued into CHAULNES where a signal office was opened.	
	19		A cable detachment was sent to "VALET" (ZRB) and laid a cable with great difficulty from there to MARCHELPOT and continued the line on thro OMMIECOURT exchange continuing to OMMIECOURT the line from CHAULNES	

Army Form C. 2118

WAR DIARY
or
INTELLIGENCE SUMMARY
(Erase heading not required.)

Place	Date	Hour	Summary of Events and Information	Remarks and references to Appendices
ALBERT	19		and on to PERTAIN where an office was opened. An cable section laid a line from ALBERT to OMMIECOURT where an advanced exchange was opened. Later in the day 2RD moved out to OMMIECOURT and 2RC to DRESLINCOURT. Both were connected to the advanced exchange. The trunk cable sections from LIHONS were moved out to OMMIECOURT.	
	To 20 24		Bde offices did not move. Lines were held and all stations etc were moved over to OMMIECOURT.	
	25		Main line from ALBERT to OMMIECOURT was continued on to MORCHAIN	
	26		Lines from OMMIECOURT to MORCHAIN were extended to VILLECOURT	
	27		Line from MORCHAIN to VILLECOURT extended to GUIZANCOURT thus from lines as follows GUIZANCOURT - CROIX MOLIGNAUX and GROIX-MOLIGNAUX - MONCHY LAGACHE and MONCHY LAGACHE - GUIZANCOURT	
GUIZANCOURT	28		Div HQs moved to GUIZANCOURT with 2RB at MERRACOURT 2RC at MONCHY LAGACHE and 2RD at ATHIES and all O SPR at HARBONNIÈRES.	

Army Form C. 2118

WAR DIARY
or
INTELLIGENCE SUMMARY
(Erase heading not required.)

Place	Date	Hour	Summary of Events and Information	Remarks and references to Appendices
GUIZANCOURT	29		Q office moved ↑ to Div HQs at GUIZANCOURT.	
	30		All lines were tested and D.A.C. D.S.C. and Train were	
	31		all put on and exchange at BETHENCOURT	

.... Captain R.E.
O.C. 61st Divl Sig. Coy.

CONFIDENTIAL

Vol 12

WAR DIARY
OF
61ST DIV. SIGNAL COY.
FOR THE MONTH OF APRIL 1917

VOLUME 12.

WAR DIARY or INTELLIGENCE SUMMARY

(Erase heading not required.)

Army Form C. 2118

Instructions regarding War Diaries and Intelligence Summaries are contained in F.S. Regs., Part II. and the Staff Manual respectively. Title Pages will be prepared in manuscript.

Place	Date	Hour	Summary of Events and Information	Remarks and references to Appendices
GUIZANCOURT	1		Div. Hdqrs. at GUIZANCOURT; R.A. Hdqrs. at CROIX MOLIGNAUX; 184 Bde. in the line on the left; 182 Bde. in the line on the right; 183 Bde. in reserve.	
	3.		An Exchange at BETHANCOURT was established with the S.S.O, Train Hdqrs., D.S.C. and D.A.C. on it.	
			183 Bde. relieved 182 Bde. in Right Sector. 183 Bde. Hqqrs. at VILLEVECQUE, and 182 Bde. Hdqrs. at MERAUCOURT.	
	4) 5) 6)		All lines were poled and improved. The weather was very bad and we had a lot of trouble with the lines. The Bde. to Battalion lines were very long and in consequence speaking was very poor.	
	7		182 Bde. relieved 183 Bde. in Right Sector.	
	8.		48 Divl. Hdqrs. were to move to BEAUVOIS, lines were laid from this place to all Bdes. when these were finished it was decided that the Division would be relieved by the 35th Division. The work of constructing the new office was proceeded with by our men on lines suitable for the 35th Division.	

Army Form C. 2118

WAR DIARY
or
INTELLIGENCE SUMMARY
(Erase heading not required.)

Instructions regarding War Diaries and Intelligence Summaries are contained in F. S. Regs., Part II. and the Staff Manual respectively. Title Pages will be prepared in manuscript.

Place	Date	Hour	Summary of Events and Information	Remarks and references to Appendices
GUIZANCOURT.	9		The 183 Bde. (In reserve) relieved by a Brigade of the 35th Division.	
	10		182 Bde. (Right Sector) relieved by a Brigade of the 35th Division. 182 Bde. moved back into rest with Hdqrs. at MONTIGNELLE Farm, near DOUILLY.	
VOYENNES.	12		Relief of Division by 35th Division completed at 11. 0.a.m. and change of Command took place at this hour. Divl. Hdqrs. established at VOYENNES at 11. 0.a.m. with 182 Bde. Hdqrs. at MONTIGNELLE FARM. 183 Bde. Hdqrs. at ENNEMAIN. 184 Bde. Hdqrs. at BUNY. The Artillery of the Division remained in the line covering the 35th Div. front.	
	13 to 22		Division in rest. Stores etc. were overhauled. No.1A Cable Section remained behind until the 15th, picking up all spare cable.	
	23		The Division relieved the 32nd Division in the line, with the French on our right and the 35th Division on our left.	
AURCIR.	30th.		164 Bde. in the Line (Left Sector). 182 Bde. " " (Right "). The Artillery covering the front was the 159, 161 & 168 Bdes. R.F.A.	

WAR DIARY
or
INTELLIGENCE SUMMARY

(Erase heading not required.)

Army Form C. 2118

Instructions regarding War Diaries and Intelligence Summaries are contained in F. S. Regs., Part II. and the Staff Manual respectively. Title Pages will be prepared in manuscript.

Place	Date	Hour	Summary of Events and Information	Remarks and references to Appendices
			German permanent air lines were still standing in the area, and all lines to the Bdes. were open wire.	
			Owing to trouble from enemy artillery fire an emergency cable line was laid from AURIOR to the two Infantry Bdes. in the line.	
			Towards the end of the month the weather improved, and as very little construction work was necessary a certain amount of training was done.	

CONFIDENTIAL

Vol 13

WAR DIARY
OF
61ST DIV. SIGNAL COY
FOR THE MONTH OF MAY 1917

VOL. 13.

Army Form C. 2118

WAR DIARY
or
INTELLIGENCE SUMMARY
(Erase heading not required.)

Instructions regarding War Diaries and Intelligence Summaries are contained in F.S. Regs., Part II and the Staff Manual respectively. Title Pages will be prepared in manuscript.

Place	Date	Hour	Summary of Events and Information	Remarks and references to Appendices
AUROIR (66L -62C)	1917 May 1st		182 Brigade in line, right section with H.Q. between SAVY and ETREILLERS (X 28 D 33 Sheet 62D) 183 Brigade in reserve H.Q. at GERMAINE (E 17 B Sheet 66D) 184 Brigade in line left section (X 18 A 44 Sheet 62 C) Artillery covering front 159 & 161 Bdes R.F.A of 32nd Divn. and 168 Bde of 35th Divn. Divisional Headquarters. AUROIR.	
	2nd		183 Brigade relieved 184 Bde in left section.	
	5th		305 Bde R.F.A. relieved 168 Bde R.F.A. as left group.	
			Draft of 12 Cable hands from Signal Depot arrived.	
	6th		Six of draft under Sergt Spicer sent to 306 Bde R.F.A. Six under Sergt Cox to 307 Bde R.F.A.	
	7th		Lateral communication on restored German route established between rear headquarters left brigade (ATTILLY) and brigade on left (MARTEVILLE)	
	9th		306 Brigade R.F.A. relieved 159 Bde R.F.A. as right group, and 158 Bde R.F.A. relieved 161 Bde R.F.A. in centre group position. Artillery covering front reduced to two Brigades.	
	13th		184 Bde moved to NESLE – traffic through 4th Corps. 121st French Regt (26th French Divn.) due to relieve them did not put in an appearance till morning of 14th. At midnight two French D.R's reported to keep touch with this Unit which was still beyond HAM.	
	14th	11 pm	121st French Regt. relieved 182 Bde in right section – 182 Bde on relief moved to GERMAINE.	

Army Form C. 2118

WAR DIARY
or
INTELLIGENCE SUMMARY

(Erase heading not required.)

Instructions regarding War Diaries and Intelligence Summaries are contained in F. S. Regs., Part II. and the Staff Manual respectively. Title Pages will be prepared in manuscript.

Place	Date	Hour	Summary of Events and Information	Remarks and references to Appendices
AUROIR	1917 May 15th		182 Brigade moved to NESLE.	
			184 Brigade moved to CAMON (2 miles East of AMIENS) by tactical train - Communication via AMIENS exchange.	
		11 pm	139 French Regiment relieved 183 Bde in left sector - French Brigade Commander established Headquarters at ATTILLY as commanding all infantry of Division - 183 Bde moved to GERMAINE.	
	16th	9 am	26th French Division relieved 61st Division in ST QUENTIN sector.	
			Headquarters 61st Division moved to VIGNACOURT (10 miles N.W. of AMIENS).	
			R.A. Headquarters remained at AUROIR.	
			Communications - Entire communications of Division ran through QUERRIEU exchange (one line)	
			Transport moved by road to NESLE.	
VIGNACOURT	17th		182 Brigade moved to FLESSELLES (VIGNACOURT area) - Direct Communication.	
			183 Bde moved to NESLE.	
			184 Bde moved to TALMAS (VIGNACOURT area) Direct Communication.	
			R.A. H.Qs remained at AUROIR.	
			Transport moved by road to ROUVROY.	
	18th		183 Bde moved to VILLERS BOCAGE (VIGNACOURT area) Direct Communication. Telephone to 184 Bde now through 183 Bde exchange.	

1875 Wt. W593/826 1,000,000 4/15 J.B.C. & A. A.D.S.S./Forms/C. 2118.

Army Form C. 2118

WAR DIARY
or
INTELLIGENCE SUMMARY
(Erase heading not required.)

Instructions regarding War Diaries and Intelligence Summaries are contained in F.S. Regs., Part II. and the Staff Manual respectively. Title Pages will be prepared in manuscript.

Place	Date	Hour	Summary of Events and Information	Remarks and references to Appendices
VIGNACOURT Contd.	1917 May 19th		R.A. H.Qs moved to NAOURS (VIGNACOURT area) - Communication via 182 Bde exchange.	
			Transport moved by road to DOMART-SUR-LA-LUCE area (S.E of AMIENS).	
			Trouble on all lines throughout day caused by Army working party making alterations.	
		2 pm	Transport reached VIGNACOURT - Casualties one horse handed over to Mobile Vetinary Section at NESLE.	
			Sub	
	20th		O.O. Cable Section and No. 39 Wireless/Section joined division from 4th Corps.	
			4th Corps opened at QUERRIEU; work passed direct to them.	
			C.S.M. F.J. Pratt mentioned in C.-in-C's despatches for service in the field.	
DOULLENS	21st	10 am	Divn. Hdqrs. moved to DOULLENS coming under 19th Corps (ST POL).	
			182 Bde. moved to GEZAINCOURT. Communication on existing lines.	
			183 Bde. moved to BEAUVAL. Communication on existing line.	
			184 Bde. moved to OCCOCHES. Single cable laid and Fullerphone worked.	
			R.A.Hdqrs. remained at NAOURS. Communication via BEAUQUESNE Exchange.	
	22nd		No.39 Wireless Sub-Section sent by lorry to 6th Corps.	
LE CAUROY	23rd		Divn. Hdqrs. moved to LE CAUROY (6 miles NNE of DOULLENS) coming under 18th Corps (FOSSEUX).	
			182 Bde. moved to IVERGNY (direct communication).	
			183 Bde. moved to SUS ST. LEGER (direct communication).	

Army Form C. 2118

WAR DIARY
or
INTELLIGENCE SUMMARY

(Erase heading not required.)

Instructions regarding War Diaries and Intelligence Summaries are contained in F. S. Regs., Part II. and the Staff Manual respectively. Title Pages will be prepared in manuscript.

Place	Date	Hour	Summary of Events and Information	Remarks and references to Appendices
LE CAUROY.	24th		184 Bde. moved to BARLY; Communication through 18th Corps. As Divisional Artillery not accompanying Division into line, Lt. BROWNING with one complete and one skeleton Cable Detachment left to join R.A. Hdqrs. on completion of their move. R.A. Hdqrs. moved from MACURS to MONFLAISIR Farm (4 miles west of DOULLENS). Communication via BERNAVILLE Exchange.	
LE CAUROY to WARLUS.	25th to 31st		Div. Hdqrs. moved from LE CAUROY to WARLUS (3 miles W of ARRAS) handing over to 12th Division, and taking over from 56th Divn. Division came under 5th Corps (DUISANS). 182 Bde. moved to BERNEVILLE. 183 Bde. moved to DAINVILLE. 184 Bde. moved to DUISANS. "OO" Cable Section left Division, reporting to advanced 17th Corps ARRAS. At WARLUS re-fitting. Advance parties sent up on various dates to see over new Sector.	

1875 Wt. W593/826 1,000,000 4/15 I.P.C. & A. A.D.S.S./Forms/C. 2118.

O. C., 61st. Divl. S.C.

CONFIDENTIAL
Vol 14

War Diary

OF

61ST DIV. SIGNAL COY RE

FOR THE MONTH OF JUNE 1917

VOL. 14.

Army Form C. 2118.

WAR DIARY
or
INTELLIGENCE SUMMARY.
(Erase heading not required)

Instructions regarding War Diaries and Intelligence Summaries are contained in F. S. Regs., Part II and the Staff Manual respectively. Title pages will be prepared in manuscript.

Place	Date	Hour	Summary of Events and Information	Remarks and references to Appendices
WARLUS. 51.G. K.36.a.	1917. June 1		Div. H.Q. WARLUS. 182 Bde. DUISANS. 183 Bde. DAINVILLE. 184 Bde. at TILLOY under 37th Division, while 112 Bde. 37th Div. had replaced 184 at BERNEVILLE. During the day 182 moved to ACHICOURT and 183 to TILLOY, 184 taking over the front line CAMBRAI ROAD Sector (51.B. 0.14 and 0.8)	
ARRAS.	2	10.0.a.m.	61st Division relieved 37th Div. in CAMBRAI ROAD Sector; 184 in line; 183 Support; 182 Reserve. Advanced Office alongside support Brigade, transmitting messages for Brigade in line, who only had a direct telephone line, one part of which was earth return. Lines in poor state and not properly known. Brigade in line had two amplifiers, 4 power buzzers, wireless Station (working to Corps directing station in ARRAS, and 14 pigeons daily. Artillery support given by 3rd and 4th Div. 184 dissed on direct line by shell fire.	
	3.		Arras shelled by 14" gun; dissed to Corps, brigade in line direct, advanced Corps office, division on left. Line to brigade in line again dissed by shell fire in afternoon, and again with advanced Corps line by bombing in the night.	
	4.		Several lines dissed by shelling of ARRAS. Major F... CLARK, Officer Commanding, awarded Military Cross.	
	5.		Normal day.	
	6.		Many lines dissed in early morning by shelling of ARRAS. New route put through to brigade in line, using permanent route. This allowed direct sounder working.	
	7.		Normal day.	
	8.		C.R.A. 61 Div. relieved C.R.A. 37 Div. in command of Artillery covering Div. front.	
	9.		Divisional front altered, one additional battalion front being taken over on right from 14th Division.	

Army Form C. 2118.

WAR DIARY
or
INTELLIGENCE SUMMARY.
(Erase heading not required.)

Instructions regarding War Diaries and Intelligence Summaries are contained in F. S. Regs., Part II. and the Staff Manual respectively. Title pages will be prepared in manuscript.

Place	Date	Hour	Summary of Events and Information	Remarks and references to Appendices
	10		This was taken over by a Battalion of 187th Bde. 56th Div. 50th Div. Artillery covered this Sub-section of front, connected to advanced Artillery Exchange. One battalion front was given up to 3rd Div. on left. 187 Bde. moved in to TELEGRAPH HILL (51.B. 0.7.a).	
	11th.		R.A. Bdes. of 61st Div. Artillery went into line, relieving 50th Divi. Artillery. 14th Div. came out of line, 18th Div. which had been on its right taking over the portion of its front not taken by 61st Div. 188 Bde. moved from TILLOY to SIMENCOURT (51.B. W.10.d.7.3). 50th Div. relieved 61st Div. in CAMBRAI ROAD Sector. 61st Div. moved to WARLUS. 17th 182 Bde. at DAINVILLE, 184 Bde. at BERNEVILLE. C.R.A. 50th Div. took over artillery command. Lieut. BROWNING with detachment therefore left in ARRAS. C.R.A. 61st Div. remained in ARRAS. Second G.S.(R.D.) wagon, complete turnout, also special draft of 6 other ranks received, consequent on expansion of Company. Capt. C.W. TWYNAM assumed command of Company during absence on leave to U.K. of Major F.W. CLARK.	
WARLUS.	12.		Training and overhauling stores. Amplifier and visual classes started.	
	13.		All messages for Brigades were sent by visual. Lecture to all Signal Officers by Lieut. REDGRAVE on the Power Buzzer and amplifier.	
	14.		R.E. Hqrs. moved from ARRAS to HABARCQ. 182 Bde. moved from DAINVILLE to DUISANS.	
	15) 16) 17)		Normal days.	

Army Form C. 2118.

WAR DIARY
or
INTELLIGENCE SUMMARY.
(Erase heading not required.)

Instructions regarding War Diaries and Intelligence Summaries are contained in F. S. Regs., Part II. and the Staff Manual respectively. Title pages will be prepared in manuscript.

Place	Date	Hour	Summary of Events and Information	Remarks and references to Appendices
WARLUS	18.		All messages not marked "Priority" sent to Bde. by Visual.	
	19		Normal day. Warning order for move of Division issued.	
	20.		Normal day.	
	21.		Normal day.	
	22		Advance party sent over to new area. Company Transport under 2nd Lieut. R.J. SPURR marched to REBREUVE. 183 Bde. moved from SIMENCOURT to BLANGERMONT.	
	23		Divl. Hdqrs. opened at 11.0.a.m. Line laid to 182 Bde. at WAIL. 184 Bde. at FROHEN-LE-GRAND put on to Exchange at DOULLENS. 183 Bde. by D.R. Company Transport under 2nd Lieut. R.J. SPURR arrived.	
WILLEMAN	24.		Line Laid to 183 Bde.	
	25.		No.20 Wireless Sub-Section arrived to join the Coy. under G.H.Q. Letter No.O.B.1026.	
	26.		C.R.E. at VAULX put on to 184 Bde. Exchange.	
	27.		184 Bde. moved from FROHEN-LE-GRAND to VAULX. They still remained on DOULLENS Exchange.	
	28) 29) 30)		Company resting and training. Power Buzzer Courses for Battalion Signallers started again. Visual Signalling Classes for the dismounted men of the Company run.	

Major, R.E.
O. C. 61st. Divl Sig. Coy.

Confidential.

Vol 15

War Diary
of the
61st Divl. Signal Coy. R. E.
for the month of
July 1917.

Volume 15.

Confidential.

Army Form C. 2118.

WAR DIARY
or
INTELLIGENCE SUMMARY.
(Erase heading not required.)

Instructions regarding War Diaries and Intelligence Summaries are contained in F. S. Regs., Part II. and the Staff Manual respectively. Title pages will be prepared in manuscript.

Place	Date	Hour	Summary of Events and Information	Remarks and references to Appendices
WILLEMAN.	1917 July 1st.		(5 miles E. of HESDIN). Div. H.Q. at WILLEMAN: 182 Inf. Bde. at WILLEMAN: 183 Inf. Bde. at BLANGERMONT: 184 Inf. Bde. at VAULX. Divl. Artillery at HABARCQ, West of ARRAS. Normal day.	Reference LENS sheet (5a) 1/100,000
	2nd		Normal day. - Capt. G.S.W. MARCON, 2/4th Oxfords, attached for month's course of instruction.	
	3rd-8th.		Normal days. Training carried on.	
	9th.		2nd Lieut. R.J. SPURR left to command A.N. Cable Section.	
	10th.		Lieut. C.B. BENNETT, with No.2 Detachment, joined Divl. Artillery at ST POL on their move northwards.	
	11th.		Capt. MARCON attached to Signals, 183rd Bde. for instruction. - Normal day.	
	12th.		Normal.	
	13th.		182 & 183 Bde. Sections inspected by O.C.	
	14th.		184 Bde. Section inspected.	
	15th-19th.		Normal days. Visual and Wireless Training carried on.	
	20th.		Route March for Headquarters and No.1 Section.	
	21st-23rd.		Normal days.	

Army Form C. 2118.

WAR DIARY
or
INTELLIGENCE SUMMARY.
(Erase heading not required.)

Instructions regarding War Diaries and Intelligence Summaries are contained in F. S. Regs., Part II. and the Staff Manual respectively. Title pages will be prepared in manuscript.

Reference Sheet 27 1/40,000.

Place	Date	Hour	Summary of Events and Information	Remarks and references to Appendices
WILLEMAN.	July 24th.		Advance party left for new Headquarters by lorry. 182nd Inf. Bde. moved to near FREVENT. Line to 182nd Bde. picked up.	
	25th.		All Brigades moved by train to the ZEGGERS Cappel area. Line to 183rd Bde. picked up.	
ZEGGERS CAPPEL.	26th.		Divl. Hdqrs. closed at WILLEMAN at 9.0.a.m. and reopened at ZEGGERS CAPPEL, with 182 Bde. at RUBROUCK (H.14.a); 183rd Inf. Bde. at ERINGHEM (B.1.a); 184 Bde. at OOST HOUCK (M.S. Central). Communication direct with 8th Corps at ESQUELBECQ, and 182nd & 183rd Bdes. 184th Bde. through 8th Corps. A.M. Cable Section joined Division, being attached for move into 5th Army area.	
	27th-30th.		Normal days.	
	31st.		A.M. Cable Section proceeded to report to A.D. Signals, 18th Corps.	

.... Major, R.E.
O. C. 61st. Divl. Sig. Coy.

CONFIDENTIAL

Vol 17

WAR DIARY

OF

61ST DIVL. SIGNAL CO.

FOR THE MONTH OF

SEPTEMBER 1917

VOL. 17.

Army Form C. 2118.

WAR DIARY
or
INTELLIGENCE SUMMARY.
(Erase heading not required).

Maps. - HAZEBROUCK 5.a. Sheet 28. 1/40,000

Place	Date	Hour	Summary of Events and Information	Remarks and references to Appendices
MERSEY CAMP. BRANDHOEK.	Sept. 1		Divl. H.Q. and Divl. Artillery MERSEY CAMP (Sheet 28 - H.1.a.Central). 182 Bde. in line WIELTJE. 183 Inf. Bde. BRANDHOEK. 184 Inf. Bde. GOLDFISH CHATEAU (28 - H.11.a.5.). Artillery covering the front. - 61st and 36th D.A., 5th & 150th Army F.A. Bdes. organized as two groups each, with two six battery groups. Under 19th Corps. 42nd Div. on Right, 58th Div. on Left. Advanced Office working at CANAL BANK (UB) (28 - I.1.b.8.4). Traffic 2006. New Corps bury from ST JEAN to WIELTJE completed. Took over working of Office at GOLDFISH CHATEAU from Corps.	
	2.		During attack on Hill 35 (28 - I.19.b.0.7) impossible to keep lines through from Brigade Forward Station (BRIDGE HOUSE, H.24.a.3.5.) to Battalion (POMMERN REDOUBT. I.19.a) owing to 5.9 barrage. - Lines cut into one yard lengths. 3 bays of Main Airline Route blown down by shell fire. Traffic.- 2099.	
	3		New Corps bury through from WIELTJE to BRIDGE HOUSE. Bury cut on both sides of WIELTJE. Traffic 2534.	
	4.		Section of buried route blown up; unable to repair as route had not been marked and no records were available. Route had to be abandoned: not very important, as only a lateral. Traffic 2394.	
	5.		No.500318 L/Cpl. HALSE C.H. awarded MILITARY MEDAL for work on August 22nd. Got Sounder Circuit through to WIELTJE and worked superimposed. 62 Hd.Q. established Hdqrs. in MERSEY CAMP as group affiliated to Division. Traffic 2549.	
	6.		Traffic 2354.	
	7.		Capt. C.S.W. MARCON, 2/4th Oxfords, had to return to his Unit, owing to casualties. Lieut. F.T.W. POWER went up to CB to replace him. 19th Corps relieved by 5th Corps.	

Army Form C. 2118.

WAR DIARY
or
INTELLIGENCE SUMMARY.
(Erase heading not required.)

Instructions regarding War Diaries and Intelligence Summaries are contained in F. S. Regs., Part II. and the Staff Manual respectively. Title pages will be prepared in manuscript.

Maps. — HAZEBROUCK, 5.A. Sheet 28. 1/40,000.

Place	Date	Hour	Summary of Events and Information	Remarks and references to Appendices
MERRIS CAMP BRANDHOEK	Sept. 7.		184 Bde. Signals relieved 182 Bde. Signals in line. G.O.C. 184 Bde. commanding with 2 battalions 184 Inf. Bde. on right, 2 Battalions of 183 Inf. Bde. on left. 183 Inf. Bde. Hdqrs. at CANAL BANK. 182 Bde. on relief moved to BRANDHOEK. Traffic 2279.	
	8.		Capt. L.S. PALMER (Sigs, Divl. Artillery) proceeded on 21 days special leave. Lieut. J.B. BROWNING took over charge of Signals, Divl. Artillery. Traffic 2224.	
	9.		Message dogs doing good work between the front and WIELTJE (BRIDGE HOUSE to WIELTJE, 1200 yards in 7 minutes). Dog goes across country at top speed regardless of tracks. Brown dog shell shock, hides in nearest dugout whenever released. 2nd Lieut. G.R. FIRTH sent from Army as supernumerary Officer while the Division is in 5th army area. Many faults on lines. Traffic 2299.	
	10.		Spur from Division to Main Corps Route being regulated. Other route dissed by shell at 8.30.a.m., did not come right till 7.0.p.m. Traffic 2330.	
	11.		Traffic 2080. Kennels built for message dogs and keepers at WIELTJE.	
	12.		Traffic 2466.	
	13.		183 Inf. Bde. moved out to POPERINGHE. Traffic 2256.	
	14.		Advance party of 55th Div. arrived and relieved most of forward personnel, changing instruments. Advance party sent to WATOU to prepare Office there. Traffic 2124.	

Army Form C. 2118.

WAR DIARY
or
INTELLIGENCE SUMMARY.
(Erase heading not required.)

Instructions regarding War Diaries and Intelligence Summaries are contained in F. S. Regs., Part II. and the Staff Manual respectively. Title pages will be prepared in manuscript.

Place	Date	Hour	Summary of Events and Information	Remarks and references to Appendices
WATOU.	Sept. 15.		No.500389 Sapper COCKLE T.G. and No.500294 Sapper CURTIS W.J. awarded MILITARY MEDALS for work on August 22nd. Closed at MERSEY CAMP and opened at WATOU with four working Offices. Circuits in WATOU areas between WATOU and POPERINGHE. Circuits to all three Brigades and 5th Corps. R.F.A. Bdes. still in line, but Divl. artillery moved to HILLHOEK. (Sheet 27 - L.21.c.8.8.) Traffic 708.	
	16		General rest, except for overhaul of Telephones and Exchanges. Lieut. L.S. PALMER in G.H.Q. Gazette as acting Captain whilst O.C. Signals, Divl. Artillery. 500406 Sapper SEALL E.A. and No.500593 Sapper VENN W.H. awarded MILITARY MEDALS for work on August 28th. Traffic 456.	
	17		182 Inf. Bde. moved to EECKE (27 - W.20.D.), 183 and 184 Inf. Bdes. to WORMHOUDT (27-c.16.c) advance party left by lorry for new Headquarters.	
	18		R... pulled out of line and arrived at WATOU. Divl. H.Q. closed down at WATOU, being replaced by 3rd Division, and reopened at DUISANS (Sheet 51c - L.7.b.) under 17th Corps, in 3rd Army. Company marched to CAESTRE (27 - W.32.d.4.2.) where they entrained in evening, reaching ARRAS at 3.30. next morning.	
DUISANS	19.		Detraining very difficult owing to train being pulled up away from platform, and only one ramp being available, which had to be pulled down and rebuilt for each truck. Company reached DUISANS at 8.30.a.m. Brigades reached destination in evening and came through on 'phone. 182 Inf. Bde. BERNEVILLE. 183 Inf. Bde. SIMENCOURT. 184 Bde. AGNEZ les DUISANS. Resting. Traffic 209.	
	20) 21)		Resting.	
	22.		182nd Inf. Bde. moved to LITCHFIELD CAMP. (51b - G.10.c.7.9) coming under orders of 17th Division.	

Army Form C. 2118.

WAR DIARY
or
INTELLIGENCE SUMMARY.
(Erase heading not required.)

Instructions regarding War Diaries and Intelligence Summaries are contained in F.S. Regs., Part II. and the Staff Manual respectively. Title pages will be prepared in manuscript.

Place	Date	Hour	Summary	Remarks and references to Appendices
DUISANS.	Sept. 23rd		182 Bde. took over Right Sector, 17 Div. Front, 183rd Bde. moving up to LITCHFIELD CAMP. R.A. Hqqrs. arrived and opened in ARRAS.	
	24		2/Lt. F.G. LEADER proceeded to Signal Depot, ABBEVILLE, on months wireless Course. at night 183rd Inf. Bde. took over Left Sector, 17th Divl front. 184 Bde. moved up to LITCHFIELD CAMP.	
ST.NICHOLAS	25.		61st Division relieved 17th Division as Left Division, Left Corps, 3rd Army, 15th Div. on right, and 63rd Division on left. Hqqrs. in ST NICHOLAS CAMP G.17.a. Headquarters of both line Brigades in GAVRELLE SWITCH, 182nd Inf. Bde. at H.16.a.1.8, and 183 Bde. at H.10.d.8.3. Reserve Bde. (184) at LITCHFIELD CAMP. 17th Divl. Artillery remained in line. Advanced Offices both for Division and Divl. Artillery in Railway Cutting, at H.14.a.1.7. To this point Division has 3 pairs permanent plus bury, and one pair sunk in River SCARPE. Forward of here all lines run in CORPS bury. wireless in FAMPOUX. 32 Pigeons per day; battalions being ordered to send messages by this means.	Appendix A
	26.		R.F.A. Bdes. arrived from WATOU and went to areas behind ARRAS. Lieut. A.V. McDOWELL proceeded to ENGLAND on 9 weeks Signal Course.	
	27.		Normal. Traffic averaging 900.	
	28.		Normal.	
	29.		First big leave party. (Lieut. L.N. ROGERS and 12 men). 47th Division relieved 63rd Division on left. Sounder superimposed to them.	
	30.		Major P... CLARK proceeded on short leave.	

Maps. 1/100,000. 5.A.
1/40,000. 51.B.

.... Captain R.E
O.C. 61st Divl Sig. Coyr

COMMUNICATIONS IN THE FAMPOUX AREA.

TELEPHONE COMMUNICATION.

Infantry. The four main Telephone Exchanges are as follows:-

(1). Divl. Hdqrs.   (G.17.a.Central).
(2) Adv. Divl. Hdqrs.   (H.13.b.9.8.)
(3) Left Bde. Hdqrs.   (H.10.d.7.1.).
(4) Right Bde. H.Q.   (H.16.d.1.6)

Divl. Hdqrs. Exchange has direct lines to the following places:-

(1) XVII Corps H.Q.   (2 lines).
(2) Adv. Divl. Ex.   (2 lines).
(3) Right Inf. Bde. H.Q.
(4) Right Inf. Bde. Rear Hdqrs.
(5) Left Inf. Bde. Hdqrs.
(6) Reserve Inf. Bde. H.Q.
(7) Division on our Right.
(8) Division on our Left.
(9) Adv. Corps Exchange.
(10) Divl. Train, ARRAS.

and local lines to G. Office, Q. Office, R.A. Hdqrs., S.S.O. Bomb Store, D.A.D.O.S. and C.R.E.

The above lines are all airlines, except the lines running to the Advanced Divl. Exchange and the Bdes. in the line, which are airline as far as H.13.a.1.8. Here the lines are coupled on to the Corps buried system that runs to H.16.d.5.9. Here the buried route splits North and South. The southern bury terminates at Right Battalion Hdqrs. of the Right Bde. and the Northern bury terminates at H.5.d.9.2.

The buried route is the only direct route we have to the two Brigades in the line, and we rely upon the R.A. Liaison lines from Infantry Bdes. to R.F.A. Groups as an alternative means of communication.

Advanced Divl. Exchange. (H.13.b.9.8) This Exchange has the following people connected to it. -

(1) Division (2 lines).
(2) D.C.L.I.
(3) Left Inf. Bde. H.Q.
(4) Right Inf. Bde. H.Q.
(5) Gas Control Post.
(6) Adv. Right Division.
(7) Adv. Divl. Artillery.
(8) Reserve Inf. Bde. of Left Div.
(9) Left Field Coy.

Left Bde. H.Q. Exchange. This Exchange has the following connected to it:-

(1) Division.
(2) Divl. O.P.   (U.C.31)
(3) Right Inf. Bde.   (U.B. 5)
(4) Right Field Coy.   (U.B.21).
(5) Adv. Divl. Exchange.
(6) Adv. Divl. Artillery Exchange (DG).
(7) Adv. Bde. Exchange (for all Battns). 2 lines.
(8) Artillery O.P. - (U.B. 2).
(9) Bde. O.P.
(10) Bde. Runner Post. (U.C.23).

(2).

All four Battalion Hdqrs. are got through the Brigade Forward Exchange at H.6.c.1.2. The lines from the Left Bde. Signal Office to this Forward Exchange are buried.

Forward of this Forward Exchange the lines are pegged into the sides of the trenches.

Right Bde. H.Q. Exchange. The following are connected to this Exchange:-

    (1). Division.
    (2) Advanced Divl. Ex.
    (3) Adv. Divl. Artillery.
    (4) Brigade on Left.
    (5) Machine Gun Coy.
    (6) 2 Bde. Report Centres.
    (7) Wireless Station.

The line to the Right Battalion H.Q. is buried; the remainder of the lines are pegged into the sides of the trenches.

S.O.S. Arrangements. Left Battalion of Left Bde. has a special direct line from its centre Company H.Q. to the Left Bn. H.Q. and on to B. & C. 306 Btys. R.F.A. A S.O.S. Call sent from the Centre Company H.Q. would be received at Battalion H.Q. and the two Battery H.Q. mentioned above.

Similarly the Right Battalion of the Left Bde. has a line running from the Left Company H.Q. to A.306 & D.306 Btys R.F.A.

The Left Bn. H.Q. of the Right Bde. has lines running from the Left and Centre Companies H.Q. through Battalion H.Q. to B.307 & C.307 Btys R.F.A., and the Right Battalion of the Right Bde. has a line running from the centre company to the Right Battalion H.Q. and on to A.307 & D.307 Btys. R.F.A.

Supplementary to the above, each Battalion has installed at one of its forward Company H.Q. a Power Buzzer, all working to either of the two Amplifier Stations - one at the Bde. Forward Station of the Left Bde. and the other at H.18.d.3.1½.

Precautions against overhearing. All communication forward of Bde. H.Q. is by Fullerphone.

Telephones are installed in Brigade, Battalion and Company Hdqrs. for the use of Officers, and they are responsible for what is spoken over the wires.

WIRELESS.

Besides the Amplifiers and Power Buzzers mentioned above there is a Trench Wireless Set at the Right Amplifier Station (H.18.d.3.1½). This Wireless Station works back to the Corps Directing Station in ARRAS, and messages are sent from this Directing Station over the 'phone to Divl. Hdqrs.

VISUAL.

The Left and Right Battalion Hdqrs. of the Left Bde. are both in Visual communication by lamp with the Left Bde. H.Q.

In the Right Bde. area the Right Battalion H.Q. is in direct Visual communication with the Right Bde. H.Q. and the Left Battalion has a Visual Station working back to the Railway arch at H.18.d.3.2. from which point there is a buried cable running back to Bde. H.Q.

PIGEONS.

The Lofts are at ARRAS and 32 birds per day are delivered to this Division, 16 being allotted to each Bde. This allows of four 2-bird Stations being sent up to each Battalion per day.

Actual Service messages are being sent each day by pigeon from Company Hdqrs. and the times taken vary from 26 minutes to 1 hour for the message to reach Battalion Hdqrs.

ARTILLERY COMMUNICATIONS.

These centre on the Advanced Artillery Exchange known as DG. There are two lines from R.A. Hdqrs. to DG, also lines to Corps Heavies, D.A.C. & Wagon Lines, and a direct line to the Left R.F.A. Bde.

From DG there are three lines to the Right R.F.A. Bde. and two to the Left R.F.A. Bde; two to the D.T.M.O. and one to the Medium & Heavy Trench Mortar Batteries; also lines to Div. Artillery and Bdes. R.F.A. on either flank of the Division.

Each Brigade has a line to each Battery, the Batteries having lateral lines between themselves. Batteries each have a line to their own O.P's: these O.P's are connected to the Brigade O.P's, which are connected with one another.

Other Liaison lines between the Artillery and Infantry are described under the Heading "S.O.S. arrangements".

................................Captain R.E.
O.C. 61st Div'l Sig. Coy.

16/

Confidential

Ist

War Diary

of the

61st Divl Signal Co

for

August 1917.

Volume 16

Army Form C. 2118.

WAR DIARY
or
INTELLIGENCE SUMMARY.
(Erase heading not required.)

Instructions regarding War Diaries and Intelligence Summaries are contained in F. S. Regs., Part II. and the Staff Manual respectively. Title pages will be prepared in manuscript.

Place	Date	Hour	Summary of Events and Information	Remarks and references to Appendices
ZEGGERS CAPPEL.	1917 AUG. 1		Divl. Hdqrs. at ZEGGERS CAPPEL. 182 Inf. Bde. at ROUBROUCK (H.14.s.) 183 Inf.Bde. at ERINGHEM (B.1.s.). 184 Bde. at OOSTHOUK (M.o.Central). Divl. Artillery at BRANDHOEK. Communication:- 182 Inf. Bde. direct. 183 Inf. Bde. direct. 184 Inf. Bde. 'phone through 8th Corps at LEDERZEELE, with sounder direct with 8th Corps intermediate. Divl. Artillery at BRANDHOEK through 19th Corps.	Ref. Sheet 27. 1/40,000.
	2 to 8.		Training. Brigade Schemes. - One Brigade Scheme for 183 Bde. Two Brigade Schemes for 182 Bde. and one for 184 Inf. Bde.	
	9.		Capt. A.C. Taylor, Officer i/c 61st Divl. Artillery Signals, evacuated sick to C.C.S. and from here to England. Lieut C.E. Bennett assumed temporary command of R.A. Signals.	
	10 to 13.		Normal days.	
	14.		Advance party under Capt. G.L. TWYNAM left for the new Hdqrs. at POPERINGHE, 16 Place Bertnen.	
	15.		Divl. Hdqrs. closed down at ZEGGERS CAPPEL at 12.noon, reopening at POPERINGHE some time. Transport of the Company moved by road and dismounted personnel by tactical train. 183 Bde. closed down at ERINGHEM and moved by tactical train to POPERINGHE. Direct communication. 184 Inf. Bde. closed down at OOSTHOEK and moved by tactical train to the western outskirts of POPERINGHE. Direct communication. Division in this area came under the orders of 19th Corps.	Ref. - Sheet. 28. 1/40,000.
POPERINGHE.	16.		182 Inf. Bde. closed down at ROUBROUCK and moved by tactical train to BRANDHOEK. Communication through 19th Corps. 183 Inf. Bde. closed down at POPERINGHE and proceeded to YPRES North (GOLDFISH CHATEAU). Communication through the Corps Sub-Office at GOLDFISH CHATEAU.	
	17.			
	18.		185 Inf. Bde. in the evening relieved 2 Bdes. of the 36th Div. holding the line, with Hdqrs. at WIELTJE.	

Army Form C. 2118.

WAR DIARY
or
INTELLIGENCE SUMMARY.
(Erase heading not required.)

Instructions regarding War Diaries and Intelligence Summaries are contained in F. S. Regs., Part II. and the Staff Manual respectively. Title pages will be prepared in manuscript.

Ref:- Sheet 28. 1/40,000.

Place	Date	Hour	Summary of Events and Information	Remarks and references to Appendices
	Aug. 19.		Divl. Hqqrs. closed at POPERINGHE at 12.noon, reopening at MERSEY CAMP (H.1.a.) Sheet 28 at the same hour. 184 Inf. Bde. moved up into support in YPRES North. 182 Inf. Bde. remained at BRANDHOEK. Communication with the front line very bad. All lines to the two main groups and Brigade in the line were in one buried route. At 2.30.p.m. this main route was blown up by a shell near YPRES. Some spare armoured cables which ran between REIGERSBERG CHATEAU and SALVATION CORNER were taken into use. Communication with 182 Inf. Bde. direct. Communication with 184 Bde. through GOLDFISH CHATEAU Exchange.	
MERSEY CAMP 19. H.1.a. Sheet 28.			Capt. L.S. PALMER R.E.(T) reported for duty as Officer i/c. 61st Divl. R.E. Signals, from the 2nd Army Signal Coy, vice Capt. A.C. TAYLOR evacuated to England sick. Lieut. C.E. BENNETT (No.1. Section Officer) wounded by shellfire at ST JEAN and evacuated to C.C.S. and eventually to England. No.500201 Sapper H. BALDWIN was fatally wounded at the same time.	
	20.		183 Brigade relieved by 184 Inf. Bde. in the line, 183 Bde. replacing 184 Bde. in support at GOLDFISH CHATEAU. Enemy aircraft bombed the main permanent line route at 2.30.p.m. Communication was maintained through the Southern loop. Lieut. HUNTER BLAIR (Seaforth Highlanders) temporarily attached for duty from 19th Corps. Signal Coy. A local bury, 150 yards long, from BRIDGE HOUSE (C.24.a.3.6, Sheet 28) was completed, with a view to forthcoming operations.	
	21.		Advanced Divl. Hqqrs. established at 2.p.m. at CANAL BANK. Advanced Divl. Hqqrs. shelled with G.s Shells from 1.30. to 3.30.a.m.	

A5834 Wt. W4973 M687 750,000 8/16 D.D. & L. Ltd. Forms/C.2118/13.

Army Form C. 2118.

WAR DIARY
or
INTELLIGENCE SUMMARY.
(Erase heading not required.)

Instructions regarding War Diaries and Intelligence Summaries are contained in F.S. Regs., Part II. and the Staff Manual respectively. Title pages will be prepared in manuscript.

Ref:- Sheet 28, 1/40,000.

Place	Date	Hour	Summary of Events and Information	Remarks and references to Appendices
	AUG. 22		At 4.45.a.m. 184 Inf. Bde. attacked, with an objective running from C.7.b.5.6. to C.14.c.6.8, with the 15th Div. on the Right and the 48th Div. on the left. (Copy of Communication Orders are attached, also a Map. - Appendix A). After heavy fighting a line was established in front of POND FARM and SOMME FARM. (report on Communications during the Operations is attached. - Appendix B).	
MERSEY CAMP	23	2.30.p.m.	Advanced Divl. Hdqrs. closed down at CANAL BANK and reopened at MERSEY CAMP at 2.30.p.m.	
	24.		Work on the forward buried routes continued.	
	25.		183 Bde. relieved the 184 Bde. in the line, 182 Inf. Bde. moving up in support at YPRES NORTH, with Hdqrs. at GOLDFISH CHATEAU. 184 Bde. moved back in Reserve at BRANDHOEK.	
	26.		A new overland pair running from CANAL BANK via SUMMER HOUSE to aD on poles, and then along GARDEN STREET to WIELTJE was laid. Heavy rain fell during the night.	
	27th.		Advanced Divl. Hdqrs. was opened up at CANAL BANK at 6.p.m. New alternative routes of 2 pairs, both backwards and forwards were available. Stormy weather with heavy showers.	
	28.		183 Bde. having withdrawn slightly from their front line to come into line with Divisions on Right and Left, attacked at 2.0.p.m. Rain had fallen intermittently during the morning and the going was exceedingly heavy. Communications to WIELTJE were satisfactory, but in front of WIELTJE the heavy going delayed the repairs to the wires and messages sent by runners took longer than they would otherwise have. Lieut. HUNTER BLAIR left to take up duty at Sub-Area Officer at 18th Corps. Lieut. F.T.M. POWER (R. Dublin Fus.) joined Company from the 16th Div. No.500123 L/Cpl. C. GARLAND accidentally killed at CANAL BANK by the falling bough of a tree.	

Army Form C. 2118.

WAR DIARY
or
INTELLIGENCE SUMMARY.
(Erase heading not required.)

Ref:- Sheet 28. 1/40,000.

Place	Date	Hour	Summary of Events and Information	Remarks and references to Appendices
MERSEY CAMP.	Aug. 29.		The gale continued. Communications behind 5th Army Area very bad, owing to routes being blown down.	
	30.		A great deal of work was done on the bury, and 19th Corps completed a new bury from ST. JEAN TO WIELTJE.	
	31.		184. Inf. Bde. relieved 183 Bde. in the line, 184 Inf. Bde. moving up in support at GOLDFISH CHATEAU. 183 Bde. in Reserve at BRANDHOEK. A line diagram (Appendix C) was prepared from information supplied by linemen at Test Points and Capt. C.B.W. MARCON, 2/4th Ox. & Bucks L.I. who during the period the Division was in the line acted as Officer i/c. the buried route.	

.... Major, R.E.
O.C. 61st. Divl. Sig. Coy.

APPENDIX A.

SECRET.   G.C.99/B.

SIGNAL INSTRUCTIONS.

TELEPHONIC COMMUNICATION FORWARD OF WIELTJE.

1. RUNNER AND LINESMEN'S RELAY POSTS.

    (1) Runner and Linemen's Relay Posts will be established as follows:-

    No. 1 Relay Post - Concrete dug-out at C.23.c.9.4.
    No. 2   do.   - Concrete dug-out at C.23.d.3½.8½.
    No. 3   do.   - Bridge House (C.23.c.c.5).

    (2) Relay Posts between No. 3 Relay Post and Left Battalion H.Q., and between No. 3 Relay Post and Right Battalion H.Q. will be selected by O. i/c. Signals, 184 Inf. Bde.

    (3) 183 Inf. Bde. will arrange for the above Relay Posts to be cleaned and marked.

    (4) Three metallic pairs of cable will be laid between WIELTJE dug-out and No. 3 Relay Post by the 183 Inf. Bde. by the night of the 20th/21st. Except where these cables are looped into the Relay Posts they will be 50 yards apart.
        Two pairs of lines will be laid between the Brigade Forward Station and the Right and Left attacking Battalions H.Q.

    (5) No.3 Relay Post will be the Brigade Forward Station, and will be equipped to transmit back any message handed in by runners or received on the Amplifier, or sent by Rocket, or Telephone.

    (6) Should the attacking Battalion Commanders decide to move forward, the 3 metallic pairs will be continued from No.3 Relay Post to the trench in front of SPREE FARM at C.18.d.5.6 with a Relay Post at SPREE FARM.

2. LOCATION OF HEADQUARTERS AND FORWARD COMMAND POSTS.

    Brigade H.Q. will be in WIELTJE dug-out.
    Advanced Brigade H.Q. will be in CALL RESERVE at C.23.c.7½.8.
    Advanced Brigade H.Q. of the Bde. on the left - CHEDDER VILLA.
    Advanced Brigade H.Q. of the Bde. on the right - MILL COTS.
    Left Battalion H.Q. - C.18.c.4.7.
    Right Battalion H.Q. - POMMERN REDOUBT.
    Left Battalion of Brigade on Right. - POMMERN CASTLE.
    Right Battalion of Brigade on Left -
    Forward Command Post of Left Battalion. - C.18.b.8.8.
    Forward Command Post of Right Battalion. - SOMME FARM.
    Forward Amplifier Station and Rocket Station - C.18.d.5.6.

3. WIRELESS AND POWER BUZZERS.

    (1) The Corps Direction Station will be at YPRES (I.8.d.0.9). This Station is in telephonic communication with 19th Corps. H.Q. One Trench Set will be installed at WIELTJE. Amplifier and Power Buzzer Stations will be at No. 2 Relay Post, No.3 Relay Post, and at the Rocket Station in the trench at C.8.d.5.6.

(2).

(2) 183 Inf. Bde. will arrange to bury the base lines of the first two of these three Stations.

(3) Power Buzzers will be taken forward by the personnel to establish the Battalion Command Posts and will work to the Forward Amplifier Set.

(4) 184 Inf. Bde. will allot 1 Officer to accompany the Forward Amplifier Station. His duty will be to encode and decode all messages, and he will be responsible for the moving of the Station from SPREE FARM to the trench at C.18.d.5.6. They will also allot a carrying party of 4 men.

(5) An officer will be detailed by the 184 Inf. Bde. to encode and decode messages at the WIELTJE Wireless Station.

4. VISUAL.

A Divisional Visual Station will be situated at C.23.c.6.8. This Station will receive messages from the Left Battalion, No.3 Relay Post, and the two Forward Command Posts of the Atacking Battalions.
On being called up, the Station when ready will give "G" and the message will be repeated by the sender until "R" is given.
The above two signals will be the only signals sent by the Divisional Station.
The Signal Officer of the 184 Inf. Bde. will arrange for all other possible signal communication in front of the Brigade Forward Station, as laid down in S.S. 148.

5. PIGEONS.

Any number of pigeons up to 60 will be available for the 184 Inf. Bde. and the Artillery.
The Officer i/c Signals, 184 Inf. Bde, and the O. i/c. Signals, 61st Divl. Artillery, will inform O.C. Signals, 61st Div. by the evening of the 20th, the number of pigeons they require.

6. SIGNAL ROCKETS.
A Rocket Station will be established in the trench at C.18.d.5.6 to work to No.3 Relay Post.
30 Rockets will be carried forward to this Relay Post.
10 Rockets will be carried forward to the Right and Left Battalion Forward Command Posts.
The Left Battalion Rocket Station will fire at the Left Battn. H.Q., and the Right Battn. Rocket Station will fire from the corner of the hedges at C.13.c.2.3 to No.3 Relay Post.

7. CODE CALLS.

5th Army Code Calls will be used.
The Forward Command Posts of the Battalions will use the Battalion Call receded by the letter "A", as laid down in S.S.148.
    No.1 Relay Post will use the Call - "A".
    No.2 " " " " " " - "B".
    No.3 " " " " " " - "C". if the Brigade Forward Station moves forward to C.18.d.5.6.
The Divl. Visual Station will use the Call - "AU".

8. CODES.
BAB Codes will be used in all messages sent by Wireless or Power Buzzer.

9. **DUMPS.**

The two main Dumps of Twisted Cable D3 will be at WIELTJE i/c Signal Officer in No.a dug-out, and the small Emergency Dump will be kept at No.3 Relay Post.

10. **CONTACT AEROPLANES.**

Separate instructions have been issued under G.C.99/6.

11. **GENERAL.**

The principles as laid down in S.S.148 - "Communication in Battle in the Forward Area", will be adhered to.
The responsibility for communication with the flanking units will be as laid down in this pamphlet.
Two operators for each of the Amplifier Stations will be found by the Divl. Signal Coy.
3 of the 9 operators for the Visual Station will be found by the Divl. Signal Coy; the remainder will be found from the Battalions of the 183 Inf. Bde.

19/8/17.

....Major, R.E.
O. C. 61st Divl Sig. Coy.

COPY.   APPENDIX B.

REPORT ON COMMUNICATIONS DURING THE ATTACK
BY THE 184TH INF. BDE. ON
AUGUST 22nd 1917.

1. **TELEPHONIC COMMUNICATION.**

    The main Cable Route laid overground between WIELTJE dug-out and BRIDGE HOUSE consisted of 3 pairs of Cable laid at least 50 yards apart, except where they were looped into the Relay Posts at C.23.c.9.5 and C.23.d.3½.9 Within 100 yards of BRIDGE HOUSE these three lines were buried 4' 6" deep with an 18" bank on top.

    BRIDGE HOUSE was equipped as the Brigade Forward Station, and two pairs of Cable were laid from here to the attacking Battalions H.Q., one in CAPRICORN TRENCH and the other in POMMERN REDOUBT.

    The 2 pairs running to the Battalion H.Q. in POMMERN REDOUBT had a Relay point at APPLE VILLA.

    4 plus 3 Buzzer Exchanges were installed at each of the Relay Posts and a man was detailed to cross connect the 3 pairs as Sections became broken by shellfire.

    On the whole Telephonic Communication was good. I estimate that after ZERO the lines were through to the Battalions approximately 60% of the time till evening. Some of these lines were so smashed that it was necessary to re-lay sections of them.

    The local bury into BRIDGE HOUSE was a success. It remained unbroken during the whole of the operations, in spite of the heavy barrages put down on this Forward Station.

    A lateral between BRIDGE HOUSE and the Forward Station of the Brigade on our Right held fairly well.

    No line was laid to the Forward Station at BRIDGE HOUSE from the Brigade Forward Station of the Brigade on our Left.

    Lines behind WIELTJE dug-out held all the time, except between Advanced Divl. H.Q. and Divl. H.Q. Here the main bury was cut by a shell at 4.10.a.m. Alternative lines, however, were available until this break was repaired.

    A certain amount of trouble resulted from the terminals in the test points on the main buried route between Advanced Divl. H.Q. and the Bde. in the line, slackening back owing to the vibration caused by the guns in the vicinity.

    The lines from WIELTJE dug-out to the Bde. on the Right and the Bde. on the left held extraordinarily well.

2. **RUNNERS.**

    The Runner Relay System was most satisfactory. At least four Runners should be at each Relay Post, to avoid a runner finding the post unoccupied and having to pass on to the next Post. Also it allows a Runner, on his return journey, to await a favourable opportunity before attempting it.

3. **POWER BUZZERS AND AMPLIFIERS.**

    Communication by this means on the whole was not satisfactory for the following reasons:-

    (1) The Forward Amplifier was in CAPRICORN KEEP, and owing to POND FARM not falling until the afternoon the Station got rather mixed up in the fighting. The proximity of some machine guns and trench mortars, combined with the bombardment, caused the valves to scream so much that tuning was impossible.

    (2). The Battery for the Power Buzzer taken forward by the Left Battalion got damaged, and the Power Buzzer of the Right Bn. was destroyed.

(2)

4. **VISUAL.**

Visual was not so successful as had been expected.

The Left Battalion Forward Visual Station had its Lucas Lamp Appartus put out of action shortly after being established.

The Right Battalion failed to establish a Forward Visual Station. During the morning of the attack the smoke of the barrage, and in the early part of the morning the mist, was very heavy and Visual was practically impossible.

5. **PIGEONS.**

These were not made very much use of.

The Pigeons worked well, but a large number of the
6. Stations were never used.

6. **MESSAGE ROCKETS.**

Only two messages were sent by Message Carrying Rockets. One of these was safely delivered; the other was lost through it landing in soft ground and burying itself.

As far as I can gather Battalions have no faith in these Rockets and fail to make use of them.

7. **CONCLUSIONS.**

(1) Relay Posts. Provided that your Relay Posts afford excellent protection to the personnel manning them, and lines are buried locally around those that are most likely to be smashed, I think it possible generally to keep the lines going most of the time.

The shelling round BRIDGE HOUSE was exceptionally heavy at times, but the cable that had been buried up to it was uncut up to the time the Brigade was relieved.

To save casualties I think it as well for all Relay Posts to be sited so that they are in view of one another. This allows of one runner being sent with a message, and then if he is seen to be hit another can be sent with a copy of the message.

(2) Visual.

Ordinary Visual Signalling is exceedingly difficult, and practically impossible when heavy shelling is going on.

The beam of the Lucas Lamp is rather too narrow and needs careful aligning, which is impossible in the middle of a battle.

(3) Signal Rockets. If the ground is hard and dry these could be used with success, but sufficient supply must be available to instruct the Infantry in their use.

The present Rocket is too clumsy and I would suggest that some form of Rocket fired from a rifle would be the only practical thing to issue to Infantry Battalions. Infantry Signallers have enough to carry without burdening them with a Rocket Firing Stand.

(4) Power Buzzers and Amplifiers. Amplifier Stations should only be installed where the Operators are not likely to be interfered with by the Infantry. I think here again the Infantry Signallers have very little confidence in the Power Buzzer. When training men in Power Buzzer work I think the Power Buzzer Station should be visible from the Amplifier Station, and after the message has been sent to the Amplifier from the Power Buzzer Station it should be repeated back by Visual to the Power Buzzer Station.

August 27th 1917.

.... Major. R.
O. C. 61st Divl. Sig. Coy.

CONFIDENTIAL

Vol 18

WAR DIARY

OF

61ST DIVL. SIGNAL COY

FOR THE MONTH OF OCTOBER 1917

VOL. 18

Army Form C. 2118.

WAR DIARY
or
INTELLIGENCE SUMMARY.
(Erase heading not required.)

Instructions regarding War Diaries and Intelligence Summaries are contained in F. S. Regs., Part II. and the Staff Manual respectively. Title pages will be prepared in manuscript.

Ref Maps:- 51B. 1/40,000. LENS 1/100,000.

Place	Date	Hour	Summary of Events and Information	Remarks and references to Appendices
ST NICHOLAS CAMP.	1917 Oct. 1.		D.H.Q. ST NICHOLAS CAMP (G.17.a): 182 Inf. Bde. - Right Sector: 183 Inf. Bde. - Left Sector: 184 Inf. Bde. In Reserve, LITCHFIELD CAMP (G.10.c.b.5). 15th Div. on Right, 47th Div. on Left: Capt. L.S. PALMER returned from leave. Traffic averaging 875. Signal School of 100 men started under Lieut. F.T.A. POWER.	
	2.		Lines laid for new positions R.F.A. Bde. Hdqrs. The same evening 307 Bde. abandoned their position and chose another.	
	3.		Authority granted for 2nd Lieuts. LEADER, MORRIS, SPURR, to wear badges of Lieutenants.	
	4.		184 Inf. Bde. relieved 183 Inf. Bde. at night in Left Sector. Lieut. F.T.A. POWER went up to be with Bde. during relief, as neither had a Signal Officer.	
	5.		Major P.W. CLARK returned from short leave. Lieut. T.H. MORRIS proceeded on leave.	
	6) 7)		Normal days.	
	8.		Lieut. J.B. BROWNING completed handing over R.A. Signals to Capt. L.S. PALMER and returned to Company.	
	9.		Accommodation for in ARRAS allotted for winter. 306 & 307 R.F.A. Bdes. moved to new Hdqrs. D.T.M.O. took over old 306 Bde. Hdqrs.	
	10 to 13		Normal days. Capt. C.D. TWYNAM proceed on leave on the 11th. Lieut. L.W. Rogers returned	
	14.		Work started on New Hdqrs. Office. - Wardens put in.	

Army Form C. 2118.

WAR DIARY
or
INTELLIGENCE SUMMARY.
(Erase heading not required.)

Instructions regarding War Diaries and Intelligence Summaries are contained in F.S. Regs., Part II. and the Staff Manual respectively. Title pages will be prepared in manuscript.

Place	Date	Hour	Summary of Events and Information	Remarks and references to Appendices
ST NICHOLAS CAMP	15 to 20		Work on lines carried on by Corps to new Office. In sewers of ARRAS, and new eight-pair route built to ST NICHOLAS. New poled lines built from test box on ST POL road for D.A.C. and 306 Bde. R.F.A. wagon lines. Lieut. BROWNING testing out existing lines in sewers.	
	16.		183 Bde. relieved 182 Bde. in Right Sector. 182 Bde. on relief moved into ARRAS.	
	17.		New Exchange put in at KB (old Reserve Bde. position) with connections to wagon lines of 183, 184 Inf. Bdes. and D.G.L.I. Capt. R.W. McKINLAY reported for duty as Officer i/c. Divl. Artillery Signals, replacing Capt. L.S. PALMER, who returned to 2nd Army Signal Coy. for duty.	
	22.		Capt. C.D. TWYNAM returned from leave. Lieut. E.G. LEADER having finished Course at Central Wireless School proceeded on leave.	
	24.		Work started on new system of O.P. Exchanges. Each Battery and Battery O.P. being connected to Exchange at Bde. O.P. instead of direct lines between Batteries and their own O.P's. Corpl. DODD laying armoured kimax cables for this. Work continued on this into November. Major P.W. CLARK proceeded on leave.	
	25 to 27		Normal days.	
	28.		Many faults on lines.	
	29.	11am.	Divl. Hdqrs. moved to 1 RUE DE LA'D HALLUIN, ARRAS: Only Office Staff, D.R's Instruments Repairers quartered in Arras. Remainder of Company stayed at ST NICHOLAS, but moved into Nissen Huts thrown spare. School remained at ST NICHOLAS, also moving into Huts. All lines U.K. except two of three Corps Circuits.	
	30) 31)		Normal days. Work continued on O.P's Exchange System and "River line" poled.	

..........Captain P.E.
O.C. 61st Divl. Sig. Coy.

CONFIDENTIAL

Vol 19

WAR DIARY
OF
61ST DIV. SIGNAL COY

For the month of November 1917

VOL. 19.

Army Form C. 2118.

WAR DIARY
or
INTELLIGENCE SUMMARY.
(Erase heading not required.)

Instructions regarding War Diaries and Intelligence Summaries are contained in F.S. Regs., Part II. and the Staff Manual respectively. Title pages will be prepared in manuscript.

MAPS:— Lens 11, 1/100,00. Sheet 51.b.1/40,000

Place	Date	Hour	Summary of Events and Information	Remarks and references to Appendices
ARRAS.	Nov. 1st.		Divl. Hdqrs. at No.1 Rue le de l'Abbe Halluin. 182 Bde. Right Sector, 184 Bde. reserve, A.H.S. 185 Bde. Left Sector, 185 Bde. Right on Left. Division under 17th Corps. 15th Div. on Right; 47th Div. By 3rd Army Orders all Telephones in front of Bde. Hdqrs. were withdrawn. This left no direct communication between Liaison Officers at Infantry Battalions and the Guns owing to the inability of the R.F.A. personnel to use Fullerphones.	
	2nd.		Poling and treeing of River Line. Lieut. E.J. Leader returned from Leave. All Horses and Mules passed through Sulphur Dip.	
	3rd.		Corpl. Fitzhenry started erecting permanent route to D.T.M.O. Good progress being made in the construction of the new Dismal O.P. at i.11.c.7.4	
	4th.		Lieut. R.T.M. POWER went on leave, Lieut. J.B. Browning taking over command of the Signal School.	
	5th.		Corpl. Fitzhenry finished 4-way permanent route to D.T.M.O.	
	6th.		The Cable thrown spare by D.T.M.O route picked up. The Forward Exchange system for R.A. finished. Corps constructed two-pair airline from CARLISLE Test Point to ST VAAST BRIDGE, replacing part of the Cable to D.A.C. & R.F.A. Bde. wagon lines. Lieut. E.G. LEADER to hospital.	
	7th.		Corps Amplifier still picking up messages, though these messages were being sent by Fullerphone. A great deal of trouble was experienced, Fullerphones being stated leaky, but as the Amplifier Loop Circuit ran pinned in to the same trench walls as the circuit from which messages were picked up for a considerable distance, it is not altogether clear that that is the true explanation. The insulation of the lines was stated to be faulty, but as Fullerphones were originally intended to be worked on earth return circuits and were said to be proof against overhearing it does not seem that badly insulated wires caused this trouble.	
	8th.		Corpl. Fitzhenry building comic pair to connect with permanent route running to Divl. Arty. on left.	

WAR DIARY
or
INTELLIGENCE SUMMARY.

(Erase heading not required.)

Army Form C. 2118.

Instructions regarding War Diaries and Intelligence Summaries are contained in F. S. Regs., Part II. and the Staff Manual respectively. Title pages will be prepared in manuscript.

Remarks and references to Appendices: LENS 11, 1/100,000. Sheet 51.B. 1/40,000.

Place	Date	Hour	Summary of Events and Information
ARRAS.	Nov. 9th.		Playing up lines in ARRAS. Comic line to Divl. Artillery on Left finished. 17th Corps Hqqrs. shifted from EIRUN to DUISANS. Special Test carried out with amplifier, to see whether Sounder Signals could be picked up, as Left Bde. amplifier at H.17.9.8.7 was getting them strong. Found that Signals were very powerful when amplifier Base was practically in the front line. The number of cells on Battery at Left Bde. Sounder cut down from 20 to 14, but Signals were still overheard. It was then discovered that the Sounder Earth was attached to an armoured Cable running forward. This was removed and a separate earth put in, but loud signals were still picked up. A separate cable pair was then run from a different test box by an entirely separate route with a separate lead into the Office, but even so the Signals were still picked up. The Same Amplifier on occasions picked up signals from the Right Bde. Sounder, and could also hear Power Buzzers working some considerable distance South of the RIVER SCARPE, the ground being extraordinarily good for Power Buzzer working. The Right Amplifier in FAMPOUX, however, did not pick up signals from either Sounder. As some of the earths of the Left Amplifier lay over the main buried route, whilst the Right Amplifier was far from anything of the sort, possibly these Signals were the result of induction from the pair on which the Sounder was working on to other pairs running forward through the bury, the Amplifier picking up the currents thrown off from this, though the amount of current passing through was not enough to interfere at all with conversation on any circuit. Major P.W. CLARK returned from leave.
	10th.		184 Inf. Bde. relieved 183 Inf. Bde. in Right Sector. Lieut. E.G. LEADER to Corps Rest Station.
	11th.		Corpl. Barton began job of laying armoured cables down CHILI AVENUE for R.A., finishing on Nov. 18th. 306 Bde. R.F.A. withdrawn from line, coming under orders of 4th Corps on the 14th. Batteries of 307 Bde. R.F.A. re-distributed to cover the whole front.
	12th.		Corpl. Lodd built comic route from River Line to Advanced Office in RAILWAY CUTTING.
	13.) 14.)		Normal days.

Army Form C. 2118.

WAR DIARY
or
INTELLIGENCE SUMMARY.
(Erase heading not required.)

Instructions regarding War Diaries and Intelligence Summaries are contained in F.S. Regs., Part II. and the Staff Manual respectively. Title pages will be prepared in manuscript.

LENS 11, 1/100,000. Sheet 51.B. 1/40,000.

Place	Date	Hour	Summary of Events and Information	Remarks and references to Appendices
ARRAS.	Nov. 15th.		At 12.15.p.m. Test Box on Main Corps Bury, through which all lines except one passed maliciously destroyed, panels being smashed with a pickaxe and all lines torn out. The culprit was not found.	
	16th.		Divl. Visual Station taken into use, but as Brigades attempted to get Company lamps aligned in daylight, none of them were through. This went on for several days, until finally a beam was shown from the Divl. Station after dark, when the outlying Lamps were aligned without the least trouble. 2nd Lieut. R.P. Martin R.E. reported from 3rd Army as supernumerary Officer.	
	17th.		Major P.W.Clark to ABBEVILLE for a weeks Wireless Course.	
	18th.		Scheme got out for new uses of lines in the event of any withdrawal and Divl. Hdqrs. moving forward. Corps finished diverting lines from the round-about route through ST NICHOLAS CAMP on to direct route from ARRAS to the bury. Lieut. E.G. Leader evacuated from C.R.S. to 8th C.C.S. and from there to No.1 Stationary Hospital, ETRETAT.	
	19th.		51st Division extended their front, taking over front of 47th Division in addition, and becoming Division on Left. No direct communication to them. In view of approaching operations Lieut. J.B. BROWNING brought in to Hdqrs., 2nd Lieut. R.P. MARTIN being sent to take charge of Signal School.	
	20th.		British attack at CAMBRAI started. From Zero use of Telephones again allowed.	
	21st.		183 Inf. Bde. relieved 182 Inf. Bde. in GREENLAND HILL (Left) Sector.	
	22nd. Signals, R.A.		Capt. R.W. MCKINLAY went on leave, Lieut. J.B. BROWNING taking over charge of Lieut. R.P. MARTIN sent on leave.	
	23rd.) 24th.)		Quiet days, with everything in readiness for forward move.	

Army Form C. 2118.

WAR DIARY
or
INTELLIGENCE SUMMARY.
(Erase heading not required.)

Instructions regarding War Diaries and Intelligence Summaries are contained in F. S. Regs., Part II. and the Staff Manual respectively. Title pages will be prepared in manuscript.

LENS 11, 1/100,000.   Sheets 51.B. & 57.C.   1/40,000.

Place	Date	Hour	Summary of Events and Information	Remarks and references to Appendices
ARRAS.	Nov. 25th.		Major P.W. CLARK returned from Course at ABBEVILLE. Circuits to 15th Division and Reserve Bde. diverted and shortened.	
	26th.		Normal.	
	27th.		Warned that Division was being pulled out of the line, 15th Division to take over front. Division to go South to the CAMBRAI area. Capt. R.W. MACKLIN and six O.R's were therefore recalled from leave. Signal School closed down without completing full Course.	
	28th.		182 Inf. Bde. moved to DAINVILLE. Relief of Brigades in the line started.	
	29th.		On completion of relief 183 & 184 Inf. Bdes. both established Reserve Bde. positions in ARRAS. Command of line passed to G.O.C. 15th Division at 10.a.m, 61st Div. Artillery taking charge of all Artillery covering the whole 15th Division front. At 8.0.a.m. Captain C.D. TWYNAM left to find new hdqrs., proposed to be North or HARLINCOURT. On arrival at 4th Corps Hdqrs. VILLERS AU FLOS the Camp Commandant was informed that Hdqrs. would be at LITTLE WOOD, YPRES, so he proceeded there. Within five minutes of arrival a telephone message was received to say Hdqrs. would not be there, so he returned to VILLERS AU FLOS and proceeded to GREVILLERS, where we were to take over the Advanced 5th Corps Hdqrs, 5th Corps relieving 4th Corps next day. Brigades were to be at BERTHAUCOURT, BERTINCOURT and LEBHELLE.	
		3.0.pm.	Captain C.D. TWYNAM informed O.C. Company where lorry with Advance Party should be sent, advised him that Division was going to consolidate and hold line which had been gained, and that accommodation was very bad, so that it was advisable to bring as much as possible from ARRAS. Lorry duly arrived at GREVILLERS, was unloaded and sent back. S	
	30th.		Sudden German counter-attack, breaking the British front on large area and penetrating to west of GOUZEAUCOURT. Guards Division thrown in to save situation, retook GOUZEAUCOURT. 61st Division rushed up as Reserve.	
		9.0.a.m.	Transport moved at 9.0.a.m. under Lieut. F.T.A. Power. Lieut. J.B. BROWNING, the other hdqr. subaltern, was at R.A.	
		11.0.am.	Relief of 4th Corps by 5th Corps was cancelled. 5th Corps returned to GREVILLERS.	

WAR DIARY
or
INTELLIGENCE SUMMARY.
(Erase heading not required.)

Army Form C. 2118.

Instructions regarding War Diaries and Intelligence Summaries are contained in F. S. Regs., Part II. and the Staff Manual respectively. Title pages will be prepared in manuscript.

Place	Date	Hour	Summary of Events and Information	Remarks and references to Appendices
	Nov. 30th.		Hqrs. 61st Division, ordered to be established at Little Wood, YTRES. O.C. Company informed, and advised would be in action immediately. No transport available to move advance Party from GREVILLERS to YTRES so Box Car commandeered and small party, with necessary instruments rushed across. General Staff at BAPAUME STATION. Despatch Riders sent there for Staff to keep touch with Units. As fast as trains with Infantry Battalions arrived at BAPAUME STATION men were loaded on motor Busses and sent forward. Transport halted outside BAPAUME until about 3.0.p.m. waiting for orders re new destination. G.O.C. & G.S.O.1 proceeded to Guards Division Hdqrs. METZ. Wire sent from there ordering 61st Division to concentrate, with 183 Inf. Bde. at TRESCAULT, 182 Inf. Bde. METZ, and 184 Bde. RUYAULCOURT area. Leading Battalions said to be arriving about 5.0.p.m.	RcH:- Sheets. LENS 11. VALENCIENNES 13. 1/100,000. 57.C. 1/40,000.
		7.0.pm. Mdnt.	O.C. proceeded to METZ to open an Office there. Orders received for Division to concentrate on the Right of the area. - 182 Inf. Bde. at HEUDECOURT, 183 Inf. Bde. at METZ, 184 Inf. Bde at FINS, Division to be available for assistance of 7th, 3rd or 4th Corps. Advance Divl. Hdqrs. to be at FINS. Soon after midnight Transport arrived at YTRES having marched 30 miles.	
	Dec. 1st.	6.30.a.m.	At 6.30.a.m. two detachments were again on the move for FINS, and the remainder of the Company left at 7.0.a.m. for the new Rear Hdqrs. at ETRICOURT. From GREVILLERS communication to all Brigades was to have been through 4th Corps. From LITTLE WOOD a pair was available to BERTINCOURT, where the 184 Inf. Bde. Hdqrs. were established. A direct pair was also put through between LITTLE WOOD and METZ. (See Appendix A) At 7.0.a.m. when the Rear Hdqrs. were moved to ETRICOURT, there were men of Hdqrs. & No.1 Section either actually working Offices or in charge of Stores at METZ, FINS, ETRICOURT, LITTLE WOOD, GREVILLERS and ARRAS.	

Major, R.E.
O.C. 61st. Divl/Sig Coy

GREVILLERS

LITTLEWOOD YTRES

FINS

METZ
on Arrival

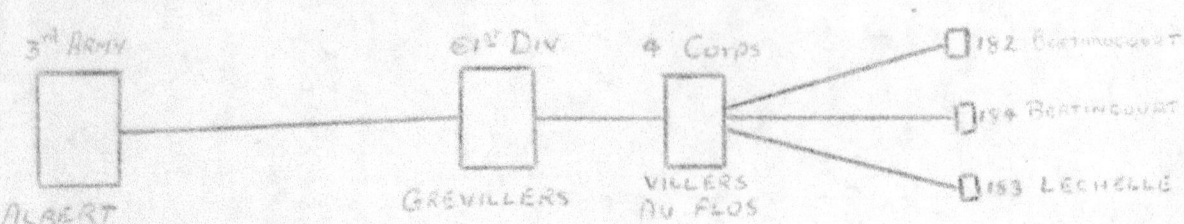

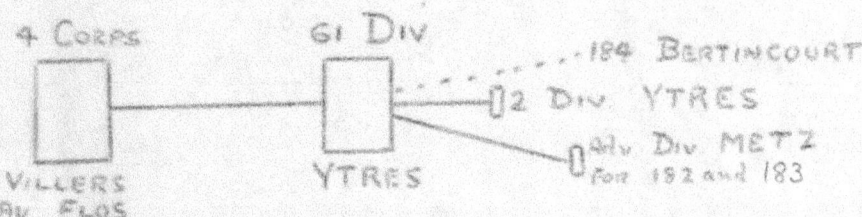

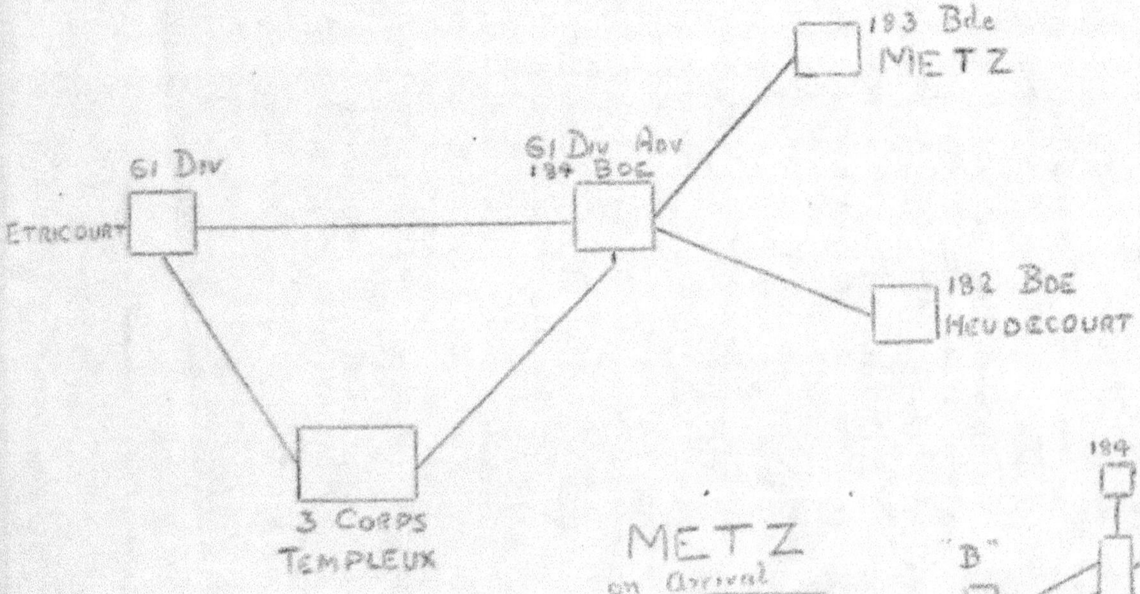

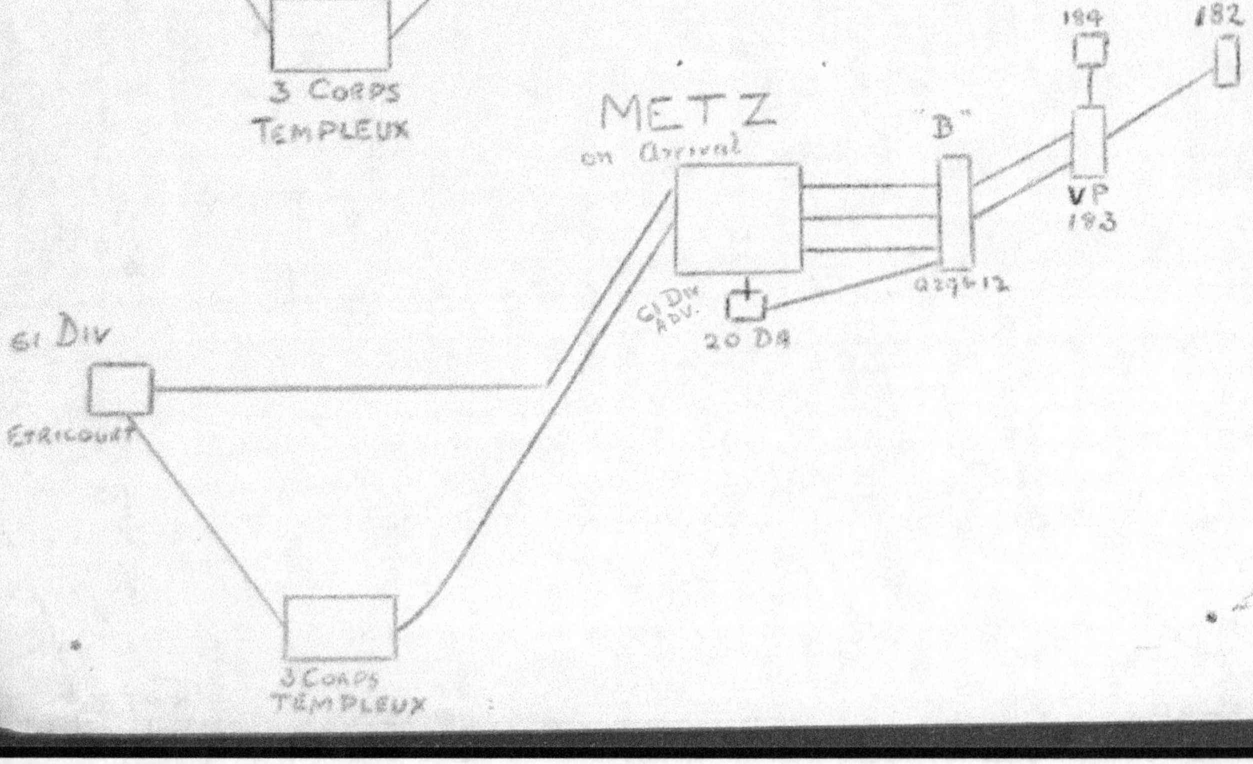

Confidential ~~Vol V~~

WAR DIARY

OF

61st Div. Signal Coy RE

For the month of DECEMBER 1917

VOL. 20.

Army Form C. 2118.

WAR DIARY
or
INTELLIGENCE SUMMARY.
(Erase heading not required.)

WAR Ref:- LENS 11, VALENCIENNES 12, 1/10,000.
Sheet No.57.C. 1/40,000.

Place	Date	Hour	Summary of Events and Information	Remarks and references to Appendices
METZ.	Dec. 1st	9.0.a.m.	61st. Div. ETRICOURT; Adv. Div. H.Q. FINS; 182 Inf. Bde. HEUDECOURT; 183 Inf. Bde. 184 Inf. Bde. FINS; under 3rd Corps. During the morning D5 pairs were laid between ETRICOURT and FINS, FINS & HEUDECOURT; and a permanent pair was loaned by 3rd Corps for communication to METZ. The Division was concentrated in this area for the purpose of:- (1) Supporting 7th Corps. (2) Assisting Counter attack by 3rd Corps. (3) Assisting 4th Corps. During the day 183 Inf. Bde. were put under the orders of 20th Division and relieves their Right Bde. on the night 1st/2nd. YF&R (Adv. Div. H.Q.) closed at FINS at 4.45.p.m., but an Exchange was kept open. 499933 Pioneer McWHIRTER R, 306 Bde. R.F.A. Signal Sub-Section wounded.	
at METZ.	Dec. 2nd		Orders received for 61st Division to relieve 20th Division, with Adv. Div. H.Q. D5 pairs were laid between YTR (20th Div). and METZ during the day, but an Exchange at YTR (Q.29.b.2.1) was kept going. The relief of the 20th Divl. Signal Coy. by 61st Divl. Signal Coy. was completed during the night of the 2nd/3rd. Traffic.- 949.	
C.R.a. 20th Div.	3rd.		Change of Command passed from G.O.C. 20th Division, to G.O.C. 61st Division at 6.30.a.m. 20th Div. continued to command the Artillery covering the front. Communication to Brigades in the line was by buried route from Q.29.b.2.1 to 'A'Test Point at R.19.b.5.3; from here to 'VP' Exchange in VILLERS PLOUICH by two cable routes,- one, part of the way in a communication trench, and the other in a sunken road. Linemen were posted at 'B' Test Point (Q.29.b.2.1); 'A' Test Point (R.19.b.5.3) and at the Left Cable Head at R.8.d. At 8.0.a.m. very heavy German attacks were launched on the whole Divisional front, particularly against La. VaCQUERIE, which the enemy succeeded in taking, though 183 Inf. Bde. hung on to the outskirts of the village and corner work. Owing to their line being driven back 182 Inf. Bde. moved their Headquarters to R.3.c.0.8. As a result of this, communication to them was impossible for a considerable time. The line to their old position had been badly cut about, and when linemen reached it with a fresh line they were found to have	

Army Form C. 2118.

WAR DIARY
or
INTELLIGENCE SUMMARY.
(Erase heading not required.)

Map Refs. Sheets - LENS 11, VALENCIENNES 12, 1/100,000
57D, 1/40,000

Place	Date	Hour	Summary of Events and Information	Remarks and references to Appendices
	Dec. 3rd.		moved, and no information could be obtained as to where they had gone. The back lines from 'VP' to 'A', and 'B' Point to Division were also frequently cut, but were never all down at the same time. C.R.E. 20th Division, moved his Hdqrs. back to METZ. Group Hdqrs. were also moved back. Wireless Station erected at VP, working to Corps Directing Station at TRESCAULT and Army Directing Station at ETRICOURT, also Station at Divl. Hdqrs. No.500299 Sapper H.E. BRINKWORTH, 183 Bde. Signal Section wounded.	
	4th.		There were no attacks by the enemy on a large scale, but considerable Artillery activity and continual bombing attacks, the chief object being to capture the forward side of WELSH RIDGE which gave observation towards CAMBRAI. The enemy failed to retain the ground which he did capture. A new line was laid to 184 Inf. Bde. approaching BEAUCAMP from the Southwest instead of running down the La VACQUERIE Valley, thus avoiding the very heavy shellfire there. A line was got through to 182 Inf. Bde. on the Left from 'VP' and communication to them could also be obtained through a couple of Battalion lines. 108 Inf. Bde., 36th Division, came under orders of 61st Division. No.223121 Pnr. Alexander T.C., 182 Bde. Signal Section wounded. Continual trouble on Corps line, causing great delay to traffic. No. 72214 Sapper G.W. Booth and No.500322 Sapper G.H. House, remained out in the open all night 'feed in' on the line from 183 Inf. Bde. to 184 Inf. Bde., under heavy H.E. and gas shell bombardment without being ordered to do so, in order to localize breaks quickly and hasten the repairs. They were awarded the MILITARY MEDAL for this on Jan.10. 1918. Traffic - 1329.	
	5th.		182 Inf. Bde. moved during the day to w.12.a.8.6. A new line was laid to this position, approaching it from the West and making use of a bury through HAVRINCOURT WOOD. Heavy German attacks took place during the afternoon gaining a little ground. 9th Division relieved the Guards on our Right. 109th Brigade took over Left Brigade front down to R.5. Central. At night 184 Inf. Bde. relieved 183 Inf. Bde. Reserve Bde. H.W. moved to METZ. Further attacks took place at 9.0.p.m. and were unsuccessful. Traffic - 1490.	

No. 500142 Pnr. W.H. Liddicoat, 182 Bde. Signal Section wounded.

WAR DIARY
or
INTELLIGENCE SUMMARY.
(Erase heading not required.)

Army Form C. 2118.

Sheets LENS 11, VALENCIENNES 13, 1/100,000.
57.C. 1/40,000.

Place	Date Dec.	Hour	Summary of Events and Information	Remarks and references to Appendices
Office.	6th.		A 'tee' off the Left Bde. Line laid the previous day was taken into the 184 Bde. By Cable Section attached to the Division. A direct cable pair was laid to Left Bde by this Section from METZ. 183 Inf. Bde. having withdrawn there was no longer any necessity to keep the lines going up the FLOUICH VALLEY; 'A' Point and 'VF' were therefore closed down. The Wireless Station was removed to 182 Inf. Bde. Hdqrs. Pigeons were obtained for the first time and sent up to Brigades. 36th Division relieved 29th Division on our Left. We had taken traffic for them for one or more of their Brigades during the previous 48 hours and continued to work the whole of their communications for the next 24 hours. This put a great strain on our Brigades, as Units of 36th Division were obtained through them. Fighting continued for the WELSH RIDGE Spur all day. At night the remainder of the 182 Inf. Bde. front was divided between 184 Inf. Bde. and 109 Inf. Bde on our Left. 182 Inf. Bde. withdrew to METZ. Traffic - 1621.	
	7th.		Much trouble on lines in the early morning. At 2.0.p.m. Adv. Div. Hdqrs. closed at METZ and re-opened at NEUVILLE BOURJONVAL. By Section laid a line between the two places and three existing lines were picked up. The METZ. Office remained open and for some time all messages had to be transmitted through it. Traffic - 1504.	
	8th.		Owing to the contraction of the Divl. front and Hdqrs. being in the neighborhood of BERTCAMP, reached by lines from the back, a large number of lines to 'B' Point were not required and two were recovered. There was a good deal of trouble on the direct 184 Bde. line from enemy shelling, but the line through 'A' and 'VF' remained through the whole time though there were no linemen to look after it. Traffic was extremely heavy and two sounders were employed continuously. Traffic:- 2092.	

WAR DIARY
or
INTELLIGENCE SUMMARY.

(Erase heading not required.)

Army Form C. 2118.

Sheets LENS 11, VALENCIENNES 12, 1/100,000.
57.C. 1/40,000.

Place	Date	Hour	Summary of Events and Information	Remarks and references to Appendices
	Dec. 9th.		6th Division were shelled out of HAVRINCOURT WOOD and retired to NEUVILLE. As they had no lines they worked through us. Our Wireless Set also worked for them. A census of the work in the YFAR office showed that 40% was for outside Units. The totals for this Office alone were averaging 1200 at this time. Traffic - 2118.	
	10th.		METZ violently shelled. Great difficulty was experienced in keeping touch with Brigades at all all day. A direct circuit to the Brigade in the line and METZ, running through the bury in HAVRINCOURT WOOD was put through. At night 182 & 183 Inf. Bdes. relieved 184 Inf. Bde., each with two weak Battalions in the front line. Traffic Traffic 1863.	
	11th.		Enemy activity slackened appreciably and all lines were O.K. at 4.p.m. and remained so the whole night. Traffic 1863.	
	12th.		Poling of the forward lines was continued.	
	13th.		61st Divl. Artillery took over from 20th D.A. There was heavy shelling around the Right Bde. Hqrs. No.500372 Sergt. B.S. Owen, 183 Bde. Signal Section wounded. Traffic:- 1839.	
	14th.		Lieut. R.J. SPURR rejoined the Company, replacing Lieut. E.G. LEADER sick to England. Lieut. F.T.A. POWER posted to 184 Inf. Bde. Signal Section. No.59448 Corpl. T.F. GLENNY & No.500314 L/Cpl. G.W. BABB, 183 Inf. Bde.Signal Section awarded MILITARY MEDALS. Traffic 1828.	
	15th.		3rd Corps was squeezed out and 61st Division came under 5th Corps. Work on poling lines continued. Traffic - 1754.	

Army Form C. 2118.

WAR DIARY
or
INTELLIGENCE SUMMARY.
(Erase heading not required.)

Instructions regarding War Diaries and Intelligence Summaries are contained in F. S. Regs., Part II. and the Staff Manual respectively. Title pages will be prepared in manuscript.

Place	Date	Hour	Summary of Events and Information	Remarks and references to Appendices
	Dec. 16th.		184 Inf. Bde. relieved 182 & 183 Bdes. One detachment of WE Cable Section was sent up by 5th Corps to replace them. The Artillery covering the front was redistributed, necessitating the laying of new lines. Traffic - 1746.	
	17th.		Heavy snowstorm. Motor Cyclist Despatch Riders doing D.R.L.S. Circuits on horseback. Traffic - 2102.	
	18th.		Nothing of special interest. 63rd Division in process of relieving 36th Division. Traffic - 2162	
	19th.		188 Inf. Bde. took over Left Battalion front, thus releasing 182 Inf. Bde. who moved back to ETRICOURT. Heavy bombing of back areas by enemy aeroplanes. Traffic - 1855.	
	20th.		184 Inf. Bde. relieved 183 Inf. Bde. making their Hdqrs. in what had been the support Battalion Hdqrs. in VILLERS PLOUICH, 1000 yards from the front line. The extent of front held by the Division was only 1000 yards. Traffic - 1832. Lieut R.J. SPURR went on leave.	
	21st.		'VP' and 'A' Point were again manned. A new direct line was laid from METZ to 'VP', striking straight across country. A new line was also laid from 'A' Point to 'VP'. 306 Bde. R.F.A. was the only Field Artillery covering our front. Detachment of WE Cable Section handed over to 63rd Division. Traffic - 1884.	

A834. Wt.W4973/M687 750,000 8/16 D. D. & L. Ltd. Forms/C.2118/13.

Army Form C. 2118.

WAR DIARY
or
INTELLIGENCE SUMMARY.
(Erase heading not required.)

Instructions regarding War Diaries and Intelligence Summaries are contained in F. S. Regs., Part II. and the Staff Manual respectively. Title pages will be prepared in manuscript.

Place	Date Dec.	Hour	Summary of Events and Information	Remarks and references to Appendices
	22nd.		Much bombing of back areas at night, with the result that Corps was 'dis' to nearly everyone. A message announcing the completion of the relief of 184 Inf. Bde. xxx by 63rd Division, which was sent off at 7.30.p.m. did not reach 63rd Division until midnight. As this relief meant that 61st Division had no troops left in the line, command of the Sector passed to G.O.C. 63rd Division on completion of the relief. 184 Inf. Bde. went to LECRELLE.	
	23rd.		Div. Hdqrs. remained at NEUVILLE, though the Division was out of action. 'P', 'A' & 'B' Test Points and METZ were all closed down, and concentrated on ETRICOURT. Advance party was sent over to new Hdqrs. at MERICOURT-SUR-SOMME. and other Offices which had been at ETRICOURT also moved over. The roads were very slippery and frost bound, with 3-ft. snow drifts in places. From MERICOURT there was no communication to anyone.	
	24th.		advanced Div. Hdqrs. NEUVILLE closed down at 8.0.a.m. Divl. Hdqrs. opened at MERICOURT-SUR-SOMME. There was no communication with 18th Corps, under whose orders the Division came, until the evening. Transport had to move by road and was at the back of a column of two Brigades transport and was delayed 2 hours at the starting point. It was found impossible to reach MERICOURT the same day, and Lieut. Browning, therefore, stopped the column for the night at CLERY. AC Cable Section joined the Division for the move. 182 Bde. Hdqrs. were at SAILLY LAURETTE. 183 " " " BRAY. 184 " " " SUZANNE. R.A. Hdqrs. remained at NEUVILLE. Traffic - 300.	

Army Form C. 2118.

WAR DIARY
or
INTELLIGENCE SUMMARY.
(Erase heading not required.)

Sheet:- AMIENS 17.

Place	Date	Hour	Summary of Events and Information	Remarks and references to Appendices
MERICOURT-SUR-SOMME	Dec. 25th.		Transport arrived in the afternoon, and the whole Company was concentrated for the first time since the advance party left ARRAS on November 29th. Traffic - 229.	
	26th.		A pair was put through to BRAY along a derelict French route, and a pair from SAILLY LAURETTE was reconnoitred. R.A. Hdqrs at TREUX, Northeast of CORBY. and	
	27th.		A line was put through to SAILLY LAURETTE from BRAY TO SUZANNE.	
	28th.		Warning Order received for Division to move to HARBONNIERES area. Captain R.W. MACKINLAY proceeded on leave.	
	29th.		Company Christmas Dinner.	
	30th.		Overhauling of Stores.	
HARBONNIERES	31st.		Divisional Hdqrs. moved to HARBONNIERES. 182 Inf. Bde. H.Q. to LE QUESNOY. 183 Inf. Bde. H.Q. to MARCELCAVE. 184 Inf. Bde. H.Q. to ROSIERES. R.A. Hdqrs. to CAIX.	

..................Major, R.E
O. C. 61st. Divl Sig. Coy.

Confidential

WAR DIARY

OF

61st DIVL. SIGNAL COY. RE.

For the month of January 1918

VOL. 21.

Vol 21

Army Form C. 2118.

WAR DIARY
or
INTELLIGENCE SUMMARY.
(Erase heading not required.)

Instructions regarding War Diaries and Intelligence Summaries are contained in F.S. Regs., Part II. and the Staff Manual respectively. Title pages will be prepared in manuscript.

Place	Date 1918.	Hour	Summary of Events and Information	Remarks and references to Appendices

	Jan. 1		61st Divl. Hdqrs. - HARBONNIERES. 182 Inf. Bde. Hdqrs. - LE QUESNOY. 183 Inf. Bde. Hdqrs. - MARCELCAVE. 184 Inf. Bde. Hdqrs. - ROSIERES. R.A. Hdqrs. - CAIX. All Brigades were put on the Telephone by repairing and putting through derelict French lines. The following Half-Yearly Awards were published.
			
			MILITARY CROSS. - Lieut. T.H. Morris.
			                              Lieut. E.G. Leader.
			MERITORIOUS SERVICE MEDAL. - 2316 C.S.M. Pratt F.J.
			DISTINGUISHED CONDUCT MEDAL - 500372 Sergt. Owen B.S.
			MENTIONED IN DESPATCHES. - Lieut. C.K. Bennett.
			                                      500130 Sergt. Fowles W.J.	

	2 - 5		All normal days.	
	6		Advance Party left for the new Divl. Hdqrs. NESLE, also party of linemen for AUBOIR, the Hdqrs. of the 5th French Infantry Division, whom we were ordered to relieve.	
	7		61st Divl. Hdqrs. moved to NESLE. 182 Inf. Bde. Hdqrs. to NESLE. 183 Inf. Bde. Hdqrs. to ROYE. 184 Inf. Bde. Hdqrs. to VOYENNES. R.A. Hdqrs. remaining at CAIX. No Brigades were on the Telephone.	
	8.		Conference with Signals, 5th French Division.	
	9.		Normal day. Lieut. J.B. BROWNING proceeded to U.K. on 14 days Leave.	
	10.		Captain C.D. TWYNAM, with some operators and linemen proceeded to AUBOIR to fix up an Exchange and get two lines forward to where the Brigade Hdqrs. were to move. 184 Inf. Bde. relieved the Left Regiment of the 5th French Division at night.	
	11.		Further work in the AUBOIR district. 182 Inf. Bde. relieved the Right Regiment of the 5th French Division. All telephone lines handed over were in a very bad state of repair and too earthy for superimposed circuits. The hard frost giving way to thaw made matters worse.	

Army Form C. 2118.

WAR DIARY
INTELLIGENCE SUMMARY.
(Erase heading not required.)

Instructions regarding War Diaries and Intelligence Summaries are contained in F. S. Regs., Part II. and the Staff Manual respectively. Title pages will be prepared in manuscript.

Place	Date Jan.	Hour	Summary of Events and Information	Remarks and references to Appendices
	11.		No.72214 Sapper G.W. BOOTH and No.500322 Sapper G.H. HOUSE awarded MILITARY MEDALS for Gallantry at VILLERS FLOUICH on the night of December 4th 1917.	
	12.		G.O.C.61st Division took over command of Sector from 5th French Division at 10.a.m. 182 Bde. holding the Right Sector with Hdqrs. at BARMEXX BOURGUET (62B - S.2.a.8.3) 183 Inf. Bde. in Reserve at RALVI (66D - C.5.a & c) 184 Inf. Bde. holding the Left Sector with Headquarters at RASPAIL (62C - R.35.d.8.4). Division on Right - 6th French Div. Division on Left - 3rd Dismounted Division. The artillery covering the front was the artillery of the 5th French Division.	
	13.		Work on overhauling the French Routes began, and continued all the month. All buried cable routes were found to be very faulty and practically useless. Field Artillery Relief completed at night. The French Heavy Artillery, however, still remained in.	
	14.		183 Inf. Bde. Hdqrs. moved to BEAUVOIS. G.O.C. 61st Divl. R.A. took over command of the artillery covering the front. This consisted of three R.F.A. Bdes organized as two Groups. Right Group Hdqrs. at RASPAIL, Left Group Hdqrs. at BOURGUYNE (62B - M.25.a.5.7). 36th Division relieved 6th French Division on our Right, and established their Hdqrs at OLIEZY (66C - R.1.)	
	15.		General overhauling of routes.	
	16.		General overhauling of routes. An Exchange at the Hdqrs. of the D.C.L.I was established for Units around ATTILLY.	
	17.		Normal day.	

Army Form C. 2118.

WAR DIARY
or
INTELLIGENCE SUMMARY.
(Erase heading not required.)

Place	Date 1918.	Hour	Summary of Events and Information	Remarks and references to Appendices
	Jan. 18.		183 Inf. Bde. relief 182 Inf. Bde. in the Right Sector. an Exchange was opened at MARTEVILLE, with lines to Left Bde; D.C.L.I.; Reserve Bde; Left Field Coy; 182 Inf. Bde. Transport Lines, 184 Inf. Bde. Transport Lines and 306 R.F.A. Bde. wagon lines.	
	19 - 25		General overhauling of existing routes, most of the available labour being put on to try to recover from fallen in trenches staked cable routes in the forward area, and digging out 'canivaux' routes which had all fallen in directly the thaw started.	
	26/27		182 Inf. Bde. relieved 184 Inf. Bde. in the Left Sector.	
	27/31		Normal days.	

.... Major,
O. C. 61st. Divl. Sig. Coy.

CONFIDENTIAL

WAR DIARY
OF
61st Div. Signal Coy RE

For the month of FEBRUARY 1918

VOL. 22

Army Form C. 2118.

WAR DIARY
or
INTELLIGENCE SUMMARY.
(Erase heading not required.)

Instructions regarding War Diaries and Intelligence Summaries are contained in F. S. Regs., Part II. and the Staff Manual respectively. Title pages will be prepared in manuscript.

Place	Date	Hour	Summary of Events and Information	Remarks and references to Appendices
AUROIR	Feb. 1		182 Inf. Brigade, Left. H.Qrs. Maison de Garde (X.35.d.9.5.) 183 Inf. Bde. Right. (S.2.a.8.3.)	
			184 Inf. Bde in reserve.	
			Dismounted Divisions on left.	
			36th Division on right.	
	2		Normal.	
	3		184 Inf. Brigade relieved the 183 Inf. Bde. in right Sub sector.	
	4			
	5			
	6			
	7		Normal.	
	8			
	9			
	10			
	11		183 Inf. Bde. relieved 182 Inf. Bde in Left Sub Sector.	
	12		Normal.	
	13			
	14		Major P.W.CLARK, R.E. to U.K. on 14 days leave. Capt. C.D. TWYNAM R.E. commanding the Company during his absence.	
	15		Buried route to Fresnoy Redoubt surveyed.	
	16		Normal.	

Army Form C. 2118.

WAR DIARY
or
INTELLIGENCE SUMMARY.
(Erase heading not required.)

Instructions regarding War Diaries and Intelligence Summaries are contained in F. S. Regs., Part II. and the Staff Manual respectively. Title pages will be prepared in manuscript.

Place	Date	Hour	Summary of Events and Information	Remarks and references to Appendices
AUROIR	Feb. 17		LT. HUNTER BLAIR appointed Officer i/c Signals, 182 Inf. Bde Signal Section Vice LT. L. N. NORRIS	
	18		ROGERS posted to 5th Army Signal Coy, attached 18th Corps.	
	19		Buried Route to Fresnoy Redoubt started.	
	20		182 Inf. Bde. relieved 184 Inf. Bde. in Right Sub Sector.	
	21		One Battalion front on the left handed over to Dismounted Division.	
	22		Fresnoy Bury completed.	
	23		One Battalion front on right handed over to 30th Division who came in the line between us and 36th Division.	
	24		Normal.	
	25		LT. HUNTER BLAIR R.E. to U.K. on 14 days leave. LT. H.S. DENTON assumed duties of Officer i/c Signals 182 Inf. Bde. Signal Section in his absence.	
	26			
	27		Normal days. Work on Battle Zone Communication.	
	28			

Army Form C. 2118

WAR DIARY
or
INTELLIGENCE SUMMARY
(Erase heading not required.)

61st. Divl. Signal Co.R.E.

Instructions regarding War Diaries and Intelligence Summaries are contained in F.S. Regs., Part II. and the Staff Manual respectively. Title Pages will be prepared in manuscript.

ST. QUENTIN 62B - 62C.

Place	Date 1918	Hour	Summary of Events and Information	Remarks and references to Appendices
UROIR	March 1st		in line as left division, XVIII Corps. All brigades in line. 182 (right) 62B.S.2.a.7.5. 183 (left) KEEPERS HOUSE. 184 (centre) ATTILLY - Division on right, 30th Division, on left Dismounted Divisions. Direct cable pair laid to ETOILE (62C.A.15.d.8.2.) put through from there by existing lines as omnibus circuit to all brigades. Work on Three Cottages bury continued daily.	
	2nd		Small allotment of lines given on new Corps lines in HOLNON WOOD area. Fresh battle circuits scheme got out. Situation quieter - Detachment recalled from ATTILLY. Signal School assembled at UGNY (62C - E.7.) Major F.W.Clark, M.C. back from leave.	
	3rd		Caniveau started along railway in HOLNON WOOD.	
	4th		Railway Caniveau finished. 182 Bde. moved back to their battle H.qrs at 62C.A.15.b.) Court of Enquiry on fire at Signal School, BEAUVOIS.	
	5th		Work of laying two armoured pairs up river from MARTEVILLE to VERMAND for brigade on left started. Digging and cable laying on Three Cottages bury finished (62C.R.35.d. to 62B.S.4.a.), jointing and filling in not finished. Caniveau dug from ETOILE to TL (62C.A.9.d.3.7.) via right brigade in X.15.b.	
	6th		Work on river lines continued. Test strips put in at TM test point on FRESNOY bury.	
	7th		Three Cottages bury finished off. River lines finished. Change of position of first line battalion H.qrs. - Right battalion moved from THREE COTTAGES (62B.S.4.d.2.2.) to (S.9.d.9.9.), centre battalion from FRESNOY QUARRIES (62B.M.26.d.9.9.) to THREE COTTAGES, both battalions now working down Three Cottages bury.	
	8-19		Fairly normal except for rumours - Buries and caniveaux being gradually finished and taken into use.	

1875 Wt. W503/826 1,000,000 4/15 J.B.C.&A. A.D.S.S./Forms/C.2118.

Army Form C. 2118

WAR DIARY
or
INTELLIGENCE SUMMARY
(Erase heading not required.)

Instructions regarding War Diaries and Intelligence Summaries are contained in F.S. Regs., Part II. and the Staff Manual respectively. Title Pages will be prepared in manuscript.

Place	Date	Hour	Summary of Events and Information	Remarks and references to Appendices
AUROIR	March 11th		183 Bde. moved back from KEEPERS HOUSE to MARTEVILLE (62B.X.3.a.2.8.) their battle H.Qrs.	
	12th		307 Bde R.F.A. (Left group) moved back alongside 183 Bde.) Lieut.T.Coats went on leave on conclusion of wireless course at ABBEVILLE. 24th.Division relieved dismounted divisions as Division on left. Work started on bury to ELLIS redoubt (62B.S.9.a.9.9) from test point on Three Cottages bury.	
	15th		232 Bde (right group) moved back alongside 182 Bde. All brigades and groups now in their battle positions.	
	17th		Bury to ELLIS redoubt completed.	
	19th		Work started on new bury from KEEPERS HOUSE to O.Ps on forward edge of HOLNON WOOD. ELLIS bury taken into use.	
	20th		Cables laid in forward end of HOLNON WOOD bury as far as dug and thence to KEEPERS HOUSE on the ground as five sources confirmed that attack would start early next morning. Allotment on all outstanding Caniveaux received and distributed. The Southern line had been badly bungled, solid joints at GERMAINE were connected to airline from AUROIR - pairs allotted in caniveau were not same as on airline, consequently the whole southern route was useless to us.	
	21st	4.35 a.m.	Bombardment opened, a large amount of gas shell being used.	
		9.0 a.m.	Attack started.	
		3.0 p.m.	Redoubts given up by order from Division who remained in touch with forward battalion Commanders the whole time, though for four hours the redoubts were isolated. Power Buzzer-amplifier men had been sent back during the morning in each case.	
		6.0 p.m.	Division still holding battle zone except on extreme left where a switch line had been constructed owing to the right flank of 24th Division being pierced. The buries held up the whole time, but permanent went everywhere, particularly in FORESTE. While caniveaux were continually cut. The omnibus line was continually cut, but save for one short spell it was always possible	

1875 Wt. W593/826 1,000,000 4/15 J.B.C. & A. A.D.S.S./Forms/C.2118.

Army Form C. 2118.

WAR DIARY
or
INTELLIGENCE SUMMARY

(Erase heading not required.)

Instructions regarding War Diaries and Intelligence Summaries are contained in F.S. Regs., Part II. and the Staff Manual respectively. Title Pages will be prepared in manuscript.

Place	Date	Hour	Summary of Events and Information	Remarks and references to Appendices
	March			ST. QUENTIN AMIENS 66D 6&C
	21st		to talk to every Unit by one way or another. Extra cable lines were laid from AUROIR to VAUX and from BEAUVOIS to VILLEVEQUE and to a point VO on the canivean system half way to ATTILLY by Corpl: Barton's detachment under Lieut: R.J.Spurr. Corps evacuated BS test point in afternoon - It was discovered just in time that the order had been given to smash the test panels and leave the place, without any warning being given to Divisions. The test panel was therefore left intact. L/Corpl: Prince did good work relaying lines to Divisional O.P's in full view of advancing Germans.	
	22nd		By midnight on 21/22nd. situation on right flank was such owing to 36th Division being driven back to SOMME Canal and 30th Division forced to form a defensive flank that it was obvious a retirement would be necessary. A Corps detachment which arrived put two extra lines through to Corps was therefore switched to lay a line from MATIGNY, the proposed Divisional H.Qrs. to BEAUVOIS where all three brigades were to be.	
MATIGNY		noon	Divisional H.Qrs opened at MATIGNY. - Brigades withdrew in early afternoon, taking up position on the Army line in corjunction with 20th Division, who came up out of reserve. 182 Bde.H.Qrs moved out of BEAUVOIS to a point midway between there and GERMAINE Division ordered to withdraw across canal leaving 20th Division to hold line. Hurried move back. Divl. H.Qrs. did not close at MATIGNY till all troops of Division had passed. H.Qrs moved to RETHONVILLERS on NESLE - ROYE road (66D.N.4.a) with advanced H.Qrs. for the night at Cross Roads 66D.1.22.d.2.5. 182 Bde. to signal box in I.23.a., 184 Bde to BILLANCOURT (H.35.c), 183 Bde to NESLE. Corps had moved from HAM to NESLE. Army from NESLE to VILLERS-BRETONNEUX. 36th Divn. had been driven across canal at St.SIMON. Div. Artillery was left in under 20th Division.	
		evening	Communications from MATIGNY were as follows:- one direct cable line to AUROIR, which had lines forward and two to BEAUVOIS, and two direct cables to BEAUVOIS, which held to evening when they got badly smashed in shelling of BEAUVOIS. Lieut. Spurr and detachment rejoined at MATIGNY. Great difficulty in ascertaining from Corps what communication we should have from RETHONVILLERS.	
RETHONVILLERS	23		Laid leads to get touch with Corps. Cable laid to BILLANCOURT for 184 Bde and rear 182 Bde.	

1875 Wt. W593/826 1,000,000 4/15 J.B.C. & A.   A.D.S.S./Forms/C.2118.

Army Form C. 2118

WAR DIARY
or
INTELLIGENCE SUMMARY
(Erase heading not required.)

Instructions regarding War Diaries and Intelligence Summaries are contained in F.S. Regs., Part II. and the Staff Manual respectively. Title Pages will be prepared in manuscript.

AMIENS SHEET

Place	Date	Hour	Summary of Events and Information	Remarks and references to Appendices
RETHON-VILLERS	March		Hurried move to the rear in afternoon owing to false reports spread by Germans who had penetrated lines, but everyone recalled and settled in again. 182 Bde and 183 Bde passed under command of 20th Division. Corps moved to ROYE. Germans penetrated through him, but were driven back by D.C.L.I.	
	24		Germans crossed river by HATTENCOURT and reached FOTIN and MORCHAIN. 183 Bde counter attacked but as their flanks were unsupported the attack broke down. French troops began to come up into line.	
PARVILLERS	25		Divl. H.Qrs. moved in afternoon to PARVILLERS (Amiens 4.I.80.95.) 2¾ miles of cable had to be laid by us to Exfinnin. gain touch with 18th Corps to whom we had to send to find out what communication we should have. All Units of the Division were by now under 20th Division, so that there was no communication to be maintained by us except S.S.O. for whom a line was laid to DAMERY. RETHANVILLERS Germans advancing rapidly, Corps moved to MOREUIL, 20th Division from PARVILLERS to CARREPUITS in morning. Divl. H.Qrs. ordered to move to LE QUESNEL (Amiens 3.n.5.3.) Detachment sent far over which again had to lay to connect with Corps - Destination then changed to BEAUCOURT (3.n.0.5) Line at LE QUESNEL was therefore picked up and detachment again put Division in touch with Corps from BEAUCOURT. Brigades withdrawn from line and came under 61 Division again.	
BEAUCOURT	26	10.pm	Divl.H.Qrs. opened at BEAUCOURT. Detachment sent out and laid cable line to LE QUESNEL where all three brigades had their headquarters. In morning Division ordered to take up a rear line of defence running S... from BEAUCOURT to MEZIERES. 182 Bde H.Qrs to be at MAISON BLANCHE (Amiens 3.G.70.55) 183 Bde at VILLERS AUX ERABLES (3.G.45.45) 184 at MEZIERES (3.G.70.45). Div. H.Qrs being fixed as MORISEL after several changes. As soon as the system was laid, the orders were changed. D.H.Qrs to remain at BEAUCOURT, all brigades at LE QUESNEL and be prepared to advance.	

1875 Wt. W593/826 1,000,000 4/15 J.B.C. & A. A.D.S.S./Forms/C. 2118.

WAR DIARY or INTELLIGENCE SUMMARY

Army Form C. 2118

(Erase heading not required.)

AMIENS SHEET

Place	Date	Hour	Summary of Events and Information	Remarks and references to Appendices
BEAUCOURT	March 27		36th Division who were on the right of 20th Division, fell back leaving a gap between them and 20th Division. 183 Bde was sent up to fill the gap, the Omnibus circuit being extended as they moved first to HANGEST and then to 3.H.Q.I. to which point a direct line was laid later from BEAUCOURT. 182 Bde. Signals reported casualties as 12 missing, 2 wounded - Later the majority of the missing men returned.	
		9.p.m	Orders received for the Division to embus at midnight and proceed to 19th Corps area (Corps on left)	
VILLERS-BRETONNEUX	28	12.30 a.m.	Reached VILLERS BRETONNEUX (2.G.5.2) establishing office in advanced 19th Corps Signal Office. The orders were for bdes. to go to MARCELCAVE (2.G.9.2) and counter attack at 5.30.a.m. against LA MOTTE (2.H.40.25) Major Clerk with a few men proceeded to MARCELCAVE to lay line with infantry as they advanced, a cable detachment also going out.to lay a line back to Division. This line was through at 6.0.a.m.	
		5.a.m	Attack cancelled as troops not in position.	
		6.30.a.m.	General stand to ordered but nothing happened.	
		8.30.a.m.	Transport moved off from DEMUIN but was stopped half way.	
		9.45.a.m	Counter attack ordered to take place at 11.0.a.m.	
		11.0.a.m.	Counter attack started but was not a success largely owing to the essence of Artillery support. It took 30 minutes for any orders to reach the artillery.	
		12.3 p.m.	heavy shelling of MARCELCAVE. Bdes all shifted their H.Qrs into the open between there and VILLERS.	
		4.20 p.m	19th Corps ordered immediate evacuation of VILLERS BRETONNEUX - Divl.H.Qrs moved to GENTELLES and on from there to BOVES (2.E.60.15) almost at once.	
BOVES		8.0.pm	Opened office at BOVES with no communication at all.	
		8.30 p.m	G.O.C decided on advanced office at GENTELLES (2.F.50.15) - Company lorry fitted up as Signal office and sent forward. Brigades did not move.	

Army Form C. 2118

WAR DIARY
or
INTELLIGENCE SUMMARY

(Erase heading not required.)

Instructions regarding War Diaries and Intelligence Summaries are contained in F.S. Regs., Part II and the Staff Manual respectively. Title Pages will be prepared in manuscript.

AMIENS SHEET

Place	Date	Hour	Summary of Events and Information	Remarks and references to Appendices
BOVES	March 29	5.30 a.m.	Through to 18th Corps at ST FUSCHIEN (2.D.8.1)	
		6.30 a.m.	Cable line through to GENTELLES - Lines also laid from there to the brigades under supervision of Lieut. Browning.	
		evening	Front line taken over by CAREY'S FORCE with 61 Division in support. Second line laid during day to GENTELLES, while Corps opened an Office in BOVES and ran a line from there to 2nd. Cavalry Division also in GENTELLES.	
	30		During morning Germans worked forward on right flank capturing DEMUIN and MOREUIL Wood. 9th Australian Infantry Brigades and Canadian Cavalry Brigade drove them out of DEMUIN area. under orders of 61 Division. Lieut. T.H.MORRIS R.E.(T.F.) wounded. Orders issued for 14th Division to relieve 61 Division at night.	
	31	6.30 a.m.	Relief reported complete but later discovered that Warwicks had not been relieved so that command did not pass to 18th Division. Our advanced Office withdrawn except for linemen on 18th Div. Signals taking over. Lieut.G.L.THORP. (The Buffs Regt.) reported for duty vice Lieut.T.H.MORRIS. Germans attacked down River Luce and towards MOREUIL making progress between there and HANGARD.	

.... Major, R.E.
O C. 61st. Divl. Sig. Coy.

61st Divisional Engineers

---o-----

61st DIVISIONAL SIGNAL COMPANY R. E.

APRIL 1918.

Army Form C. 2118

WAR DIARY
or
INTELLIGENCE SUMMARY
(Erase heading not required.)

Vol 24

61st Div. Signal Coy. R.E.

War Diary

April 1918

Volume 24.

Army Form C. 2118

WAR DIARY
or
INTELLIGENCE SUMMARY
(Erase heading not required.)

Instructions regarding War Diaries and Intelligence Summaries are contained in F.S. Regs., Part II. and the Staff Manual respectively. Title Pages will be prepared in manuscript.

61st DIVL SIGNAL CO. R.E. OFFICE
Date   No.

Place	Date 1918	Hour	Summary of Events and Information	Remarks and references to Appendices
BOVES.	April 1st.		Divl. HQ. BOVES (2.e.60.15); Adv. D.H.Q. GENTELLES (2.f.50.15) under 19th Corps (2.d.75.10). Brigades grouped round GENTELLE.	AMIENS 17.1/100,000
		2.30.a.m	Relief of war.icks complete at 2.30.a.m, and command of Sector handed over to G.O.C. 18th Division.	
		8.0.am	Division ordered to occupy part of GENTELLES - BERTHAUCOURT reserve line instead of moving to back areas.	
			It was decided to form a composite Brigade if Division ordered into action again before re-organizing.	
LONGEAU	2nd.		Divl. HQ. moved to LONGEAU (2.B.25.50) at 3.0.p.m. Brigades remaining at GENTELLES.	
			at 6.0.p.m. decided to move to PISSY (2.B.55.35) on arrival found village full, so Div. H.Q. had to remain at LONGEAU till next morning, when other troops moved out.	
PISSY.	3rd.		Transport arrived about 12.30.a.m. having left LONGEAU at 6.30.p.m. Brigades moved by bus to new area – 182 Inf. Bde. HQ. to SAUX (17 – 2.B.3.5) 183 Inf. Bde. HQ to HEUCOURT (16 – 1.K.6.2) 184 Inf. Bde. HQ. to TAILLY (16 – 1.L.3.2). 61st Divl. Arty. moved from QUEVAUVILLERS to GUIGNEMICOURT (17 – 2.C.10.35) rejoining Division.	
			Got line through to Advanced 4th Army (late 5th Army) at DURY (17 – 2.D.25.20), but no communication with Brigades.	
	4th.} 5th.}		Checking and overhauling Stores and Equipment.	
	6th.		Visual communication established with 182 Inf. Bde.	
	7th.		Through to 19th Corps at MOLLIENS VIDAME (17 – 2.A.25.6.0) with Sounder superimposed. Great uncertainty as to whether Division under 18th or 19th Corps. Visual chain extended half way to distant Brigades.	
	8th.		Visual established right through to 183 Inf. Bde. with three transmitting Stations. Divl. Arty. moved to Army Artillery Area POIX (16 – 3.L.8.3).	DIEPPE 16) 1/100,000 AMIENS 17)

1875 Wt. W593/826 1,000,000 4/15 J.B.C. & A. A.D.S.S./Forms/C. 2118.

WAR DIARY
or
INTELLIGENCE SUMMARY

(Erase heading not required.)

Army Form C. 2118

Instructions regarding War Diaries and Intelligence Summaries are contained in F.S. Regs., Part II. and the Staff Manual respectively. Title Pages will be prepared in manuscript.

Place	Date APRIL	Hour	Summary of Events and Information	Remarks and references to Appendices
PISSY	9th		Warning order for move by train. Germans attacked, making deep salient between FLEURBAIX (5a - 5.K.0.8) and GIVENCHY (5A - 6.J.05.35.)	
	10th.		Sergt. Young's detachment proceeded to join Divl. Artillery at FOLA. Div. moved by train to become G.H.Q. reserve under Second army in First Army area, detraining at CALONNE (5.H.3.5) and ST VENANT (4.A.55.45) advance party arrived to find these railheads had been put out of action, and that Division was to detrain at BERGUETTE (5.F.55.35) and STEENBECQUE (4.F.8.1) going into billets in AIRE area. In afternoon orders came through that Division was under 11th Corps in First Army. Lorries were sent to meet the first trains and the Battalions were rushed up into the line near ST VENANT under 51st Division. Division ordered to construct a rear line on Rivers CLARENCE and NOE, 184 Inf. Bde. on the Right with Hdqrs. at ST VENANT, 182 Inf. Bde. in the Centre, with Hdqrs. at P.10.c.4.5. 183 Inf. Bde. on the left, Hdqrs. ST VENANT. Div. Hdqrs. established by the Cathedral in AIRE, with a line to AIRE M.O.	
AIRE.) F.L)	11th.		It was decided to open an Advanced Hdqrs. West of ST. VENANT. The Company, which detrained at BERGUETTE at 6.0.a.m., waited there till adv. Hdqrs. fixed at P.l.d.5.0, when Lieut. J.B. Browning with two detachments moved there and laid line to 183 Inf. Bde. in ST. VENANT and 182 Inf. Bde. HQ. at P.10.c.4.5. Remainder of Company proceeded to AIRE.	
	12th.		50th Division on our Left gave ground near MERVILLE in face of German attacks, but situation restored by 5th Division counter attack. 5th Division relieved 50th Division. Division came into the line between 50th & 51st Divisions. Preparations made for moving advanced Hdqrs. to MOLINGHEM. (0.14.a)	
AIRE MOLINGHEM	13th.	4.0.pm	Enemy shelling ST VENANT - GUARBECQUE Road, ½-mile West of Adv. Hq. heavily during the morning. Wireless Set sent up to Advanced Hdqrs. Advanced Div. Hdqrs. moved to MOLINGHEM, but Office at P.l.D. kept on as Forward Exchange.	
	14th.		154 Bde, 51st Div. came under orders of 61st Div., 51st Div. Hdqrs. withdrawing. 4th Div. now on our right. Line through to 154 Bde. via 'P' Forward Exchange.	

Army Form C. 2118

WAR DIARY
or
INTELLIGENCE SUMMARY
(Erase heading not required.)

Instructions regarding War Diaries and Intelligence Summaries are contained in F.S. Regs., Part II and the Staff Manual respectively. Title Pages will be prepared in manuscript.

Place	Date APRIL	Hour	Summary of Events and Information	Remarks and references to Appendices
AIRE MOLINGHEM	15th		2nd Lieut. F. POTTAGE R.E. reported for instruction (supernumerary). 184 Inf. Bde. advanced our line about 400 yards.	
	16th		Brigade transport lines moved to neighbourhood of LA LACQUE and LA ROUPIE (I.31.D) and were put on telephone.	
	17th	8.30.pm.	182 Inf. Bde. moved Hdqrs. to HeMET BILLET (P.14.a.4.5).	
	18th		184 Inf. Bde. moved Hdqrs. to P.9.d.1.6	
			Protective barrage put down as prisoners stated an attack would be made at 4.0.am. No attack developed except on BACQUEROLLES FARM which was beaten off, 20 prisoners being taken.	
	19th	2.15.am.	Heavy enemy shelling. 6 lines forward from 'P' down.	
	20th		Military Medals awarded to No.500554 Spr. LLEWELLYN H, 500544 Spr. SMITH A, of 184 Inf. Bde. Section, and three attached Orderlies.	
			11th Corps moved from NORRENT FONTES to ROQUETOIRE. One line through to 11th Corps. Through to 51st Div. at NORRENT FONTES on old 11th Corps Line.	
			Tidying lines to BARGUETTE. Corps lines faulty all day.	
	21st		Tidying lines to BERGUETTE. Considerable trouble with Corps lines.	
	22nd		F.B.A Stations installed. Lieut. G.L. THORP came back for a rest. Military Medals awarded as follows:- Hdqrs.- 500332 L/Cpl. HAGGIS G.L. 500281 L/Cpl. PRINCE R. 183 Section. No.500334 Sergt. Robinson S.J. 500330 Spr. Nash H.E. 500566 Spr.Coster A.W. also to two orderlies of 182 Bde. Section and two orderlies of 183 Bde. Section. Sounder line put through to 182 Inf. Bde. Hq.	
	23rd		Successful minor operation by 5th Glosters in conjunction with a Battalion of the 4th Div., resulting in our line being shortened by 1000 yards. Over 100 prisoners taken. Sounder lines to 182 & 184 Inf. Bdes. through. Enemy shelling caused considerable trouble on forward lines.	

Army Form C. 2118

WAR DIARY
or
INTELLIGENCE SUMMARY

(Erase heading not required.)

Instructions regarding War Diaries and Intelligence Summaries are contained in F. S. Regs., Part II. and the Staff Manual respectively. Title Pages will be prepared in manuscript.

Place	Date APRIL	Hour	Summary of Events and Information	Remarks and references to Appendices
AIRE MOLINGHEM.	24th.		Counter attack against 5th Gloucesters resulted in capture of another 80 prisoners, our line being maintained intact.	
	25th.		154th Inf. Bde. withdrawn except for one Battalion.	
	26th.		Battalion of 154th Inf. Bde. withdrawn. 184 Inf. Bde. moved to Hdqrs. of 154 Inf. Bde. 61st Divl. Artillery rejoined Division, going to LIETTRES. Cable detachment under Lieut. R.J. SPURR rejoined the Company. Lieut. G.L. THORP to C.C.S.	
	27th.		New office prepared for Forward Exchange and lines got ready.	
	28th.		New 'P' Exchange opened at O.18.b.0.2. Direct lines to Bdes. from YFAR. 182 Inf. Bde. moved to near old 'P' (enemy shellfire).	
	29th.		183 Inf. Bde. moved to old 'P', keeping report centre open at old Hdqrs. L/Cpl. Babb and Sapper C.D. Webb of 182 Bde. Section wounded.	
	30th.		Nothing to report.	

Major, R.E.
O. C. 61st Divl Sig. Coy.

Vol 25

War diary
of 61st Divl. Signal Coy. R.E.
May 1918
Volume 25

WAR DIARY or INTELLIGENCE SUMMARY

Army Form C. 2118

Ref:- Sheet 36.A. 1/40,000.   HAZEBROUCK 5A. 1/100,000.

Place	Date	Hour	Summary of Events and Information	Remarks and references to Appendices
MOLINGHEM. AIRE	MAY 1		Divl. Hdqrs. at AIRE, with G. Branch at MOLINGHEM (N.14.a) - 182 Inf. Bde. holding Centre Sector (Hdqrs. at P.W.c.1.7); 183 Inf. Bde. on Left (Hdqrs. F.1.d.5.0); 184 Inf. Bde. on Right (P.27.a.1.3). Artillery covering Divl. front - 16th & 51st Divl. artilleries and 12th Australian Army F.A. Bde, under command of C.R.A. 51st Division. Division under 11th Corps (ROQUETOIRE G.6.a), with 4th Div. on Right (B.G RIEUX U.24.b) and 5th Div. on Left (THIENNES I.6.a). Lieut. C. "RIGHT, R.F.A. left to rejoin 315 A.F.A. Bde. on conclusion of attachment. Great deal of trouble on lines.	
	2.		Quiet day.	
	3.		Quiet day. G.R.A. 16th Div. took over command of Artillery covering Divl. front from G.R.A. 51st Div.	
	4) 5) 6)		Nothing of interest to report.	
	6.		61st Divl. artillery moved into 13th Corps area, Brigades coming under 4th D.A. 2nd Lieut. POTTAGE, with Sergt. Young's detachment, accompanied them. 61st Divl. Artillery Hdqrs. not functioning. Trouble on Right Bde. lines.	
	7.		Lieut. D.J. CAMERON, R.E. joined from 16th Signal Coy. and took over 1A Section.	
	8.		Direct line to Right Bde. relaid in part to avoid shelled area.	
	9.		Sounder line to Centre and Left Bde. giving trouble all day.	
	10		Distinguished Conduct Medals awarded to No.500017 Sergt. W.G. LAY and 500154 Corpl. W.R. BARTON	
	11) 12)		Nothing of interest.	

Army Form C. 2118

WAR DIARY or INTELLIGENCE SUMMARY

(Erase heading not required.)

Instructions regarding War Diaries and Intelligence Summaries are contained in F.S. Regs., Part II and the Staff Manual respectively. Title Pages will be prepared in manuscript.

Ref:- Sheet 36.A. 1/40,000. HAZEBROUCK 5A 1/100,000

Place	Date	Hour	Summary of Events and Information	Remarks and references to Appendices
MOLINGHEM AIRE	MAY 13		Lines to 182 & 183 Inf. Bdes. converted to ring; 184 unable to change over owing to exchange falling into canal. Successful raid by 184 Inf. Bde. Work started on new main route forward (7 pair armoured running across country to railway at O.16.c.0.7; along railway to 'F' Exchange (O.18.b.0.2), thence by railway and streams F.7.c. and a, f.1.c. and d, and on to P.4.a.3.4, thence in canal to P.5.b.c.6)	
	14		Successful raid by 182 Bde. Shell entered 184 Signal Office, wounding three men.	
	15.		Normal day.	
	16.		Quiet day. Severe bombing of AIRE at night, dissing lines.	
	17.		Lieut. G.L. THORP (Gen. List & Buffs) returned from Base Hospital and took over 1B Section.	
MOLINGHEM LAMBRES.	18.		Rear Div. Hdqrs. moved from AIRE to LAMBRES. Line had to be laid between LAMBRES and MOLINGHEM, as line Corps proposed to give us was found to be in use. 7 pair armoured route completed as far as 'F' Exchange.	
	19.		Normal day.	
	20.		Armoured quad laid by boat in canal from F.13.a.3.3. to P.20.d.	
	21.		Armoured quad extended to 4th Div. Cable Head in P.29.c.	
	22.		Corps closed down BERGUE. The Exchange and stationed their linemen at MOLINGHEM. 50TH M.G. Battalion left area.	
	23		The following were mentioned in the Birthday Honours List :- Captain C.D. Twynam M.C. Lieut. J.B. Browning. No.72377 Sergt. Williamson M.	

1875 Wt. W593/826 1,000,000 4/15 J.B.C. & A. A.D.S.S./Forms/C. 2118.

Army Form C. 2118

WAR DIARY
or
INTELLIGENCE SUMMARY
(Erase heading not required.)

Instructions regarding War Diaries and Intelligence Summaries are contained in F. S. Regs., Part II. and the Staff Manual respectively. Title Pages will be prepared in manuscript.

Ref:- Sheet 36.A. 1/40,000. HAZEBROUCK 5A 1/100,000.

Place	Date	Hour	Summary of Events and Information	Remarks and references to Appendices
MOLINGHEM LAMBRES.	MAY 24		New Signal Office opened at 1.30.p.m. 282 A.F.A. Bde. relieved 12 Aus. A.F.A. Bde.	
	25		7 pair Cable finished to test point at F.4.a.3.4. Line put through to 45 Mobile Pigeon Loft at HERGUETTE.	
	26		"Silent day". - Telegraph and telephone not allowed to be used. Very great drop in traffic, which was handled by W/T, Pigeons and two extra D.R.L.S. runs. Corps spoilt working of W/T by putting on a man who had never done wireless. New Battalions for 183 Inf. Bde. arrived from 34th Division (9th(N.F) Northumberland Fusiliers, 11th Suffolks, 1st East Lancs.)	
	27		Large quantities of permanent line stores salved from ST FLORIS dump (East of ST VENANT) for Corps. German attack started between SOISSONS & RHIEMS.	
	28		Batteries of 61st Divl. Artillery began relieving Batteries of 51st Divl. Artillery.	
	28		183 Inf. Bde. Hdqrs. moved back to La LACQUE (I.32.a.9.8), command of their Scottish Battalions being taken over by 182 Inf. Bde.	
	29		C.R.A. 61st Division took over command of artillery covering Divisional front from C.R.A. 16th Division.	
	30		One Battalion of 182 Inf. Bde. relieved the Scotch Battalions and Divl. front was re-organized as a two Brigade front. Communications were altered to do away with the Exchanges and personnel which had been left at F.1.d.5.0 when 183 Inf. Bde. moved out. Major General Sir Colin Mackenzie evacuated to Base, his wound having become worse.	
	31.		Preparations began for intended move of 184 Bde. Hdqrs. to BUSNES Chateau.	

.... Major R.E.
O. C. 61st. Divl. Sig. Coy.

1875 Wt. W593/826 1,000,000 4/15 J.B.C. & A. A.D.S.S./Forms/C. 2118.

WAR DIARY or INTELLIGENCE SUMMARY

Army Form C. 2118

Place	Date 1918 June	Hour	Summary of Events and Information	Remarks and references to Appendices
MOLINGHEM LAMBRES	1st		D.H.Q. LAMBRES (N.10), Adv. D.H.Q. MOLINGHEM (O 14 a), 182 Inf. Bde. on left (P 7 d 25) 183 Inf. Bde. in reserve in LACQUE (O 2 a), 184 Inf. Bde. on right (P 27 b 23). Artillery covering divisional front 61st and 66th D.A's and 282 A.F.A.Bde. under C.R.A. 61st Division. Division under XI Corps, 4th Division on right, 5th Division on left. Scotch Battalions which had formed 183 Bde. left to join 15th Division.	
	2nd		183 Bde. moved to HAM EN ARTOIS with battalions at HAM, LA MIQUELLERIE and GARBECQUE. 9th Canadian Inf. Bde. left area being replaced two days later by 229th Bde., 74th Div. 184 Bde. moved back from P 27 b 23 to BUSNES Chateau O 36 d 93. New line laid from P Exchange (O 18 central) and old direct line split at Chateau. Great trouble on lines owing to leakage from H.T. Transformer. 'A' Section went to rear hqrs for training under Lieut. Cameron.	
	3rd		Quiet day.	
	4th 5th 6th		Nothing of interest to report.	
	7th		198147 Sergt. FOWLER J. awarded D.C.M. in Birthday Honours List. Line laid from P exchange to reserve Bde. in HAM EN ARTOIS.	
	8th		Normal day.	
	9th		183 Bde. relieved 182 Bde. in Left Section at night, 182 Bde. moving to HAM.	
	10th		'B' section went back to rear hqrs under Lieut. Thorp replacing 'A' Section.	
	11th		Work on lines in HAM area picking up disused cables.	

Army Form C. 2118

WAR DIARY
or
INTELLIGENCE SUMMARY
(Erase heading not required.)

Instructions regarding War Diaries and Intelligence Summaries are contained in F. S. Regs., Part II. and the Staff Manual respectively. Title Pages will be prepared in manuscript.

Place	Date	Hour	Summary of Events and Information	Remarks and references to Appendices
	12th		Demonstration of Fewer Buzzer and Loop Set working. It was intended also to demonstrate overhearing but the leakage from the MoLiNGHEM transformer was so bad that nothing could be heard of speech though the Station was 4,000 yards away. 306 Bde. R.F.A. moved their hqrs back alongside 184 Inf. Bde.	
	13th		Normal.	
	14th		Normal. Major-General F.J.Duncan C.M.G., D.S.O. arrived to command Division vice Major-General Sir Colin Mackenzie.	
	15th		Lieut. Thorp took over charge of D.A.Signals from Capt. Mackinlay who proceeded on leave. 282 A.F.A. Bde. withdrew from line prior to moving into 5th Div'n area.	
	16th		Wave of fever started. All Officers down.	
	17 - 20th		Large number of men down with fever including complete office relief. 436024 Sergt. Smith F. of No.4 Section and 500927 Corpl. Webber T.G. of Hqrs. awarded M.S.M's in Birthday Honours List.	
	21st		Examination of 61st Div. Artillery Signal School at end of six weeks' course. Three passed as First Class and three as Second Class out of 20 examined.	
	22nd		Quiet day.	
	23rd		Line laid from LAMBRES to FONTES (N 35 b 04) for new reserve brigade hdqrs.	
	24th		182 Inf. Bde. relieved 184 Inf. Bde. in Right Section, 184 Bde. moving back to FONTES. Owing to fever 182 Bde. had to be strengthened by 7 men from headquarters.	
	25th		Picking up lines round HAM. Successful raid by 183 Bde.	
	26th		Quiet day.	

1875 Wt. W593/826 1,000,000 4/15 J.B.C. & A. A.D.S.S./Forms/C. 2118.

Army Form C. 2118

WAR DIARY
or
INTELLIGENCE SUMMARY

(Erase heading not required.)

Instructions regarding War Diaries and Intelligence Summaries are contained in F. S. Regs., Part II. and the Staff Manual respectively. Title Pages will be prepared in manuscript.

Place	Date	Hour	Summary of Events and Information	Remarks and references to Appendices
	27th		Second batch of fever cases started; other office relief down, also P exchange.	
	28th		Normal. Successful attack on 3-mile front East of NIEPPE FOREST by 5th and 31st Divisions; greatest depth gained nearly a mile. Operators loaned to 5th Division for this as they had had a number gassed.	
	29th		Line laid from LAMBRES to LINGHEM as two battalions of Reserve Bde. there as well as Divisional Reception Camp and communication very roundabout.	
	30th		Nothing of special interest.	

.... Major, R.E.
O. C. 51st. Div. Sig. Coy.

1875 Wt. W593/826 1,000,000 4/15 J.B.C. & A. A.D.S.S./Forms/C.2118.

WAR DIARY or INTELLIGENCE SUMMARY

Army Form C. 2118

Place	Date	Hour	Summary of Events and Information	Remarks and references to Appendices
Mollinghem	July 1		D.H.Q. LAMBRES (N21c); Adv. D.H.Q. Mollinghem (O 14 a); 182 Bde on Right R.27 b 2 3; 183 Bde Left R 7 d 2.5; 184 Bde in reserve at FONTES. Artillery covering Division -61st and 66th Bde's under G.R.A. 61st Division. Division under XI Corps, 4th Division on right, 5th Division on left. Capt MacKinlay resumed charge of D.A.Sigs.	
	2		Salving Hop pole route from 'A' Exchange to Lys Canal.	
	3		Quiet day: continued salving hop pole route.	
	4		Normal.	
	5		Lieut. Browning went on leave. Lieut. Cameron took over charge of Sigs., 183 Brigade.	
	6		'P' Exchange personnel relieved. L/Cpl Booth took charge vice L/Cpl Haggis.	
	7		Normal.	
	8		HAM Signal Office overhauled for the reserve Brigade to return there.	231 Bde moved to HAM
	9		Normal. 74th Division preparing to take over from 61st Div.	
	10		Line laid from HAM to LE WILDEMONT for Battalion of Reserve Brigade. 231 Brigade of 74th Div. relieved 183 Brigade in left sector. 230 Brigade moved into reserve area - Hqrs in HAM.	
	11		Started to lay 7-pair route in stream from Mollinghem to Lilette Chateau for 74th Div. 230 Brigade relieved 182 Brigade in Right sector. 229 Brigade moved up to HAM area.	
	12		Continued with 7-pair route to Lilette. 183 Brigade at St.Hilaire; 182 Brigade at St.Andre Farm (N 2 d 4 8). Artillery relief commenced. Communication through 74 Divn at NORRENT FONTES	
	13		Completed 7-pair route to Lilette Chateau. Remainder of Artillery relieved during the night 13/14.	

WAR DIARY
or
INTELLIGENCE SUMMARY

(Erase heading not required.)

Army Form C. 2118

Instructions regarding War Diaries and Intelligence Summaries are contained in F. S. Regs., Part II. and the Staff Manual respectively. Title Pages will be prepared in manuscript.

Place	Date	Hour	Summary of Events and Information	Remarks and references to Appendices
Norrent Fontes	14		Command of the Sector passed to G.O.C. 74th Division at 10.0 a.m. Company marched to NORRENT FONTES at 9.15 a.m. Billets and accommodation good except for Picquet lines. Direct lines to all Brigades.	
	15		Fatigues and erecting harness sheds etc.	
	16		Baths all morning. Training programme: 1 Detachment in each Cable Section Cable drill - remainder jointing. 1 Wagon in each Section stripped in preparation for XI Corps Horse Show.	
	17		183 Brigade and 184 Brigade changed places at 11 a.m. 183 Brigade now at FONTES, 184 Bde at ST.HILAIRE. Training continued.	
	18		Normal Day. Training continued.	
	19		184 Brigade closed at ST HILAIRE and re-opened at MOULIN-LE-COMTE 3.30 p.m. Communication via XI Corps and RINCQ.	
	20		57 Brigade opened at St Hilaire 3.30 p.m.	
	21		Nothing to report. XI Corps had a "Silent Day" but as no official intimation was received no action was taken.	
Wardrecques	22		Division moved into the XV Corps and 2nd Army area. Div. Hqrs WARDRECQUES; Div. Arty. and 184 Brigade PONT ASQUIN; 182 Brigade Chateau BAMBECQ; 183 Brigade HEURINGHEM; M.G.Battalion at BLARINGHEM; 1/5 D.C.L.I. at STAPLE. Direct lines to all Brigades and Artillery, except 183 Brigade which is through BAR.	
	23		Very wet. Day spent in draining horse lines and erecting shelters.	
	24		Weather again interfered with training. Detachment Commanders reconnoitred Army line north of Hazebrouck which 61st Division is detailed to hold in case of attack.	
	25		Fatigue work on Sports Ground. Weather again bad.	

Army Form C. 2118

WAR DIARY
or
INTELLIGENCE SUMMARY
(Erase heading not required.)

Instructions regarding War Diaries and Intelligence Summaries are contained in F. S. Regs., Part II. and the Staff Manual respectively. Title Pages will be prepared in manuscript.

Place	Date	Hour	Summary of Events and Information	Remarks and references to Appendices
	26		Company Sports held at 2.30 p.m. No. 5 Section (M.G.Bn.) win the Inter-Section competition.	
	27		Weather again hopeless. Nothing of interest to report.	
	28		One cable wagon and one limbered R.E. wagon again placed under shelter and stripped for the 2nd Army Signa Horse Show. XI Corps Horse Show held at ACQUSTGIRE but only the wrestling team competed as it was impossible to enter wagon owing to the move and condition of picquet line.	
	29		Nothing to report. Work on snow wagon continued. Warning order received that 61st Divn. will return to XI Corps area.	
	30		Inspection by G.O.C. 61st Division at 10.0 a.m. of Headquarters, Wireless, and No.1 Sections, in drill order with transport.	
	31		Advanced party left at 2 p.m. for NORRENT FONTES to establish report centre. Brigades moved during night 31 July/1 August. 182 Brigade at ST ANDRE Farm; 183 Brigade to FONTES; 184 Brigade to ST PIERRE; Divl Arty. to Estree Blanche; M.G.Bn. to WITTERNESSE. Advanced office opened 7 p.m.	

Captain R.E
O.C. 61st Divl Sig. Cov.

Army Form C. 2118.

WAR DIARY
or
INTELLIGENCE SUMMARY.
(Erase heading not required.)

Vol 26

Place	Date	Hour	Summary of Events and Information	Remarks and references to Appendices
	1918 Aug 1		Division in 15th Corps Reserve but moved from WARDRECQUES to NORRENT FONTES at 10.0 a.m. into 11th Corps reserve. 182 Brigade at ST ANDRE FARM, 183 Brigade at FONTES, 184 Brigade ST HILAIRE, 61st D.A. ESTREE BLANCHE, C.R.E. HAM (36a, M 5). Lieut. L.B.G.Cunningham (G.L.) reported for duty as Officer i/c 307 Brigade R.F.A. sub-Section vice Lieut. a.V.McDowell to 79 H.A.B.	
	2		Heavy rain. No training possible.	
	3		Detachments trained in laying village cable.	
	4		Warning that Division would relieve 5th Division in Left Sector, 11th Corps, by 7th.	
	5		Inspection of 5th Division area. Very few lines and those in extremely poor condition. 184 Brigade took over Left Section.	
	6		Conferences re proposed attack on 2-mile front to take place on 12th. 182 Brigade took over Right Section. Relief of wireless sets. advance party sent over.	
	7		Command passed to G.O.C. 61st Division at 10.0 a.m. 182 Brigade at J.16 c 7 1, 183 Bde STEENBECQUE, 184 Brigade J 4 c 7 5. Artillery covering the front - one Brigade 5th and two Brigades 59th D.A's, other Brigade 5th D.A. being under 74th Division. 74th Division on Right and 31st Division on Left. In morning enemy withdrew on 74th Division front and in evening on 61st Division front. At night line laid in hurry from STATION INN to DOLLS HOUSE to put 183 Brigade who were ordered to act as Advance Guard in touch with their supporting artillery (307 Brigade J. 21 a 3 5 with advanced headquarters at DOLLS HOUSE J. 23 a O O).	

Army Form C. 2118.

WAR DIARY
or
INTELLIGENCE SUMMARY.
(Erase heading not required)

Instructions regarding War Diaries and Intelligence Summaries are contained in F. S. Regs., Part II. and the Staff Manual respectively. Title pages will be prepared in manuscript.

Place	Date	Hour	Summary of Events and Information	Remarks and references to Appendices
	8		In early morning 183 Brigade opened Headquarters at STATION INN. Speaking to them practically impossible as we had to use lines Division - THIENNES, THIENNES to Left Brigade, Left Brigade to Left Battalion stepped through. Five slight casualties in No. 4 Section from gas shelling. 183 Brigade attacked in morning and advanced line on right and centre but were held up on left.	
		6 p.m.	Line ran K 33 b 3 2, K 22 c 37, K 22 a 8 0, K 16 d 0 5. Speaking was possible by the evening but as 183 Brigade had not taken up a ring phone or sounder no through line was possible. This threw a big strain on 184 Brigade who had to transmit all messages.	
	9		No further advance took place and at night 183 Brigade was relieved and brought back into Divisional reserve. Comic pair mostly derelict along south side of Forest overhauled.	
	10		Direct line to Left Brigade overhauled and cable extension laid putting comic pair through to Right Brigade. Right Brigade existing line also relaid from where it left Canal in J 26 d to CAMOUFLAGE HOUSE J 21 a 7 6.	
	11		Lines laid on 10th poled. Lieut. Hunter Blair went on Paris leave. Lieut. Cunningham admitted to Hospital.	
	12		Started to make new office in THIENNES to replace hovel with inches of stagnant water on floor. This meant 10 pairs comic for 150 yards and 400 yards 8-pr armoured. Faulty section of Right Brigade line relaid.	
	13		D.A. established separate Signal Office. Examination of candidates for Corps Signal School by 2/Lieut. Pottage. Lieut. G.F.Box (5 Essex) posted to Company vice Lieut. Cunningham.	
	14		Examination continued. At night 183 Brigade relieved 184 Brigade in Left Section.	

Army Form C. 2118.

WAR DIARY
or
INTELLIGENCE SUMMARY.
(Erase heading not required.)

Place	Date	Hour	Summary of Events and Information	Remarks and references to Appendices
	15		Line put through from Reserve Brigade to D.C.L.I. giving a means of getting Left Brigade without passing through THIENNES. new office at THIENNES completed.	
	16		Direct Right Brigade line improved and labelled.	
	17		Labelling and improving lines. 59 D.A. in STEENBECQUE put through on permanent and cable picked up.	
	18		Left Group moved up to LA MOTTE CHATEAU. New direct Brigade lateral laid and old one recovered.	
	19		Indications of further German withdrawal. Right Brigade said they would move to CORBIE SOUTH (J 36 a 8 1). A pair was laid there from VIA ROMa teed off STATION INN - DOLLS HOUSE line.	
	20		Germans withdrew East of MERVILLE. 182 changed their minds and arranged to go to Right Battalion Headquarters. Brigade Section re-arranged all lines to suit this but Brigade did not move at all. 183 Brigade again went to STATION INN to act as advance Guard. Good speaking using comic pair and STATION INN - DOLLS HOUSE line. Front line ran by evening - K 36 a 5 5, K 29 b 7 5, K 17 b 6 2, K 11 c 9 3. Major Clark returned from leave.	
	21		Line laid to SACHET FARM (K 23 a 1 5) as 183 proposed to move there. Line through wood relaid and put up on trees. Line to CORBIE SOUTH recovered. Front line pushed out to about ROBERMETZ where opposition stopped movement.	
	22		Direct line put through to STATION INN for D.A. Route reconnoitered in morning for Army scheme of buried cables. In evening scheme was cancelled and Corps got out proposals for ditched cable.	

Army Form C. 2118.

WAR DIARY
or
INTELLIGENCE SUMMARY.
(Erase heading not required.)

Instructions regarding War Diaries and Intelligence Summaries are contained in F. S. Regs., Part II. and the Staff Manual respectively. Title pages will be prepared in manuscript.

Place	Date	Hour	Summary of Events and Information	Remarks and references to Appendices
	23		Reconnoitred routes for ditched cable scheme. 40th Division relieved 31st Division on left.	
	24		Corps ditched cable scheme vetoed by Army. 15-way route being built to about J 28 b 4 9. Decided to run three cables forward from there and make test point. Railhead moved to THIENNES. Front line roughly MEURILLON - NEUF BERQUIN road, L 31 a - L 13 b.	
	25		Pairs laid from J 28 b 4 9 to STATION INN (YFA 26) and to Support Brigade atold Right Brigade Headquarters DEVON CAMP.	
	26		59th Division relieved 74th Division on right. 184 relieved 183 as Outpost Brigade in early morning, 183 moving to DEVON CAMP.	
	27		Poled cable started to run from J 28 b 4 9 to STATION INN moved South of wood (YFA 29). Picking up cable round La MOTTE.	
	28		Running through cable; work on southern line continued.	
	29		Work on southern line. Corps decided to stop airline route at J 27 a so our centre at J 28 b 4 9 useless and all pairs there had to be diverted to run direct to proposed Divisional Headquarters at B.BY FARM J 21 c 4 3.	
	30		Preparations for move of D.H.Q. lines being split and led in to BABY FARM under Lieut. THORP. 184 moved forward to PAUTERY A 23 c 6 4; YFA 26 extended to there and YFA 28 diverted to run there instead of to STATION INN.	
	31	10 a.m.	Advanced D.H.Q. opened at BABY FARM. Preparations for move of rear Headquarters. Front line ran roughly L 32 b - L 21 a - L 14 a.	

.... Major, R.E.
O.C. 61st. Divl. Sig. Coy

Army Form C. 2118.

WAR DIARY
or
INTELLIGENCE SUMMARY.
(Erase heading not required.)

Instructions regarding War Diaries and Intelligence Summaries are contained in F. S. Regs. Part II. and the Staff Manual respectively. Title pages will be prepared in manuscript.

Place	Date	Hour	Summary of Events and Information	Remarks and references to Appendices
CROIX MARRAISE	Sept. 1		Div. in XI Corps. 182 Brigade STEENBECQUE; 183 Brigade STATION INN (K 8 d 5.2) MERVILLE FACTORY (K.23 c 6.4). 59th Div. on Right; 40th Div. on Left. 184 Brigade Rear D.H.Q. moved from WIDDEBROUC (I.20 a) to TANNAY (I 29 a). Trunks YFA 26 and 28 were extended via GREVE FARM (K 24 d) CHAPELLE DUVELLE (L 27 a 03) ESTAIRES captured.	Sheet's X 36.A Hazebrouck 5A
	2.		184 Brigade established advanced headquarters at CHAPELLE DUVELLE.	
	3.		Lieut. Thorp with Cable Section stationed at GREVE FARM to extend trunks as necessary. YFA 26 and 28 extended to L 11 d 3.7 where Brigade expected to go, but lines had to be diverted to L 24 a 1.5 as soon as laid. 183 Brigade relieved 184 Brigade as Outpost Brigade. Divisional boundary was extended 2,000 yards Northwards. YFA 20 laid from Factory via CHAPELLE DUVELLE to L 11 d 3.7. No. 500406 L/Cpl Seall E.A. awarded Bar to M.M.	
	4.		182 Brigade moved up to G 14 a 2.1 laying spurs to connect with main forward route at L 24 a 1.5 (Sheet 36A) (LF Test Point). YFA 26 & 28 extended to HOLYHEAD G.27 a 0.3 (Sheet 36) 307 Brigade R.F.A. relieved 306 Brigade R.F.A. as Outpost Artillery.	36
	5.		184 Brigade moved up to CHAPELLE DUVELLE, 183 Brigade moving up from STEENBECQUE to the FACTORY. Preparations started for opening Advanced D.H.Q. at RILL WORKS (L.33 b 3.7 Sheet 36 A). D.H.Q. to move on the 6th.	
	6.		Move of D.H.Q. postponed to 7th. Trunks all extended across River LYS to G 28 a 8.6 (Sheet 36); 20 from L 11 d 3.7 (36A); 26 and 28 from HOLYHEAD. Lieut. Power proceeded on leave to U.K.	
	7.		183 Brigade relieved 182 Brigade as Outpost Brigade. 182 Brigade on relief went further still off main route to G 8 d 4.2 and also opened a new rear Brigade office in L 12 d. No through line to their new headquarters. Move of D.H.Q. put off till 9th.	

Army Form C. 2118.

WAR DIARY
or
INTELLIGENCE SUMMARY.
(*Erase heading not required.*)

Instructions regarding War Diaries and Intelligence Summaries are contained in F. S. Regs., Part II. and the Staff Manual respectively. Title pages will be prepared in manuscript.

36A. 36.
HAZEBROUCK 5A.
Mayo

Place	Date	Hour	Summary of Events and Information	Remarks and references to Appendices
	Sept. 8.		Recovering spare cables.	
RILL WORKS	9.		Advanced D.H.Q. moved to RILL WORKS at 10 a.m., Rear Headquarters moving to CROIX MARAISE at 3.0 p.m. Line laid from 183 Brigade to 182 and through Fullerphone working to 182 obtained through telephone still through 183 exchange. New line (YFA 41) laid from Div.direct to LF Test point. Corpl. Barton left behind to recover cable.	
CROIX MARAISSE	10.		YFA 41 poled and extended to 183 where it was put through to the inter-brigade line laid on 9th giving direct line Division to 182 Bde.	
	11.		184 Brigade relieved 183 Brigade as Outpost Brigade, 183 withdrawing to CHAPELLE DUVELLE. Poling of forward lines.	
	12.		Poling continued.	
	13.		Corps installed exchange at MERVILLE to deal with minor units there. Communications nowwere:- Corps .. .. 2 lines and 1 via Rear Hqrs. Rear Headquarters .. 1 direct line ad 1 via Merville Exchange, Outpost Brigade .. 1 line, Support Brigade .: (G 8 d 4 2) 1 line, (CH.DUVELLE).. 2 lines, Outpost Artillery .. 1 line, Support .. 1 line.	
	14.		YFA 20 and 26 recovered between MERVILLE and CD. Cpl Barton rejoined picking upYFA 26 from CM to MERVILLE en route Lines straightened out and poled from LF to Outpost Brigade Headquarters.	
	15.		2/Lieut. J.S.Kippen R.E. reported for attachment as supernumerary Officer under lnstuction. 182 Brigade relieved 184 Brigade as outpost Brigade.	

Army Form C. 2118.

WAR DIARY
or
INTELLIGENCE SUMMARY.
(Erase heading not required.)

Instructions regarding War Diaries and Intelligence Summaries are contained in F. S. Regs., Part II. and the Staff Manual respectively. Title pages will be prepared in manuscript.

Maps:- 36A : 36
HAZEBROUCK 5A.

Place	Date	Hour	Summary of Events and Information	Remarks and references to Appendices
RILL WORKS	Sept. 16.		Test Box at forward communication centre G 28 a 9.7 blew up. Several other houses blew up the same day. 182 Brigade headquarters shifted out into fields under shelters. 306 Brigade R.F.A. relieved 307 Brigade R.F.A. as Outpost Artillery	
CROIX MARAISSE.	17.		Work started on putting through old XV Corps bury from SAILLY to ROUGE DE BOUT. 10 pairs through from G 17 d 0.2 to G 36 b 7.0, butroute at Northern end could not be proved further back, all lines seeming diss in section which would pass under cemetery of 4,300 Germans.	
	18.		Missing section discovered to lie to East of cemetery and route traced North across river.	
	19		Work started on proving Northern end of bury.	
	20		10 pairs through from G 11 c 5.5 to G 36 b 7.0. Bury had been used by Germans who had put 16 pairs through ad left remainder diss. Army area detachment working on main route PC 1 (L 27 b 5.1 sheet 36 A) - PC 2 (L 29 b 0.9 sheet 36A) - PC 3 (G 20 b 3.1 sheet 36) - PC 5 (G 11 a 1.5 sheet 36) with which this bury connected still on West side of PC 3 so that we did not gain full advantage of the bury.	
	21		183 Brigade relieved 182 Brigade as Outpost Brigade. 182 Brigade on arrival at CHAPELLE DUVELLE went out into tents. As usual began teeing off all lines and dissed lines all round.	
	22		Lieut. J. Hunter-Blair left to take up Instructor's post at S.S.T.C. BEDFORD.	
	23		LE DRUMEZ bury reconnoitred (G 20 b 2.1 - G 33 a 1.0).	
	24		Work started on putting through pairs in LE DRUMEZ bury.	
	25		Lines laid from PC to tee into main forward trunks with view to using bury from D.H.Q. BARTLETT FARM and JUNCTION POST captured and lost.	
	26		Work began on suspending 2 7-pair lead cable to Canal Box to pick up buried system.	

Army Form C. 2118.

WAR DIARY
or
INTELLIGENCE SUMMARY.
(Erase heading not required.)

Instructions regarding War Diaries and Intelligence Summaries are contained in F. S. Regs. Part II. and the Staff Manual respectively. Title pages will be prepared in manuscript.

Maps:- 36A: 36.
HAZEBROUCK 5A

Place	Date	Hour	Summary of Events and Information	Remarks and references to Appendices
	Sept			
RILL WORKS	27.		7-pair cables through in evening and four strapped tight through to PC 3 to pick up main forward trunks there.	
CROIX MARAISSES	28.		Two Brigades put into line relieving 183 Brigade which withdrew to CHAPELLE DUVELLE. 184 Brigade on Right (HQ G 13 a 5.4), 182 Brigade on Left (HQ G 8 a 8.1). YFA 20 relaid to run to G 8 a 8.1 as support artillery group moved up to Left Brigade Hqrs. New Group lateral also laid.	
	29.		Bury taken into use as far as PC 2, tees off PC 2, tees off 26, 28, 41 being brought in there. Cables on the Division side of the tees picked up. Enemy withdrawal seemed imminent so both groups were put on YFA 26 and YFA 20 was picked up the whole way owing to shortage of D8 cable in case of an advance. Fifth battle of YPRES opened.	
	30		JUNCTION POST captured. Breakdown of all communication with Battalion concerned caused great commotion. It was found that the Battalion had been shelled and had evacuated its headquarters taking its Loop Set with it and not going to Cable head 300 yards away where they could have remained in touch. Lieut. F.T.A.Power wrote to say he was being admitted to Hospital in Dublin and would not be back for months.	

.... Major, R.E.
O. C. 61st. Divl. Sig. Coy.

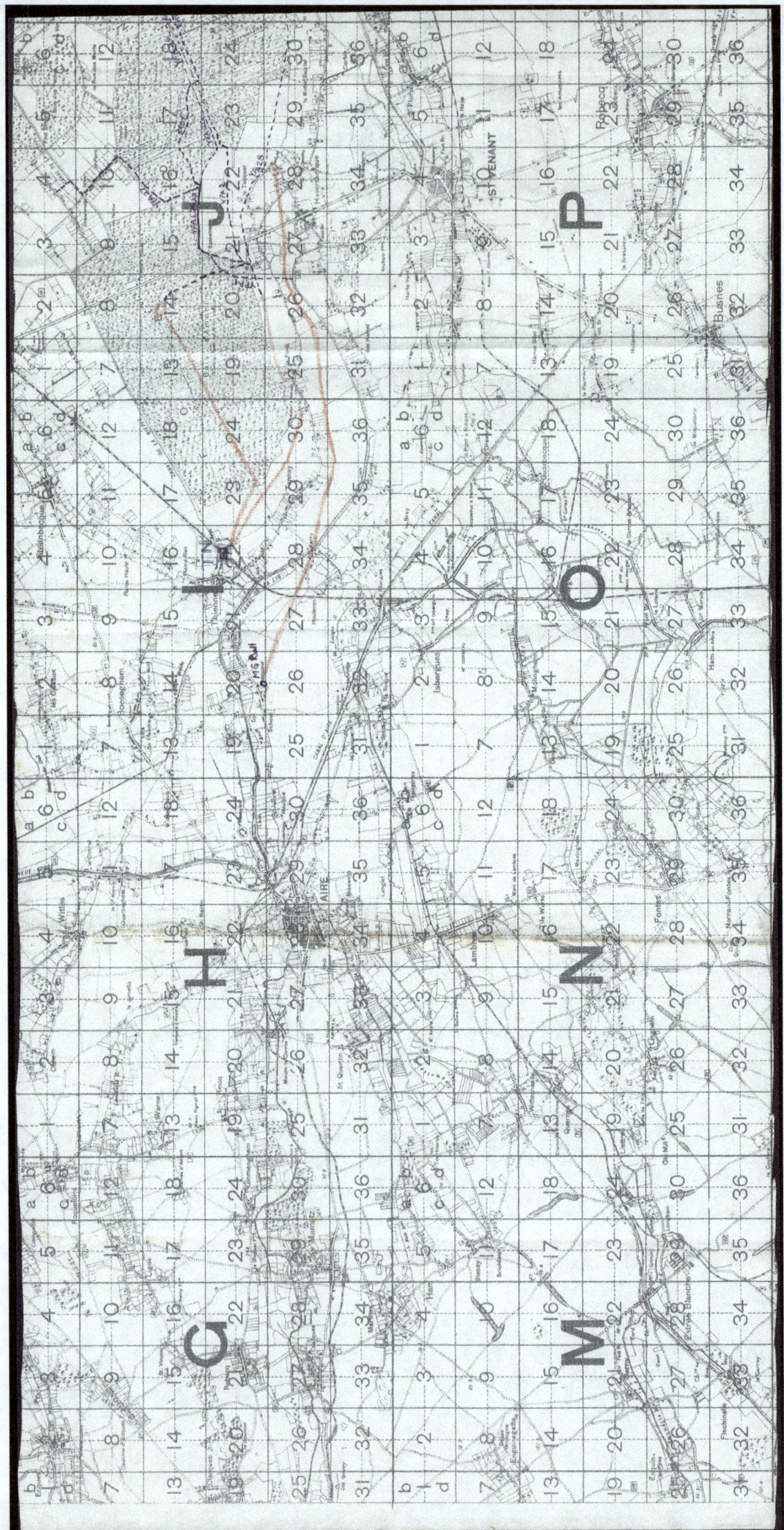

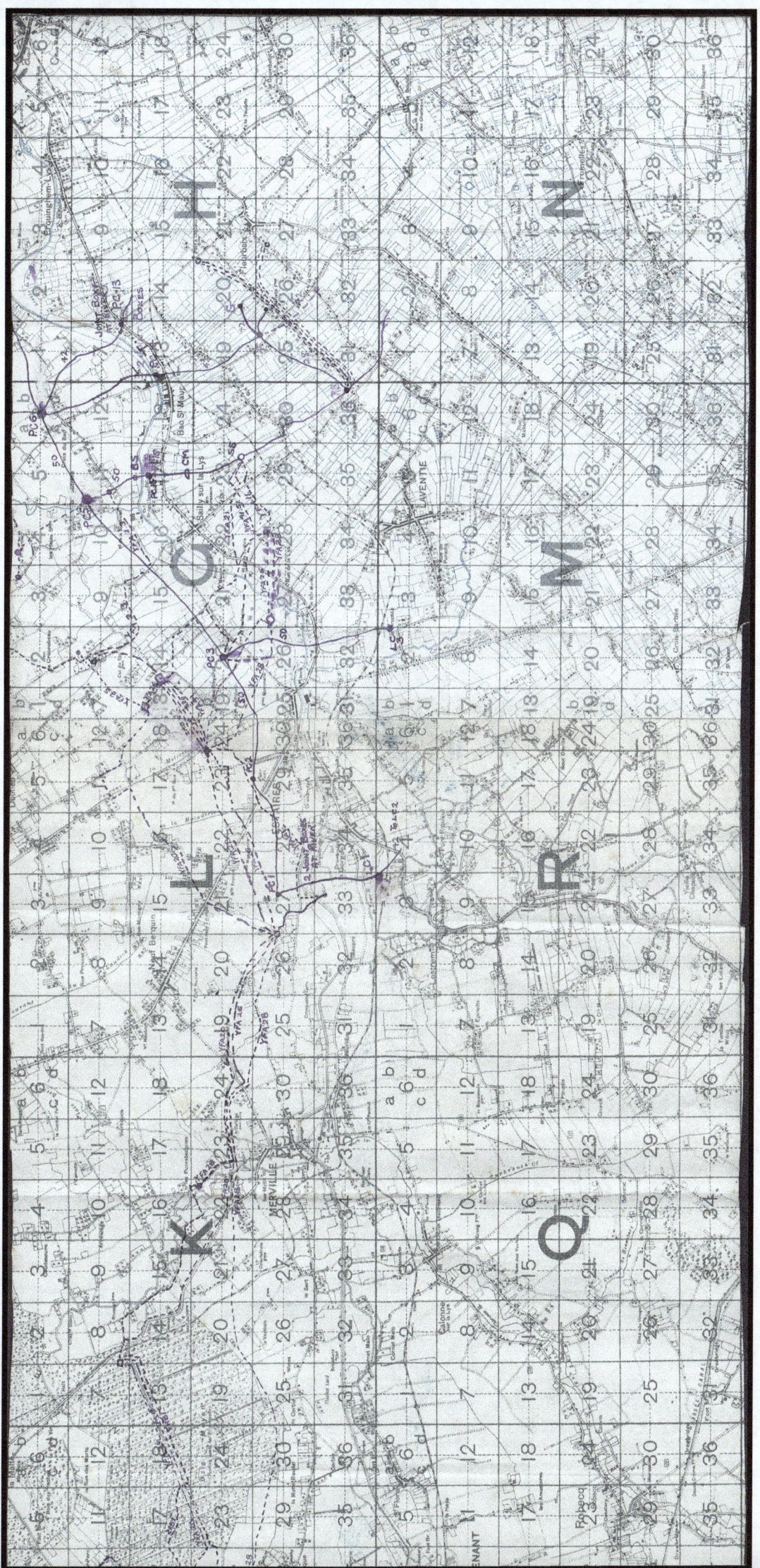

CONFIDENTIAL

WAR DIARY
OF

61st DIV Signal Coy

For the month of OCTOBER 1918

Army Form C. 2118.

WAR DIARY
or
INTELLIGENCE SUMMARY.
(Erase heading not required.)

61st. Divl. Signal Company R.E.

Place	Date	Hour	Summary of Events and Information	Remarks and references to Appendices
Rill Works. CROIX MARAISSE	1918. Oct. 1st.		Division holding left sector, 11th Corps front. 182 Bde on left,36.G.8.a.7.1. 183 Bde in reserve CHAPPELLE DUVELLE 36a.L.27.a.0.3. 184 Inf. Bde on right G.13.a.3.5. 61 Div. Arty. covering front. 59 Div. on right. 40 Div. on left. Two pairs laid from F.C.3 to SS Test Point G.23.d.5.4. YFA 20 extended to SS from G.22.c.4.5 and YFA 26 from G.28.a.9.7. to same place, then giving four pairs to SS. Continental time came into force.	1/40,000 Sheet 36 & 36A. 1/100,000 HAZEBROUCK 5A. APPENDIX B "A"
	2nd		Enemy retired: by evening line ran H.36. H.30. H.24. H.18. H.12. 17. At night 176 Bde relieved 182 Bde going to G.23.c.7.7.	
	3rd		Enemy still retiring. 178 Bde taking over from 184 Bde who had moved up to G.29.a.8.6. Hurried preparations for further move. Cables laid from end of bury and allotted to Brigades. 59 Div. preparing an advanced H.Qrs. near BARTLETT FARM H.26.a. Great confusion owing to two Brigades and another division all trying to fix lines to suit themselves. Both Brigades suddenly jumped forward without warning with their supporting artillery. Three of the four out of touch owing to lines having been changed about.	
LA LACQUE CROIX MARRIASSE	4th		59 Division relieved 61 Division; advanced hdqrs. moved to LA LACQUE but "Q" remained at CROIX MARRIASSE. Through to all brigades and Corps 182 MOLINGHEM, 183 STEENBECQUE, 184 THIENNES, Div Arty. FONTES.	
	5th		Advanced party sent to DOULLENS by lorry.	
	6th		D.H.Q. moved to DOULLENS - 182 Bde ST SULPICE 5.E.3.8. 183 Bde POMERA 4.F.3.1. 184 Bde BEAUVAL 5.E.0.3. Div. Arty AMPLIER 5.E.8.6. under 17th Corps, 3rd Army. Company roused at 03.30 hrs, at station 06.30 hrs. Train drew in 09.30 hrs left 10.30 hrs. Reached DOULLENS 17.30 hrs. Went on 10 miles up hill to ROSEL, arrived there 22.00 hrs. Company marched back into DOULLENS and got into billets 03.00 hrs next day. Winter time came into force.	
	7th		At DOULLENS. Company attended the "Frolics". 2/Lt. Kippen took over 307 Sub-section on 2/Lt Philp being withdrawn.	

LENS 11.
1/100,000

Army Form C. 2118.

WAR DIARY
or
INTELLIGENCE SUMMARY.

(Erase heading not required.)

Instructions regarding War Diaries and Intelligence Summaries are contained in F. S. Regs., Part II. and the Staff Manual respectively. Title pages will be prepared in manuscript.

Place	Date	Hour	Summary of Events and Information	Remarks and references to Appendices
DOULLENS	Oct. 8.		Advance party sent to LAGNICOURT 5.L.5.9. Brigades to be in area west of Canal du Nord. One line to rear 17th Corps, no lines for brigades. Transport moved by road to BRETENCOURT 4.I.3.8.	LENS 11. 1/100,000
LAGNICOURT	9		D.H.Q opened at LAGNICOURT 10.30hrs Party sent by train due in about 23.00 hrs did not arrive till 04.30 hrs. 182 Bde E.29.a.7.8. 183 Bde E.21.a.1.2. 184 Bde J.6.c.8.8. Artillery sent forward. Transport to BOYELLES Lens 4.J.8.4. CAMBRAI captured, very big advance S.E. of town.	57C 1/40,000
	10		Transport reached LAGNICOURT at midday. In evening brigades moved up, 183 as leading brigade to CANTAING L.3.b. 182 Bde to ANNEUX F.25.a. 184 Bde to SUGAR FACTORY L.29.a. Front line by evening LE CATEAU – ST HILAIRE – RIEUX. Organisation of Corps in depth throughout 24th Division leading, 19 Division in support, 51 Division in reserve; Corps front 3500 yds parallel to and south of CAMBRAI –SAULZOIR – BAVAI road. Lieut. F.T.A.Power struck off strength. 2/Lieut. Scott reported he was being sent to the Base.	
	11		Lieut Thorp proceeded on leave. Capt R.W.Mackinlay left for 3rd Corps H.A.Signals.	
	12		Lieut. A.Turnbull reported from Guards Division to take over Div. Arty Signals. D.H.Q. ordered to move forward but order then cancelled. Stores split to allow of forward instrument shop and minor motor cycle repairs, bulk of both kits remaining with Rear Office in event of rapid moves.	
NOYELLES	13		D.H.Q. moved to NOYELLES L.11.b.0.4. replacing 19 Division who replaced 24 Division at CAUROIR the latter going to AVESNES. Brigades did not move. Corps now at NINE WOOD L.10.d. Div. Arty. went up to relieve 40th Div Arty. in leading group of Corps. C.R.A. 61 Div. taking over command.	
	14		Running through salved cable.	

Army Form C. 2118.

WAR DIARY
or
INTELLIGENCE SUMMARY.
(Erase heading not required.)

Instructions regarding War Diaries and Intelligence Summaries are contained in F.S. Regs. Part II. and the Staff Manual respectively. Title pages will be prepared in manuscript.

Place	Date	Hour	Summary of Events and Information	Remarks and references to Appendices
Noyelles	Oct. 15		2 Detachments out for cable drill. Lieut. Baly rejoined from Course at 5th Army Signal School.	
	16		2 Detachments on cable drill. 2/Lt Pottage left for 37th Div. Signals, 2/Lt E.C.Hicks joined from that Company. 2/Lt Scott wrote that he had been transferred to England.	
	17		Cable drill.	
	18		Brigades moved up, 182 to S.W. corner of CAMBRAI, 183 to S.E. Corner, 184 to CANTAING, all on wire.	57C 1/40,000
	19		D.H.Q. moved to Rieux U.20.c. 182 Bde to RIEUX, 183 Bde to AVESNES-L'S-AUBERT U.22.a. (via 19 Div.) 184 Bde to CAGNONCLES T.28.d. (via Corps)	
	20		19 Division attacked after violent bombardment to find enemy had retired. Line advanced to River HARPIES. Corps Cable Detachment attached under Lt. Exelby (TT Section).	
	21		Warning order for moving up. Trouble over rations owing to trains being over 24 hours late.	
	22		2/Lt. A.W.May joined from 3rd Division for temporary duty attachment. Test Point at V.4.b. constructed and lines laid from ST AUBERT.	
ST AUBERT RIEUX	23		Advanced D.H.Q. opened at ST AUBERT at 14.30.hrs alongside 19 Div. "G". All Brigades moving up for attack on 24th. Advanced "G" office prepared at MONTRECOURT V.3.b.8.7. This to open at Zero while "C" still remained at RIEUX till 11.00 hrs 24th. Thus three offices had to be run, two of which had to be fitted up and the personnel conveyed from place to place. 182 Bde moved to V.5.c.6.2. with advanced Hdqrs at P.30.c.4.5. 183 Bde to ST AUBERT and V.5.a.7.2. with advanced Hdqrs at Q31.a.0.6. 184 Bde replaced 183 in ST AUBERT in evening and early next morning moved up to MONTRECOURT.	51A 1/40,000.

Army Form C. 2118.

WAR DIARY
or
INTELLIGENCE SUMMARY.
(Erase heading not required.)

Instructions regarding War Diaries and Intelligence Summaries are contained in F. S. Regs., Part II. and the Staff Manual respectively. Title pages will be prepared in manuscript.

APPENDIX B.
51A 1/40,000

Place	Date	Hour	Summary of Events and Information	Remarks and references to Appendices
ST AUBERT RIEUX	Oct 23		19 Division carried out a minor operation to give us a straight start - Finding opposition slight they pushed on and captured our first objective - The final objective therefore set further away. Lieut. Wilson and 9 men of No.5 Section called in to Headquarters for active operations.	
	24		Zero 4.a.m., 183 Bde got on on right capturing BERMERAIN (Q.22) but 182 Bde held up, short of VENDEGIES (Q.14) though their left got through SOMAING (Q.7) - in afternoon 184 Bde were put in to work round VENDEGIES from the S.E. and the final objectives were captured. Advanced "G" did not open at MONTRECOURT till noon. 183 Bde moved up to Q.23.c.o.0. and 184 Bde also made their headquarters there when they were put in. Communications are shown in Appendix "B". 2nd Division, VI Corps was on the right and 4th Division XXII Corps on the left	
MONTRECOURT ST AUBERT	25		Line was pushed forward across the VALENCIENNES - LE QUESNOY road on the whole divisional front.	
VENDEGIES ST AUBERT	26		Advanced D.H.Q. opened at VENDEGIES Q.14.d.5.5. at 5.p.m., the MONTRECOURT office being closed down, also M.G. test point. Through to all Brigades though only four hours notice was given. 182 Bde moved to Q.9.c.2.7., 183 and 184 to Q.22.a. BERMERAIN.	
	26		Rear D.H.Q. moved up to VENDEGIES - Left flank found ARTRES unoccupied and 4th Div. then moved up. 3rd Div. relieved 2nd Div. on right. 182 Bde left support 183 Bde right support, 184 in line, Hdqrs Q.22.a.5.5. with T.P. at LARBLIN Q.16.a.5.2. - in afternoon 184 suddenly moved their Hdqrs to opposite flank and went straight away to Q.4.c.6.7. giving no warning. At night 183 Bde relieved 184 Bde in line making their Hdqrs at Q.4.c.6.7.	
	27		Direct line laid to 183 Bde working Divn. Battn and Staff Captain all through one line to LARBLIN. LARBLIN taken over as Divisional Test Point in charge of L/Cpl.Tooth C.W. and tidied.	
	28		2/Lt May sent to 306 Bde R.F.A. to replace Lt. Baly while on leave.	

Army Form C. 2118.

WAR DIARY
or
INTELLIGENCE SUMMARY.
(Erase heading not required.)

Instructions regarding War Diaries and Intelligence Summaries are contained in F. S. Regs., Part II. and the Staff Manual respectively. Title pages will be prepared in manuscript.

51A. 1/40,000

Place	Date	Hour	Summary of Events and Information	Remarks and references to Appendices
VENDEGIES	Oct 29		Heavy shelling mixed gas and H.E. on night 28/29th - Direct hit on Div. Arty Signal Office. 9 men of Div. Arty Section became casualties. 182 Bde very heavily shelled. Lieut. H.F.Box buried by a shell and killed. Funeral at 3.p.m. He was buried at the CRUCIFIX 51A.Q.19.b.8.8. 182 Bde moved their Hqrs to SOMMAING Q.7.d.6.4. 183 Bde withdrew to old Hqrs in BERMERAIN keeping a Test Point at Q.4.c.6.7. 7 of 182 Bde Section to hospital gassed including all N.C.Os except Sgt. Williamson who remained on end of line to Division while rest were digging out Lieut. Box. Lieut. Thorp returned from leave. Lieut. Baly proceeded on leave (31/10 - 14/11)	
	30		6 Signallers borrowed from D.C.L.I. to help 182 Bde Section. 2nd Division in on right again splitting 6th Corps front with 3rd Division. Line laid from Q.4.c.6.7. to railway in K.34.b. as eventual third trunk also a lateral to brigade of 4th Division in QUERENAING. 2/Lt. Hicks to 182 Bde for temporary duty.	
	31		A second line laid form Q.4.c.6.7. to railway. Military Medals awarded to:- No.500367. Sgt. Gaut. H.G. D.A. H.Q. Section. No.500401. M.C.Corpl. Troy W. do. do. No.499937. 2/Cpl. Pople H. 306 Sub-section. No.499935. Sapr. Hucker V.W. do. do. Armistice with TURKEY.	

Signature .... Major R.E.
O. C. 61st. Divl. Sig. Coy.

Vol 31

War Diary
of
61st Div. Sig'nl Coy. R.E.
for
November 1918

V. Greene ?t.

WAR DIARY

OF

61st Divl. Signal Coy

FOR THE MONTH OF MARCH 1918

VOL 23

Army Form C. 2118.

WAR DIARY
of
INTELLIGENCE SUMMARY.
(Erase heading not required.)

Instructions regarding War Diaries and Intelligence Summaries are contained in F. S. Regs., Part II. and the Staff Manual respectively. Title pages will be prepared in manuscript.

Maps:- VALENCIENNES 1/100,000. Sheet 57A 1/40,000.

61st DIVL. SIGNAL Co. R.E. OFFICE

Place	Date	Hour	Summary of Events and Information	Remarks and references to Appendices
VENDEGIES.	1918 Nov. 1		Divl. HQ. at VENDEGIES Q.4.c.9.u. with Report Centre at K.34.b.6.3: 182 Inf. Bde. - LA JUSTICE at LARBLIN W.16.a.5.3: 183 Inf. Bde. - BERMERAIN, with advanced HW. covering front (7 R.F... Bdes). 184 Inf. Bde. in Reserve at BERMERAIN. C.R.A. Commanding Artillery attack began at 05.15 from small bridgehead North of River RONELLE in K.29.a.b.d. with objective a North & South line east of FRESEAU and MARESCHES. All objectives were taken, except on left, where failure of 4th Division to capture FRESEAU. Over 800 prisoners taken, including 27 officers. A counter attack drove us back off crest. A further attack at night did not gain all objectives as FRESEAU was still untaken. Over 1000 prisoners in the 24 hours. Sappers VENN & BURDETT wounded. L/Cpl. SH.RWOOD wounded at duty.	
	2		Further attack made in early morning by 184 Inf. Bde., who established their Hdqrs. at K.34.b.6.3., took us well out beyond objectives, final line running L.14.b.0.5., L.15.d.2.8.-L.21 Central - L.27.a.a.4. - L.32.b.2.7 - R.2.b.2.7 - Prisoners taken from 27 Battalions.	
ST. AUBERT.	3		Division was relieved by 19th & 24th Divisions, the latter taking the night. H.Drs. moved to ST. AUBERT U.24.b.5.3. 182 Inf. Bde. ST. AUBERT; 183 & 184 Inf. Bdes. at AVESNES les AUBERT U.28.8. Artillery Bdes. remained in action. Lieut. COATS went on leave.	
	4		19th Div. & 24th Div. attacked at dawn, but found enemy had gone. 182 Inf. Bde. moved to HAUSSY V.12. Advanced Corps Hdqrs. moved up to VENDEGIES. By evening front line had reached "ARGNIES ETH BRY. Lieut. WILSON went on leave. Lieut. J.F. SIMPSON reported for duty and took over 182 Inf. Bde. Signals. Lieut. HICKS returning to Hdqrs. Armistice signed with AUSTRIA.	

Army Form C. 2118.

WAR DIARY
or
INTELLIGENCE SUMMARY.
(Erase heading not required)

Instructions regarding War Diaries and Intelligence Summaries are contained in F.S. Regs., Part II. and the Staff Manual respectively. Title pages will be prepared in manuscript.

Maps. — VALENCIENNES 1/100,000. Sheet 57A 1/40,000

Place	Date 1918	Hour	Summary of Events and Information	Remarks and references to Appendices
ST AUBERT.	Nov. 5		Rain all day. Warned to be ready to move, but move cancelled later.	
	6.		Rain all day. Front line reached outskirts of BAVAI.	
	7.		SEDAN and BAVAI captured. German plenipotentiaries reached allied front line near GUISE.	
VENDEGIES.	8.		Advanced Div. Hdqrs. moved to VENDEGIES; 182 Inf. Bde. to SOMAING; 183 Inf. Bde. to BERMERAIN; 184 Inf. Bde. to SEPmERIES. Corps Hdqrs. moved to BAVAI.	
	9.		'B' Branch moved up to VENDEGIES. MAUBEURGE captured.	
	10.		Picking up cable in village.	
	11.		Hostilities ceased at 11.0.a.m. - Impromptu Concert in evening.	
	12.		281693 Sapper BLACKETT H no.3 Section) awarded MILITARY MEDAL.	
	13.		Normal day.	
RIEUX	14.		D.H.Q. moved to RIEUX; 182 Inf. Bde. to AVESNES; 183 Inf. Bde. to ST AUBERT; 184 Inf. Bde. to HAUSSY. Move only ordered at midnight, so everything was disorganised on arrival. No lines to Brigades.	
CAMBRAI	15		Division started to concentrate in CAMBRAI, Div. Hdqrs, 182 & 183 Inf. Bdes. reaching there. 184 Inf.Bde. stayed at CAGNOCLES, T.28. No billeting done before arrival of Division. Line to 'ACTAR' Exchange, with Morse extended to 3rd Army.	
	16.		No.199864 Sergt. BURCHETT J.H. (No.4 Section) awarded MILITARY MEDAL.	
	17.		Very cold. Special Church Parade cancelled owing to weather.	

Army Form C. 2118.

WAR DIARY
or
INTELLIGENCE SUMMARY.
(Erase heading not required.)

Instructions regarding War Diaries and Intelligence Summaries are contained in F. S. Regs., Part II. and the Staff Manual respectively. Title pages will be prepared in manuscript.

Map: — LENS 1/100,000.

Place	Date	Hour	Summary of Events and Information	Remarks and references to Appendices
	1918 Nov. 18 to 22		Special Service in English Church for Signal Company at 10.a.m. Rifle exercises, physical exercises, route marches and games. Wet, cold and misty.	
	19.		MILITARY MEDAL awarded to No.500149 Sergt. Cox L.C., 495333 Spr. Jewl R.J., 325589 Sapper Sandham W.A., 503097 Fnr. Barlow A.M. all of 307 R.F.A. Bde. Sub-section.	
	21.		Artillery Bdes. reached CAMBRAI from MAUBEUGE.	
CAMBRAI.	23		Transport moved off under 2nd Lieut. HICKS for new area, staging in HAPLINCOURT - BERTHINCOURT area (Lens 5 L)	
	24		Transport reached ALBERT. Advance party sent over by lorry.	
	25.	3.p.m.	D.H. closed at CAMBRAI at 9.0.a.m. and re-opened at BERNAVILLE (5.c.0.6) at Train party under 2nd Lieut. HAY due to leave at 10.a.m., but whole railway system disorganized, and at 9.0.a.m. notice was given that train would be at least 10 hours late. Transport made a 25 mile march, reaching BERNAVILLE at 5.0.p.m. Billets bad, but slightly better than in Jan. 1917. The attitude of the inhabitants was also hostile.	
	26.		Train party left CAMBRAI at 15.00.	
	27.		Train party reached CONTEVILLE at 09.00 and were lorried to destination. Divis on concentrated in BERNAVILLE area, 182 Inf. Bde. at MAISON PONTHIEU (4.x.6.5), 183 Inf. Bde. DOMLEGER (5.b.0.9); 184 Inf. Bde. DOMART (6.b.5.9), Divl. Artillery WAVANS (4.c.0.6) all on 'phone.	
	28/30.		Improving Billets in BERNAVILLE.	

.... Major. R.E.
O. O. 61st. Divl. Sig. Coy

Headquarters,
   61st.Division.

   The Diary of the Divisional Signal Coy. as shewn on the attached schedule was not received with the other Diaries; please cause same to be rendered without delay.

G. H. Qrs.,
3rd.Echelon.
6th.February, 1919.

Y. Yates
Major,
D. A. A. G.,
for D. A. G.

No. 140/3449

O.C. 61/Div. Signal Coy.

Please forward copy of your War Diary for month of December '18.

H. M. Taylor
Captain
S.A.A.
61st. Divn.

14.2.19.

B.M. 2nd H.Q.
21/2
Instruction.
Forwarded.

[stamp: HEADQUARTERS HIGHLAND MOUNTED DIVISION No. 236/1]

H. A. Taylor Capt.
for Major General
Commanding 61st. Divn.

18.2.'19.

Army Form C. 2118.

WAR DIARY
or
INTELLIGENCE SUMMARY.

(Erase heading not required.)

Instructions regarding War Diaries and Intelligence Summaries are contained in F. S. Regs., Part II. and the Staff Manual respectively. Title pages will be prepared in manuscript.

61 D Signals
Vol 32

Place	Date	Hour	Summary of Events and Information	Remarks and references to Appendices
Bernaville	1.12.18.		Dec.1st. to 7th.. Time spent maintaining permanent lines in the area.	
St.Riquier	8.12.18.		Dec.1st. to 7th.. Time spent maintaining permanent lines in the area. Divisional Hqrs. moved to St.Riquier. Infantry Brigades at Domart (184), Ailly (MB 3) and Hiermont (182). Remainder of month spent in maintaining and patrolling lines in new area. Number of messages and D.R.L.S. packets averaged 550 per day except Xmas Day, when number was 150. Company Dinner and Concert on Xmas Day.	

W.Browne
Lieut.R.E.,
for O.C.61st.Divl.Signal Company.

Army Form C. 2118.

WAR DIARY
or
INTELLIGENCE SUMMARY.
(Erase heading not required.)

61st. Divl. Signal Co. R.E.

Place	Date	Hour	Summary of Events and Information	Remarks and references to Appendices
ST RIQUIER	January 1919		Month spent at ST. RIQUIER in maintaining permanent routes in the Area, checking stores etc. Lieut. G.L.Thorp demobilised January 19th. Major P.W.Clark, D.S.O. M.C. demobilised January 20th. Command of Company taken over by Major G.R.Smallwood, M.C. on January 28th. 55 other ranks demobilised.	

G.R.Smallwood
Major.
O.C. 61st. Divl. Signal Co. R.E.

Army Form C. 2118.

WAR DIARY
or
INTELLIGENCE SUMMARY.

(Erase heading not required.)

61 D Signals
Vol 34

Instructions regarding War Diaries and Intelligence Summaries are contained in F. S. Regs., Part II. and the Staff Manual respectively. Title pages will be prepared in manuscript.

Place	Date	Hour	Summary of Events and Information	Remarks and references to Appendices
St. Riquier	1919 February		Month spent at St.Riquier maintaining permanent routes in the area. Capt.A.Turnbull M.C. 182 Brigade moved to DIEPPE and 184 Brigade to ETAPLES during month. Capt. G.D.Twynam M.C. demobilized Feb.1st. Capt. G.D.Twynam M.C. demobilized Feb.3rd. 24 other ranks demobilized.	
			J.R.Smallwood Major, O.C.61st.Divl.Signal Company.	

Army Form C. 2118.

WAR DIARY
or
INTELLIGENCE SUMMARY.
(Erase heading not required.)

Place	Date	Hour	Summary of Events and Information	Remarks and references to Appendices
LE TREPORT	April 1919.		Month spent at LE TREPORT taking care of communications of the Division, and assisting L. of C. at the LE TREPORT locality exchange. All animals have been transferred from this unit, also all Motor Transport except the Box Car. All surplus stores checked and ready for handing over. 60 O.Rs. demobilized during month. 15 O.Rs. transferred to L.of C. Battn. 30.4.19.. Major G.R.Smallwood left unit to take over Signals, Calais 23.4.19.. His place taken by Capt. E.W.Benson.	

E.W.Benson
Captain,
O.C. 61st. Divl. Signal Co. R.E.

Instructions regarding War Diaries and Intelligence Summaries are contained in F. S. Regs., Part II. and the Staff Manual respectively. Title pages will be prepared in manuscript.

Army Form C. 2118.

WAR DIARY
or
INTELLIGENCE SUMMARY.
(Erase heading not required.)

Summary of Events and Information

WAR DIARY _____ 61st. DIVL. SIGNAL CO. R.E.

Place	Date	Hour		Remarks and references to Appendices

LE TREPORT. JUNE 1919.

Month spent in assisting Dieppe Signals in maintaining communications in the Area;
also in getting all stores ready for final departure to the U.K.
Last man on the Cadre was demobilized on the 3rd. of the month, only the Equipment
Guard now remaining.

Capt.E.W.Benson M.C.demobilized on 17th.;
Lieut.J.D.Cameron   do   on 3rd.
Lieut.J.F.Simpson R.G.A.now in charge.

The Equipment Guards of 306 and 307 Brigades R.F.A. left for U.K.on the 22nd.and 23rd.
respectively and Equipment Guard of 315 A.F.A.Brigade on the 16th. of month.

J.F.Simpson Lieut.
O.C.61st. DIVL. SIGNAL CO.R.E.

WO95/3049/2
61 Battalion Machine Gun Corps

61ST DIVISION

61 BN. MACHINE GUN CORPS
~~267TH MACHINE GUN COY.~~

JAN 1918 - SEP 1919

CONFIDENTIAL

WAR DIARY

of

267th Machine Gun Company

From 13 January to 31 January, 1918.

1.

Army Form C. 2118.

WAR DIARY
or
INTELLIGENCE SUMMARY.
(Erase heading not required.)

Instructions regarding War Diaries and Intelligence Summaries are contained in F. S. Regs., Part II. and the Staff Manual respectively. Title pages will be prepared in manuscript.

Place	Date	Hour	Summary of Events and Information	Remarks and references to Appendices
SOUTHAMPTON	13/1/18	7 p.m.	Sailed from SOUTHAMPTON in "ARCHIMEDES"	MM
HAVRE	14/1/18	10.30 a.m.	Berthed and proceeded to disembark personnel, horses vehicles. Disembarkation completed 3.30 p.m. & company	MM
			proceeded to No. 2 Rest Camp.	MM
	15/1/18		Cleaning up and training carried out.	MM
	16/1/18	6.30 p.m.	Proceeded to GARE des MARCHANDISES entrained. Left HAVRE 9.32 p.m.	MM
VILLERS ST CHRISTOPHE	17/1/18	1.45 p.m.	Arrived TILLERS ST. CHRISTOPHE and proceeded to billets. Billeted in Huts by Station.	MM
FORESTE	18/1/18	2.30 p.m.	Proceeded by road to FORESTE and billetted.	MM
	19/1/18		Cleaning up.	MM
	20/1/18		Company inspected by Major General commanding 61st Division.	MM
		2.30 p.m.	Nos 3 & 4 Sections relieved two Sections of 90th Machine Gun Company in PRESNOY & at S4 & c.27.33.d. Strongpoints at MM	FRANCE 62.B.SW ⅟20,000.
	21/1/18 -27/1/18		Work carried out at strongpoints, improving emplacements, preparing trenches, building alternative emplacements &c.	MM
			Nos 1 & 2 Sections carried out training in immediate action, mechanism repairs, drill, revetments &c.	MM
			Inspections were attended from each section for instruction to instructors to teams of 1&3 & 1&4 off per Coy Front MM	MM
	28/1/18	9 p.m.	Nos 1 & 2 Sections relieved 3 & 4 Sections who returned to billets at FORESTE.	MM
	29/1/18		Cleaning up. Training carried out by 3 & 4 Sections, Work at alternative emplacements & improvements carried out by 1 & 2 Sections	MM

Army Form C. 2118.

WAR DIARY
or
INTELLIGENCE SUMMARY.
(Erase heading not required.)

Instructions regarding War Diaries and Intelligence Summaries are contained in F. S. Regs., Part II. and the Staff Manual respectively. Title pages will be prepared in manuscript.

Place	Date	Hour	Summary of Events and Information	Remarks and references to Appendices
FORESTE	30/1/18		3 & 4 sections carried out training & gun drill, musketry, aiming, further practice, gunlayers & inspecting drills.	
	31/1/18		1 & 2 sections improving gun positions & dugouts, making alternate emplacements &c.	

HWilliams Major.
O.C. 267 M. G. COY.
1/2/18.

267th Machine Gun Company.

	Officers	W.O's	Sgts	Other Ranks
Strength 31/1/18.	10	1	9	167

Drafts during Month   Nil.

Officers struck off strength   Nil.
or reinforcements.

A.W.Hannay

O.C. 267 M.G. Coy.

31/1/18

CONFIDENTIAL.

War Diary

of.

267th Machine Gun Company.

From 1 February to 28 February, 1918.

2.

Army Form C. 2118.

WAR DIARY
or
INTELLIGENCE SUMMARY.
(Erase heading not required.)

Instructions regarding War Diaries and Intelligence Summaries are contained in F. S. Regs., Part II. and the Staff Manual respectively. Title pages will be prepared in manuscript.

Place	Date	Hour	Summary of Events and Information	Remarks and references to Appendices
FORESTE	1/2/18		1 + 2 Sections improved gun positions, constructed alternative emplacements, &c.	Appx
	–4/2/18		3 + 4 sections carried out training	Appx
	5/2/18		3 + 4 sections relieved 1 + 2 sections who returned to billets at FORESTE. Gun position moved from M.27.A.95.70 to M.27.d.80.95 within PRESNOY STREAM POINT	FRANCE 62 S.M. 1/20,000 Appx
	6/2/18		3 + 4 sections improved gun positions and constructed positions at M.27.d.80.95. 1+2 Sections cleaned up, letters, pay &c.	Appx
	7/2/18		do. 1+2 sections carried out training &c.	Appx
	8/2/18		3 + 4 Sections building alternative positions, improved troops, together &c. 1+2 Sections carried out training exercises and gun-fire practice, route march, tactical schemes &c.	Appx
	9/2/18 – 10/2/18		as on 8/2/18	Appx
	11/2/18		1 + 2 Sections relieved 3 + 4 sections, who relieved to billets at FORESTE.	Appx
	16/2/18		1 + 2 sections worked improved emplacements, 3 + 4 sections training	Appx
	–21/2/18		do	at PRESNOY Pt No 2 Section relieved
	22/2/18		by section of 152 Company & Section returned to FORESTE	Appx
	23/2/18		N° 1 Section at PRESNOY Pt relieved by section of 152 Coy at 11pm. Section returned to FORESTE	Appx

T.131. Wt. W708–776. 500000. 4/16. Sir J. C. & S.

Army Form C. 2118.

WAR DIARY
or
INTELLIGENCE SUMMARY.
(Erase heading not required.)

Instructions regarding War Diaries and Intelligence Summaries are contained in F. S. Regs., Part II. and the Staff Manual respectively. Title pages will be prepared in manuscript.

Place	Date	Hour	Summary of Events and Information	Remarks and references to Appendices
FOLKESTONE	24/7/16		Church parade 10.40.	FRANCE 62.C.SE & 62.C.SW 1/20,000
	25/7/16	9pm	No. 2 Section relieved guns of 183 Company at M.35.A.45.25 (Tr. DAKAR) and M.35.C.5.5, and guns of 183 Company at M.35.a.4.7, and occupies new position at M.34.d.95.40.	
		9.30pm	No. 3 Section relieved hub guns of 183 Company at M.33.a.4.8.1 & occupies two new positions M.33a.85.15 Moved H.Q. Moved to ATTILLY and took over billets. Inspected temporarily No. 1 & 4 sections & Company HQ.	
			Relieved at ATTILLY and held themselves in readiness to man positions in BATTLEZONE as follows: 2 guns S1.6.16.35 2 guns X.1.c.85.65, 2 guns S.7.b.45.50, 2 guns X.12.c.35.00.	
	26/7/16		1 & 2 Sections carried on training, 2 & 3 sections improved positions, constructed new positions ie rest of do	
	27/7/16		do	
	28/7/16	6.5pm	manning BATTLEZONE positions carried out.	
		7.55pm		
		10pm	1 - 4 Sections moved to BATTLEZONE positions for permanent occupation.	

A.D. Mann
Major
Commanding
207 Machine Gun Company.

1/8/16.

267 Machine Gun Company

	Officers	Other Ranks
Strength on 28/2/18.	10	204
Decrease during month.		
Increase " "		
	—	8 to C.C.S.
	—	18 reinforcements.
	1	20 posted from inf. Batt⁰⁵
		4 " " 2/5 R. War. Regt.
		4 " " 2/4 Glos. Regt.
		4 " " 2/6 " "
		4 " " 2/1 Bucks.
		4 " " 2/8 R. War. Regt.

H.W.N. Anan
Major

1/3/18

Army Form C. 2118.

WAR DIARY
or
INTELLIGENCE SUMMARY.
(Erase heading not required.)

VOL. I.

WH 2

61 Bn M.G.C.

Place	Date	Hour	Summary of Events and Information	Remarks and references to Appendices
PPUX	1/3/18		The Battalion at present under organisation. Officers of 61st Bn. are:- Commanding Officer Lt Col R.E. Scott D.S.O., 2nd in Command Major S. Oldham. Adjutant Lieut J Lynde & Transport Officer Lieut J Shepherd. Four Companies & 2 sections manning the divisional front. B & D Coys. & No 4 Section at PPUX. No Battalion Staff yet arrived & the companies not yet made up to the new establishment. Guns not arranged on the divisional front into three groups distributed in depth, each under a group commander. (tactical purposes under the orders of the G.O.C. Bde. of their sub-sectors.) Twelve guns in the forward zone - 30 in the near zone for purposes & 34 in the battle zone. In addition as part of the divisional artillery scheme on a large barrage front of heavy artillery cover. 12 emergency barrage guns are held in reserve. Training carried out by sections in reserve. Casualties Nil.	

WAR DIARY
or
INTELLIGENCE SUMMARY.
(Erase heading not required.)

Army Form C. 2118.

61/B. M.G.C.

Place	Date	Hour	Summary of Events and Information	Remarks and references to Appendices
VAUX	2/3/18	Nil	Front quiet. Increased aerial activity. Training carried out by reserve sections & gun teams in battle zone. Casualties Nil.	
"	3/3/18		Front quiet. Suspected enemy relief during night - M.G.s on right division fired on ST QUENTIN. Training as usual. Casualties Nil.	
"	4/3/18		Nothing to report. Training as usual - losses this Nil.	
"	5/3/18		Heavy enemy trench mortar activity & approaching our lines, but ran down off by M.G. & rifle fire. One official casualty.	
"	6/3/18		Front quiet. Our M.G.s fired on E.A.s during day - they were more active than usual. No casualties. Capt A.T.H. Edmunds joined BN as R.M.O. R.A.M.C.	
"	7/3/18		Nothing to report. Training as usual. Casualties Nil. B# Coy relieved A# Coy in the right front. Relief satisfactorily carried out.	

Army Form C. 2118.

WAR DIARY
or
INTELLIGENCE SUMMARY.

(Erase heading not required.)

Instructions regarding War Diaries and Intelligence Summaries are contained in F. S. Regs., Part II. and the Staff Manual respectively. Title pages will be prepared in manuscript.

Place	Date	Hour	Summary of Events and Information	Remarks and references to Appendices
VAUX	8/3/18		Front quiet. Aerial activity above normal. Several fights took place. Training as usual. Casualties Nil.	61 Dn M.G.C.
"	9/3/18		Slightly increased hostile artillery activity. Training as usual. Casualties Nil.	
"	10/3/18		Nothing to report. Casualties Nil.	
"	11/3/18		Day & night quiet. Long dump behind enemy lines near HERCOURT was hit by our artillery shrewd from 7.15 PM until 10.0 PM. Casualties Nil.	
"	12/3/18		Enemy artillery below normal. Training as usual. Casualties Nil.	
"	13/3/18		Fnt quiet. Training carried out as usual. Personnel komplete Dn H.Qrs arriving in odd ments. No casualties.	

Army Form C. 2118.

WAR DIARY
or
INTELLIGENCE SUMMARY.
(Erase heading not required.)

Vol. I   61 Bn N.G.C.

Place	Date	Hour	Summary of Events and Information	Remarks and references to Appendices
VAUX	14/9/18		Front quiet. Aerial activity normal. Training carried out by recent drafts. Casualties nil.	
	15/9/18		Front normal. Aerial activity slightly more flying by our squadrons. Relief of Batalion carried out satisfactorily by relief "C" Coy in left Sub sector carried out satisfactorily. Front quiet. Aerial activity normal. Training carried out by recent drafts. Casualties nil.	
	16/9/18		Front quiet. MG fire on E.A. during day. Casualties nil.	
	17/9/18		Front normal. Nothing to report. Casualties nil.	
	18/9/18		Normal quiet. Training carried out by recent drafts. Casualties nil.	
	19/9/18		Very quiet. Aerial activity nil. Casualties nil. 51 accessory rounds.	
	20/9/18		Enemy started an intense bombardment at 11.40 PM our forward & back areas. His Infantry advanced to the attack at 9.30 am. The day was very foggy till about noon when it turned sunny & clear. The order to man battle stations was issued about 2.15 AM. Owing to the thick fog little is known of the fighting in the front lines but ELLIS and ENGHEIN redoubts were still holding out at about 11 AM and FRESNOY redoubt was surrounded & being attacked from all sides at that hour. When the fog lifted about noon large numbers of the	

Army Form C. 2118.

WAR DIARY
or
INTELLIGENCE SUMMARY.
(Erase heading not required.)

Place	Date	Hour	Summary of Events and Information	Remarks and references to Appendices
			Enemy were seen advancing over MANCHESTER HILL and were effectively engaged by B, Z guns 5, 6, 7, 8, 9 & 10 guns took cover behind ROUND HILL. At about 3pm the same guns fired on him while moving in column of route westwards along the HOLNON – SAVY road and inflicted very heavy casualties. The attacks died down about 5pm and the night was quiet except for a little shelling. A section of C company under Lt.Moon from ISSUE was sent up to C.O.C. 183 Inf Bde at MARTEVILLE railway cutting about 2.30pm to assist in a counterattack on high ground on R 30 a + c. They took up a position on MILL HILL and very effectively engaged the enemy advancing BN from MAISSEMY. Later they took up a position at the Railway cutting MARTEVILLE (Sheet 62c R 33 c,d,5?) and from there on the following day did good work covering the retirement to rear line. At about 10pm the last section of C company was ordered up to 182 Inf Bde in quarry at X 15 central. Two guns under Lng. Smith being sent to OO of HARMAR Regt. to support at MDJ (X 16.57) or indicated by Lng. Smith being the other two guns at X 15 d 3.1. These two new guns did great execution the following day. 19th Transport arrived NOSEO at 3pm. to move from VAUX to DOUILLY.	
	28/3/14		Another enemy morning. Enemy had attacked the Battle Zone about 4am. Posts were in the Battle Zone suffered very heavy casualties till they were knocked out or surrounded. The whole line open to all posts withdraw thro' HOLNON WOOD soon after midday as the enemy were getting round the flanks of the division. N.line was taken up running N & S through BEAUVOIS by 5pm. All M.G. personnel without guns were ordered to rendezvous at DOUILLY.	

WAR DIARY or INTELLIGENCE SUMMARY

Army Form C. 2118.

Place	Date	Hour	Summary of Events and Information	Remarks and references to Appendices
	22/3/18		At this time (5pm) there were only two guns left, the remainder having been either disabled or captured. Two of the above 4 were out of action. At 7pm contact aeroplane wanted to MATIGNY but on arrival there received further orders to go on to RETHONVILLERS. At midnight the Garrison fell back from the BEAUVOIS line to the west of the SOMME canal without interruption. Casualties for the previous 48 hours were:- 14 Officers missing. Lt A.E. KER; Lt E.R. FORWARD; Lt E.C. DOUGLAS; Lt S.C. GOODE; Lt F.M. CASWELL; Lt W.O. JONES; Lt H. KAY; Lt J. EDGAR; 2/Lt P.R. ORGILL; 2/Lt S.P. GREER; 2/Lt L.N. FENN; 2/Lt G.H. FARROW; 2/Lt W.E. WICKS; 2/Lt G. EARL. 3 Officers wounded. Lt E.G. WARDROP; Lt E.R. RICHARDS and 2/Lt A.G. JONES. 320 (approx) O.R. missing.	
RETHONVILLERS	23/3/18		A quiet day without fighting. The division held the line BREUIL to a point about 1000 yds west of ROUY-le-PETIT. Whilst troops held the passages over the SOMME canal.	
RETHONVILLERS	24/3/18		The enemy had got across the SOMME canal at BETHENCOURT and had pushed guns under NOON took part in a counter attack by 183 Inf Bde on the high ground E of MESNIL St NICASSE and inflicted exceptional heavy casualties on the enemy. Lt & Q.M. W.H. GREEN reported for duty with the Bn. 4 new guns & tripods & 56 Lot boxes received from Ordnance and issued to D Coy. The Bn (less subsection under 2/Lt MOON) & transport marched at 4.30 pm to BOUCHOIR arriving there about 9.30pm.	

Army Form C. 2118.

WAR DIARY
or
INTELLIGENCE SUMMARY.
(Erase heading not required.)

Instructions regarding War Diaries and Intelligence Summaries are contained in F. S. Regs., Part II. and the Staff Manual respectively. Title pages will be prepared in manuscript.

Place	Date	Hour	Summary of Events and Information	Remarks and references to Appendices
BOUCHOIR	25/3/18.		The division fell back from vicinity of NESTLE fighting a rearguard action in which the guns under 1/Lt MOON did very good work. 10 more new guns were received from ordnance but no Tripods or belt boxes. The B². & Transport moved at 6 pm to VILLERS-AUX-ERABLES arriving about 9.30 pm.	
VILLERS-AUX-ERABLES.	26/3/18.		Div. H.Q. was established at BEAUCOURT EN SANTERRE. The East of the division was to block the main ROYE–AMIENS road in the vicinity of MEZIERES and BEAUCOURT. All M.G. personnel not required for manning guns were formed into an infantry Company & attached to 183 I.B with Captain LECK M.C. in command. The six available MGs were allotted to defy. & positions prepared. 2 guns C coy to 104 I.B. on the right, 2 turn guns (salvaged by C coy on 24th) to 183 I.B. on centre & 2 vickers Day to 182 I.B. on left. At 11pm orders were issued for the division to advance and to take over from 20th Divn. a line of defences E of LE QUESNEL & to in corp. reserve.	App.ˣ B App.ˣ C
—	27/3/18.		The occupation of the new position E of LE QUESNEL was completed about 8 am. A quiet day & no attack made on our front. Tripods & belt boxes having arrived The 10 new guns were sent into the line during the afternoon, teams to man them being withdrawn from the personnel acting as infantry. About 6 pm orders were received to send up limbers to pick up guns in the line & to hold the transport ready to move at midnight. The division was relieved by elements of FRENCH 133 Divn and moved to XIX Corps area. Personnel by bus to MARCELCAVE. B" H.Q & transport to CACHY. Fighting limbers with guns from the line to VILLERS BRETONNEUX & then sent on to MARCELCAVE.	App.ˣ D App.ˣ E App.ˣ F

Army Form C. 2118.

WAR DIARY
or
INTELLIGENCE SUMMARY.
(Erase heading not required.)

Instructions regarding War Diaries and Intelligence Summaries are contained in F.S. Regs., Part II. and the Staff Manual respectively. Title pages will be prepared in manuscript.

Place	Date	Hour	Summary of Events and Information	Remarks and references to Appendices
CACHY	28/3/18		Divnl HQ opened at VILLERS BRETONNEUX about 8am and 3rd Cav. took up a line running N + S through the E edge of MARCEL CAVE with the 3rd Cav division on the left + 39th division on the right. 183 + 184 Bde were ordered to attack + recapture the village of LAMOTTE-en-SANTERRE at 11 a.m. The Machine guns attached to these brigades cooperated but the attack was not successful. MARCELCAVE very heavily shelled from noon onwards. Brigades took up a line just E of MARCELCAVE in the evening. Our casualties during the day were 25 or killed, wounded, or missing. Divnl advance HQ + 8" advance HQ were established at GENTELLES at 6pm + the 8" transport moved to FUEN CAMPS. Copy of orders from Army Commander received showing the defence put up by the Divn.	Appx G Appx H
Line just W of MARCEL CAVE	29/3/18		A quiet day. The enemy did not attack and there was only desultory shelling.	
"	30/3/18		Enemy attacked our right + the division on our right. The machine guns with our right Bde under Lt EVANS m.c. frustrated the enemy's attempt to advance + caused them heavy casualties. During the day the division on our right being forced to fall back our right flank eventually had to conform. Casualties during the day 10 or wounded.	
GENTELLES	31/3/18		The division was relieved between midnight 30/31 + dawn 31st by 18th Divn and the 9th 10th 3rd Aust" BMs + guns + personnel rendezvoused in GENTELLES. Transport moved from FUEN CAMP to BOUILLERIE.	

JD CDent Lt/Col.
Comdg 61st Bn. M.G.C.

Identification Trace for use with Artillery Maps.

App.ᵈ A

NOTE.—(1). These traces are intended to facilitate the communication of information as to the position of targets, which have been located on a squared map.
(2) The squares on this trace are 500 yards in length on the 1/10,000 scale, 1,000 yards in length on the 1/20,000 scale, and 2,000 yards in length on the 1/40,000 scale.
(3). The squares on the trace are fitted to the squares of the map showing the targets, which are then drawn on the trace. Sufficient letters and numbers must also be added to enable the recipient to place the trace in the correct position on his own map. A little detail may also be traced, but this is not essential. The name and scale of the map to which the trace refers must be always given. The trace can be used for the 1/10,000, 1/20,000, or 1/40,000 scale.

G.S.G.S. 3083.

Tracing taken from Sheet 42ᵈ S.W. – 62ᵈ S.E

of the 1:20,000 map of ....

Signature .... Date ....

"A" Form
MESSAGES AND SIGNALS.

Army Form C. 2121
(In pads of 100)

Prefix	Code	m.	Words.	Charge.	This message is on a/e of:		Recd. at	m.
Office of Origin and Service Instructions			Sent				Date	
			At	m.		Service.	From	
			To					
			By		(Signature of "Franking Officer.")		By	

TO { 182 Inf. Bde.   1/5 Cornwalls.
     183 Inf. Bde.   C.R.E.
     184 Inf. Bde.   M.G.Bttn.

Sender's Number.	Day of Month.	In reply to Number.	
G.958	26		AAA

Information has been received of enemy advance on NOYE - AMIENS Road aaa Enemy last located about BOXENCOURT aaa Orders are being issued with regard to move of transport beyond destination given today aaa Fighting portion of all units including surplus personnel will stand to at once and be ready to take up position as may be ordered aaa This position will probably be astride road on line BEAUCOURT - MEZIERES aaa A mounted officer from each Bde. Pioneer Bn, Fld.Coy.,R.E., and M.G.Bn. will report at Div. H.Q. BEAUCOURT forthwith aaa Pending receipt of orders units will make arrangements for local protection aaa Acknowledge aaa
         Added Inf. Bdes 1/5 Cornwalls C.R.E. and

From	61 Div.M.G.Bn.		
Place	61 Div.		
Time	1.15 p.m.		

The above may be forwarded as now corrected. (Z)

Censor.   Signature of Addressor or person authorised to telegraph in his name.

* This line should be erased if not required.

MESSAGES AND SIGNALS.

Prefix	Code	Words / Charge	This message is on a/c of:	Recd. at ... m
		Sent		Date
Office of Origin and Service Instructions	At ... m	APM	Service	From
	To Div Sig Coy	By	(Signature of "Franking Officer")	20 DIV 30 DIV

TO	OC MG BN	Pioneer BN	ADMS	Camp Comdt
	CRA	132 }	OADVS	DGO
	CRE	173 } BDEs	OADOS	18th Corps
		174 }	TRAIN	36 DIV

Sender's Number	Day of Month	In reply to Number	AAA
*G960	26		

The enemy is known to be in the vicinity DAMERY aaa 36 DIV have orders to block roads between GUERBIGNY and ERCHES aaa 30 DIV to block ROYE – AMIENS Road at BOUCHOIR and the junction of roads at HANGEST-EN-SANTERRE aaa 20 DIV to block roads at LE POINT HANGEST on the main ROYE-AMIENS Rd and LE QUESNEL aaa the task of the Division is to block the main ROYE-AMIENS road in

From
Place
Time

The above may be forwarded as now corrected. (Z)

Censor. Signature of Addressor or person authorised to telegraph in his name.

* This line should be erased if not required.

MESSAGES AND SIGNALS.

West of MEZIERES and BEACOURT EN SANTERRE aaa For this purpose the troops at the disposal of the GOC will be organised as follows aaa 152 Bde — Bde personnel plus Pioneer Battalion plus 16 machine guns aaa 153 Bde — Bde personnel plus machine guns personnel not required for manning MG's plus 4 machine guns aaa 154 Bde — Bde personnel plus 6 machine guns aaa 1 Field Coy RE will be attached to each Inf Bde aaa OC Machine Gun Battalion will arrange to hand over the machine guns aaa

MESSAGES AND SIGNALS.

named above to Brigade Commanders aaa The line to be taken up extends from Farm Buildings D27a44 (inclusive) to small wood about D16a33 (inclusive) This line is unsupported N of the ROYE-AMIENS Road by Three small woods aaa Disposition — 183 Bde astride the ROYE-AMIENS Road for a distance of 350 yds either side of the road aaa 184 Bde from farm buildings at D27a44 (inclusive) to right of 183 Bde aaa 182 Bde from left of 183 Bde to wood at D16a33 (inclusive)

182 4 MG'S   Left
183 2 Lewis Centre
184 2 MG   Right

MESSAGES ...

It is not known at present what artillery will be in support there are no troops on our immediate right or left flanks aaa it is essential that every effort be made to delay the enemy as long as possible aaa an Advanced Dressing Station will be established at VILLERS-AUX-ERABLES aaa Bearer will report locations of battle stations aaa Div HQ closes at BEAUCOURT at 5.0 pm and will re-open at [a] place that will be notified later aaa Map

MESSAGES AND S[IGNALS]

Code	m	Words. Charge.	This message is on a/c of:	Recd. at ... m.	
e of Origin and Service Instructions.		Sent		Date	
		At ... m.	... Service.	From	
		To		By	
		By	(Signature of "Franking Officer.")		

TO

Sender's Number.	Day of Month.	In reply to Number.	**A A A**

Addressed Div Sig Coy – OC MG Bn
– CRA CRE Pioneer Bn –
152 Bde – 153 Bde 154 Bde
ADMS DADVS DADOS APM
TRAIN "Q" Camp Comdt DGO
repeated 36 Div 30 Div 20 Div
15th Corps

From 51 Div
Place
Time

The above may be forwarded as now corrected. (Z) R.H. Lively Lt

Censor. Signature of Addresser or person authorised to telegraph in his name.

MESSAGES AND SIGNALS.

TO: CRE — 182
OC MG Bn — 183 } Infy Bdes —
OC Pioneer Bn — 184

Sender's Number: G 967 Day of Month: 26

The Division will move forward tonight take over defences E of LE QUESNEL from 20th Division and be in Corps Reserve. — GO'sC Brigades with Battalion representatives OC Pioneer Battn and CRE will report to Divisional Headquarters forthwith.

From Place: 61st Div
Time: 7.0 p

"A" Form
MESSAGES AND SIGNALS.

Army Form C. 2121
(In pads of 100)

TO: Divl Signal Co - MG Battn - CRA - CRE - Pioneer Battn - 182 Bde, 183 Bde, 184 Bde - ADMS - DADVS - DADOS - Div Train - Camp Comdt - Q

Sender's Number: G968
Day of Month: 26
In reply to Number: DGO - 20th Div - 30th Div - 24th Div - 36th Divn - 18th Corps -

Information with regard to the enemy unchanged AAA 20th Divn are advancing and taking up a line E of ARVILLERS and FOLLIES AAA Roll of 30th, 36th & 24th DIVS unchanged AAA The Divn will move forward at once and take over from 20th Div the line of defences E of LE QUESNEL and be in Corps reserve AAA Composition of Brigades will remain as ordered in G960 AAA Line to be taken up extends from road at approximately K13a02 along Eastern edge of wood in K8c thence E of cemetery in K2a and b to E26 central AAA dispositions 183 Bde astride the ROYE - AMIENS road for a distance of 350 yards on each side of the road AAA

"A" Form.
MESSAGES AND SIGNALS.

Army Form C. 2121.
(In pads of 100.)

| TO | ② |

* Sender's Number | Day of Month | In reply to Number | AAA

184 Bde. from road at K.13.a.0.2 to right of 183 Bde AAA 182 Bde. from left of 183 Bde. to E.26 central AAA The line will be held by a line of outposts but arrangements will be made to man it at very short notice AAA Bdes will in addition push forward patrols along the main roads running towards the enemy in order to keep touch with the situation AAA It is not known whether there are any troops on our immediate left flank AAA Bdes will report locally p. H. Qrs AAA Divl. Hd. Qrs. does not move AAA Acknowledge AAA Addressed Div Sig Co M.G. Baton C.R.A. C.R.E. Pioneers 182 183 184 Bdes A.D.M.S. DADVS. DADOS. APM. Train Camp Comdt. Q. DGO. 30 36 Divs 18th Corps

From: 61st Divn
Place:
Time:

(Z) [signature]

"A" Form.
MESSAGES AND SIGNALS.

Army Form C. 2121.
(In pads of 100.)

Sender's Number.	Day of Month.	In reply to Number.	AAA
B10	27		

The following additional guns will
move into the line this afternoon.

A Coy 4 guns ~~will remain in battery~~

B - 4 - } Belt boxes are to
C - 2 - } be equalised
          } between companies
          } to 8 per gun.

Two guns of B Coy are allotted
to 183 Inf Bde (right Brigade).

Two guns of C Coy are allotted
to 184 Inf Bde (centre Brigade).

~~Two~~ guns A Coy are allotted to
182 Bde (left Brigade).

(Z)

"A" Form.
MESSAGES AND SIGNALS.

Army Form C. 2121.
(In pads of 100.)

The teams for these guns will be found by the respective companies from the personnel at present acting as infantry.

Company Commanders concerned will make arrangements with G.O.C 183 Bde. as to the withdrawal of these men.

Capt Lick will hand over the command of the men acting as infantry personnel to Lieut ~~Stokes~~

Capt Leech will take command of the four guns attached to the right Brigade.

"A" Form.
MESSAGES AND SIGNALS.

Army Form C. 2121.
(In pads of 100.)

The Transport of "D" Coy will take up 20 boxes S.A.A.

Rations will be dumped as follows at a time to be notified later.

Left Brigade — LE QUESNEL K.8.B.3.9 (the most easterly house in K. village)

Centre Brigade — LE P? HANGEST.

Right Brigade — B.H.Q. HANGEST.

"A" Form.
MESSAGES AND SIGNALS.

Army Form C.2121
(in pads of 100).

This message is on a/c of:
Appx E

TO: 61 MG Bn

Sender's Number: G 980
Day of Month: 27
AAA

Please send limbers up forthwith to pick up guns of 3 Bdes who are being relieved tonight. Personnel are moving to 19th CORPS Area by bus aaa guns will be conveyd by limber aaa destination probable VILLERS-BRETONNEUX aaa Personnel embuses midnight 27/28

GS. 61 Div

"A" Form.
MESSAGES AND SIGNALS.

Army Form C. 2121.
(In pads of 100.)

TO: 61 M. C. Battn.

Sender's Number: G.979. Day of Month: 27th.

AAA

The 61st Div. will be relieved tonight by xxxxx
elements of 133 French Div. as follows aaa
The 3rd Battn. 401st French Regt. now in
LA QUENNEL will relieve the 182 and 184 Bdes.
in LA QUENNEL aaa Arrangements to be made
direct between Battn. Commander and Brigade
Commanders aaa A Battn. of 321st French Regt.
is already moving to HAMMEL to relieve 183
Bde aaa Arrangements to be made direct between
Battn. Commander and Brigade Commander aaa
On relief 61st Div. will bus to 19 Corps area
as follows :-
    183 Bde - 42 busses. Head of column at
        J.21.a.1.6 (road junction N.E.
        of PLESSIERS) at midnight 27/28th.
    182 Bde - 57 busses) Head of column at
    184 Bde - 32 busses) J.28.a.3.9 (X Rds.S.W.
                        of BEAUCOURT-en-SANTERRE)
                        at midnight 27/28th

"A" Form.
MESSAGES AND SIGNALS.

Army Form C. 2121.
(In pads of 100.)

Sender's Number.	Day of Month.	In reply to Number.	AAA
G 979	27		

All dismounted personnel now with Brigades will embus including Pioneers R.E. and machine gunners aaa ~~dismounted personnel will embus including pioneers with~~ Limbers are being sent up to pick up the Vickers machine guns aaa Div.H.Q. closes on completion of relief and will reopen at a place to be notifed later aaa Added 182 183 184 Inf Bdes C.R.A. C.R.E. Train Sig.Coy. M.G.Bn. 1/5 Cornwalls Q A.D.M.S. Camp Comdt D.A.D.V.S. A.P.M. D.A.D.O.S. D.G.O. 18 Corps 20 24 and 30 Divs 133 French Div General SIMON PLESSIERS Col.HOFF VILLERS AUX ERABLES.

From 61 Div.

"A" Form.
Army Form C. 2121.
(In pads of 100.)

MESSAGES AND SIGNALS.

No. of Message..........

Prefix........ Code........ in	Words.	Charge.	This message is on a/c of:		Recd. at .... m.
Office of Origin and Service Instructions.		Sent			Date..........
		At........m.	...........Service.		From..........
		To........	(Signature of "Franking Officer.")		By..........
		By........			

TO 182 Inf.Bde.   Maj.WHITWELL, 478 Fd.Co.RE.
    183 Inf.Bde.   O.C. M.G.Bn.   Corps
    184 Inf.Bde.   A.D.M.S.   CAREY'S FORCE
                                      39 Div. AAA

Sender's Number: 981   Day of Month: 29   In reply to Number:

(1) The G.O.C. does not wish the effort to
    sieze LAMOTTE persisted in.

(2) Troops can be withdrawn at earliest and
    most opportune moment. G.O.C. suggests
    just after dusk and in a westerly
    direction.

(3) Whole force will bivouac or billet
    tonight in the vicinity of, or in,
    MARCELCAVE and 182 Inf.Bde. will be
    responsible for local protection.

(4) Acknowledge.

        Added 182 183 184 Inf.Bdes. reptd
C.R.E. Maj.WHITWELL 478 Fd.Co.RE.
O.C. M.G.Bn. A.D.M.S. Q.   Corps
CAREY'S FORCE 39 Div.   19

From: 61 Div.
Place:
Time: 3.40 p.m.

"A" Form
MESSAGES AND SIGNALS.

Army Form C. 2121.
(In pads of 100.)

TO	182 Inf.Bde. 1/5 DCLI 61 Sig.Co. 183 Inf.Bde. 61 Bn.MGC. A.D.M.S. 184 Inf.Bde.

Sender's Number.	Day of Month.	In reply to Number.	
G 984	28		AAA

Following from 19 Corps aaa The following has been received from the Army Commander aaa By the grand and stubborn way you are holding out and delaying the advance of the enemy the British and French Reserves are being given the necessary time to come up and assume the offensive aaa Your great exertions and sacrifices are not being thrown away they are of immense importance and your resistance and your deeds in this great battle will live for all time and will save our country aaa Ends

From: 61 Div.
Time: 5.10 p.m.

O. Anderson Major

Clean clothing
Bathing
[illegible]
[illegible]

List of missing effects
to Q.M.

SECRET G.S. 79.

61st DIVISION.
Locations of Units – 27th March, 1918.

61 DIV. H.Q.	BEAUCOURT-EN-SANTERRE.
182 Inf. Bde.)	
2/6 Warwicks.)	
2/7 Warwicks.)	Northern half of LE QUESNEL.
2/8 Worcesters.)	
183 Inf. Bde.)	
1/5 Gordons.)	
1/8 Argylls.)	HANGEST-EN-SANTERRE.
1/9 R.Scots.)	
184 Inf. Bde.)	
2/4 Oxfords.)	
2/4 R. Berks.)	Southern half of LE QUESNEL.
2/5 Glosters.)	
Transport Lines.) of all 3 Bdes.)	
Q.M. Stores.) & 1/5 D.C.L.I.)	HAILLES.
61 Bn. M.G. Corps.	VILLERS-AUX-ERABLES. (Guns with Bdes.).
C.R.A.	BEAUCOURT-EN-SANTERRE.
306 Bde. R.F.A.)	
307 Bde. R.F.A.)	In action under orders of 20th Div.
61 D.A.C. (less S.A.A. Section)	– under orders of 20th Div.
S.A.A. Section.	CASTEL.
C.R.E.	BEAUCOURT-EN-SANTERRE.
476 Field Coy. R.E.	with 182 Inf. Bde.
478 do.	with 183 Inf. Bde.
479 do.	with 184 Inf. Bde.
Transport Lines.	CASTEL.
1/5 Cornwalls (P).	LE QUESNEL (with 182 Inf. Bde.).
A.D.M.S.	BEAUCOURT-EN-SANTERRE.
2/1 Field Amb.	COTTENCHY.
2/2 do.	MORISEL (A.D.S. VILLERS-AUX-ERABLES).
2/3 do.	HAILLES.
61 Div. Train H.Q.	BEAUCOURT-EN-SANTERRE.
No. 1 Coy.)	
No. 2 Coy.)	
No. 3 Coy.)	DOMMARTIN.
No. 4 Coy.)	
Supply lorries of 61 M.T. Coy.	– DOMMARTIN.
61 Mob. Vet. Sec.	DOMMARTIN.
Ammunition Refilling Point	– MONIMEN, Cross-roads South of ROUVREL.
Railhead.	LONGUEAU.

27.3.18. G.S., 61st. Div.

SECRET.   61st Division No. G.1186/13/54

The Division is being relieved in the Line at midnight to-night and is proceeding by bus route to VILLERS BRETONNEUX Area.
All fighting troops must be equipped with rations on the man for consumption to-morrow. If any Quartermasters have failed to deliver rations these must be taken to embussing points which are as follows :-

    183rd Inf. Bde.)   Head of Column at J.21.a.1.6. (Road junction
    and attached   )   N.E. of PLESSIER) at midnight.
    troops.   )

    182nd Inf. Bde.)   Head of Column at D.28.a.4.9. (Cross Roads
    184th Inf. Bde.)   S.W. of BEAUCOURT-en-SANTERRE). midnight.
    and attached   )
    troops.   )

The Divisional Train will not move.
The 2/2nd Field Ambulance will remain with the French under arrangements of the A.D.M.S.
Transports will be held in readiness to march northwards about midnight. Details as to destination and routes will be issued later.

D.H.Q.
27th March, 1918.

                                                Lieut-Colonel,
                                                A.A. & Q.M.G.,
                                                61st Division.

                DISTRIBUTION.

    182nd Inf. Bde. Rear H.Q.   2/1st Field Ambulance.
    183rd Inf. Bde. Rear H.Q.   2/2nd Field Ambulance.
    184th Inf. Bde. Rear H.Q.   2/3rd Field Ambulance.
    1/5th D.C.L.I.   S.A.A. Section, 61st D.A.C.
    61st Bn. M.G.Corps.   A.P.M.
    C.R.E.   Camp Commandant.
    Div. Train.   Copy to 61st Div. Art.
    A.D.M.S.

61st Divisional Troops

61st BATTALION

MACHINE GUN CORPS

APRIL 1918.

Army Form C. 2118.

WAR DIARY
or
INTELLIGENCE SUMMARY
(Erase heading not required.)

Vol II

Instructions regarding War Diaries and Intelligence Summaries are contained in F. S. Regs., Part II. and the Staff Manual respectively. Title pages will be prepared in manuscript.

Place	Date	Hour	Summary of Events and Information	Remarks and references to Appendices
GENTELLES	1.4.18		Transport remained at BOUTILLERIE. Battalion less transport at GENTELLES.	Reference map
			Positions were reconnoitred for defence of GENTELLES.	AMIENS 1/...
	2.4.18		Orders were received at 2.30 P.M. to form a Composite Company. This was done	
"			and Major J.O. COOK put in command vice O.O.	
			At 7.30 P.M. orders were received that the Division would be taken out of the	
			line by bus at 3 A.M. on April 3rd. H.Q. and transport were ordered to move	
			to GUIGNEMICOURT early on 3rd. H.Q. moved at 10 P.M. to BOUTILLERIE.	
BOUTILLERIE	3.4.18		Transport moved at 1 A.M. by march route SALOUEL to GUIGNEMICOURT arriving	
			at 10.30 A.M. Balance of personnel from GENTELLES with R.G. FRYER and A.S. O.R.	
			moved by motor bus and arrived about noon.	
			Parking for 16 guns were manned by Composite Company on a line AUBIGNY,	
			GENTELLES, BERTEAUCOURT (see Appendix). These parties were manned from	
			9 P.M. onwards. Battalion less Composite Company proceeded with training and	
			reorganization.	
GUIGNEMICOURT	4.4.18		Training and reorganization. Composite Company's Appearance of parking and controls	
			of shelters. Casualties Lieut. R. MOON 2 O.R. wounded.	

Army Form C. 2118.

WAR DIARY
or
INTELLIGENCE SUMMARY.
(Erase heading not required.)

Instructions regarding War Diaries and Intelligence Summaries are contained in F. S. Regs., Part II. and the Staff Manual respectively. Title pages will be prepared in manuscript.

Vol. II

Place	Date	Hour	Summary of Events and Information	Remarks and references to Appendices
GUIGNEMICOURT	5.4.18		Training and reorganization. Composite Company's improvement of position and construction of alternative emplacements. Casualty 1st Lieut E. OLIVER wounded	Reference map AMIENS 1/20,000
"	6.4.18		Training and reorganization. Composite Company's Exploration of alternative emplacements.	
"	7.4.18		Training and reorganization. Composite Company. Construction of alternative emplacements. Orders were received that positions occupied by the Company would be relieved by the 14th and 18th Divisions.	
"	8.4.18		Training and reorganization. Composite Company sections proceeded independently from 9 A.M. onwards to LONGEAU, where the Company concentrated and proceeded by march route BOUTILLERIE, SALOUEL to GUIGNEMICOURT, arriving 2 P.M. Warning order received by Battalion H.Q. to proceed by train on the 10th inst.	
"	9.4.18		Training and reorganization. Draft of reinforcements, 19 Officers, 241 O.R. arrived	
		12.30 P.M.	and were posted to Companies.	
"	10.4.18		Battalion proceeded by march route to AMIENS, ST ROCH station. Battalion less A Company and details entrained + leaving at 7.47 P.M. and 9.47 P.M. for	
BERGUETTE				Reference map 36A 1/40,000

Army Form C. 2118.

WAR DIARY
or
INTELLIGENCE SUMMARY.
(Erase heading not required.)

VOL II

Place	Date	Hour	Summary of Events and Information	Remarks and references to Appendices
GUARBECQUE	11-4-18		Battalion has H.Q. established at GUARBECQUE. Battalion arrived in position during the day. Orders were received at 1 P.M. that the Division would hold a line from ROBECQ to MERVILLE along the line of rivers NOE and CLARENCE. 184 Brigade on right, 182 in centre, 183 on left. One Company was to be attached to the LEFT and CENTRE Brigades respectively. D Company moved up to the LEFT Brigade 183, and B Company to the CENTRE Brigade 182. Fighting limbers and 2 S.A.A. limbers were placed at the disposal of each company. Lieut Colonel B.C. DENT D.S.O. appointed to the command of 47th Brigade. Major F.C. ALDOUS assumed command of the Battalion temporarily from this date.	Reference map 36A Vol. 1110
ST. VENANT	12-4-18		Headquarters established at ST. VENANT P.1.d.91. The enemy attacked heavily during the morning and the line was driven in to approximately a line two miles east of ST. VENANT. Orders were received at 8.15 A.M. for A Company to reinforce the RIGHT Brigade, 184. This was done by C Company. Centre Company. The infantry were driven back and after covering the withdrawal, guns were moved back to new positions in rear of 8 forward guns and was surrounded and cut off. The remainder were	

Army Form C. 2118.

WAR DIARY
of
INTELLIGENCE SUMMARY.
(Erase heading not required.)

Vol. II

Instructions regarding War Diaries and Intelligence Summaries are contained in F. S. Regs., Part II. and the Staff Manual respectively. Title pages will be prepared in manuscript.

Place	Date	Hour	Summary of Events and Information	Remarks and references to Appendices
			withdrawn. Most of the belt boxes had to be abandoned, owing to heavy casualties. Enemy targets were engaged throughout the day.	
			Left Company. There nothing were attached to the two battalions in the line by order of G.O.C. Left Brigade. The whole of these guns were thus at 11 a.m. the front section of these Company was pushed up, two guns to K 31 D 51, two guns to K 31 B 51. These guns inflicted heavy casualties on the enemy and a hostile party advancing along the road through Q 2 B 90, in column of route was annihilated. At the conclusion of the battle, these guns were withdrawn to positions conforming with a line from K 31 D 16 to Q 12 AC from which they engaged hostile machine guns during the night.	
			Casualties 4 O.R. killed, 10 O.R. Died of wounds, 8 O.R. wounded Reinforcements 61 arrived	
ST. VENANT	13.4.18		A local attack was launched against our Left Brigade about 8.0 p.m. but was driven off by machine gun and artillery fire, and heavy casualties inflicted. Fighting continued during the day, hostile parties being engaged with good results. Targets were engaged during the day by guns of the Right	

WAR DIARY or INTELLIGENCE SUMMARY

Army Form C. 2118.

VOL II

Place	Date	Hour	Summary of Events and Information	Remarks and references to Appendices
			Company instituting two heavy Field gun many raids from R152 D V VINAGE. Just shoulders but disappeared to enemy shelter. Estimate covered fire tubes.	
			Casualties: 2nd Lieut C. SEYMOUR killed, Lieut W.R. STONES, 2nd Lieut G. W. BOURNE, 2nd Lieut P.H. WILSON, 2nd Lieut J. HILL wounded, 7 O.R. missing, Lieut W.R. STONES, 2nd Lieut W.H. HILL wounded, 1 O.R. missing	
ST VENANT	10.9.18		Three hostile attacks on the left Brigade were driven off. A further attack succeeded in penetrating our lines near the LYS canal at about K.31 Central. The enemy were subsequently ejected and the situation restored.	
			During the above attacks very heavy casualties were inflicted on the enemy by direct fire at ranges from 500 yards to 1070 yards.	
			A counter attack was made by the Rifle Brigade on the ground in 9.20C, and was supported by direct fire from one of our machine guns. This attack was unsuccessful.	
			Casualties: 2nd Lieut P. RICHARDS wounded. 12 O.R. wounded, 1 O.R. missing	

Army Form C. 2118.

WAR DIARY
or
~~INTELLIGENCE SUMMARY~~

(Erase heading not required.)

Instructions regarding War Diaries and Intelligence Summaries are contained in F.S. Regs., Part II. and the Staff Manual respectively. Title pages will be prepared in manuscript.

VOL II

Place	Date	Hour	Summary of Events and Information	Remarks and references to Appendices
ST. VENANT	15.4.18		An attack was made by the Right Brigade to make good the line of the road south of BAQUEROLLES FARM from G.20.a.5.8 to G.20.c.9.6. Three of our machine guns cooperated, one from BAQUEROLLES FARM fired 300 rounds sweeping the ground in G.14.D and G.20.B. Two guns at G.12 acted fire 650 rounds on G.20 acted and LA. PIERRE AU BEVRE. This attack was not successful. The four guns of D Company were relieved by one section of A Company. Casualties 1 OR killed, 1 OR wounded, 1 OR missing.	
ST. VENANT	16.4.18		Front was comparatively quiet. Two sections of B Company were relieved by two sections of A Company. The line was now held by C Company Right Sector, A Company Centre and Left Sectors, B and D Company being withdrawn for reorganizing. Major H. MORRISON, Captain V. JOYCE, Captain R.H. COULINSON, 73 OR were posted to battalion.	
ST. VENANT	17.4.18		Comparatively quiet during the day. About 8.30 P.M. the enemy raided the post at BAQUEROLLES FARM, G.20.a.5.8, and at 10.30 P.M. occupied the farm at G.14.c.9.9. An unsuccessful counter attack was made by the Right Brigade. A further hostile attack was met by direct machine gun fire at close range from the guns at G.12 acted	

Army Form C.2118/5

Army Form C. 2118.

WAR DIARY
or
INTELLIGENCE SUMMARY
(Erase heading not required.)

Vol II

Instructions regarding War Diaries and Intelligence Summaries are contained in F. S. Regs., Part II. and the Staff Manual respectively. Title pages will be prepared in manuscript.

Place	Date	Hour	Summary of Events and Information	Remarks and references to Appendices
			Heavy casualties were inflicted on the enemy, 25 being left dead on the ground, and the remainder was scattered. Firing on hostile parties was continued at intervals during the next day.	
			Casualty 2nd Lieut SHARPE killed.	
			Reinforcements 91 OR arrived.	
ST. VENANT	18.2.18		At 3.30 am a hostile patrol of about 40 with a machine gun attacked a post in the Centre Brigade. This attack was completely repulsed by our machine gun fire, a number of enemy being killed and the machine gun captured. Remainder of front comparatively quiet. One section A Coy was relieved by one section B Coy.	
			Casualties 8 OR wounded	
ST. VENANT	19.2.18		Front was comparatively quiet. Harassing fire was carried at during the night bursts of fire being opened on roads and approaches.	
			Casualties 7 OR wounded	
ST. VENANT	20.2.18		Front was comparatively quiet. One section A Coy was relieved by one section B Coy.	
			Front was MG'd by three Coys in see Appendix. Casualties 1 OR wounded.	

Army Form C. 2118.

WAR DIARY
or
INTELLIGENCE SUMMARY
(Erase heading not required.)

VOL II

Instructions regarding War Diaries and Intelligence Summaries are contained in F. S. Regs., Part II, and the Staff Manual respectively. Title pages will be prepared in manuscript.

Place	Date	Hour	Summary of Events and Information	Remarks and references to Appendices
ST. VENANT	21.4.18		Front was comparatively quiet. Heavy fire was carried on during the night on roads and approaches.	
ST. VENANT	22.4.18		Front was comparatively quiet. 20 guns were sent up in the evening, and layed for barrage fire in support of an attack by the Rifle Brigade, together with 12 guns already in position. Casualties 2 O.R. wounded.	
"	23.4.18		The Rifle Brigade attacked at 4.30 am in cooperation with the 4th Division on our right. Objective for Rifle Brigade cross roads G.20.B.80 to G.14.C.58. This attack was a complete success on our front and 100 prisoners and 6 machine guns being captured. The attack was supported by 32 machine guns from 61st Bn. M.G.C. evening hostile approaches, 200,000 rounds being fired down the approaches. Fire was opened at 4.30 am for 1 hour and at 6.30 am for 15 mins. Four machine guns were sent up in the afternoon to consolidate and to protect the R. flank, from the situation was still obscure, two guns to G.20.C.90.75, two guns to G.20.D.48. Casualties Major H. MORRISON missing.	

Army Form C. 2118.

WAR DIARY
or
INTELLIGENCE SUMMARY.
(Erase heading not required.)

Instructions regarding War Diaries and Intelligence
Summaries are contained in F. S. Regs. Part II.
and the Staff Manual respectively. Title pages
will be prepared in manuscript.

Vol II

Place	Date	Hour	Summary of Events and Information	Remarks and references to Appendices
ST. VENANT	24.4.18		A hostile counter attack made on the Right Brigade at 5 AM was repulsed, heavy casualties being inflicted on the enemy by machine gun and artillery fire, their being estimated at 200 killed + 200 wounded. 10 prisoners were taken.	
"	25.4.18		The front was comparatively quiet. D Company behind the guns on the right. A protective barrage was maintained along the front of the Rifle Brigade. Lieut. E.G. WARDROP returned to duty.	
"	26.4.18		Front was comparatively quiet. Losses of the men quite exhausted with heat and exposure.	
"	27.4.18		Front was comparatively quiet. Training for use carried on during the morning and afternoon. Casualties 2 O.R. wounded.	
"	28.4.18		Front was comparatively quiet. Harassing fire continued.	
"	29.4.18		Front was comparatively quiet. Lieuts G.F. HALE, Lieut J. SHEFFIELD arrived from the Company and quite Capt. G.T. HALE, Lieut J. SHEFFIELD arrived at un this to the Staff from this date.	

Part of Sheet 36ᵃ N.E. & 36ᵃ S.E.

Scale 1:20,000.

Batteries of 4 Guns shewn thus:-

SECRET.   M.G.321.

Headquarters,

   61st. Division (G).

Herewith War Diary for the Month of May 1918.

Please acknowledge.

                                            [signature]
                                       Capt.& Adjt.,for Lt-Col.
                                  cmdg.61st.Battalion Machine Gun Corps.

BN.H.Q.
3/6/18.

WAR DIARY.
61st BN. M.G.C.
MAY 1918.

Army Form C. 2118.

WAR DIARY
or
INTELLIGENCE SUMMARY.
(Erase heading not required.)

Instructions regarding War Diaries and Intelligence Summaries are contained in F. S. Regs., Part II. and the Staff Manual respectively. Title pages will be prepared in manuscript.

61 Bn MGC ojo

Place	Date	Hour	Summary of Events and Information	Remarks and references to Appendices
ST. VENANT.	1/5/18.		Artillery fairly active on both sides. During night enemy massing at Q.2.central were dispersed by our Machine Gun fire. Casualties 4 O.R. killed in action.	Ref.Map. 36.A. 1/40,000.
Do.	2/5/18.		Moderate shelling on both sides. Machine Guns co-operated with artillery in area shoot. 40,000 rounds fired. Casualties 4 O.R.wounded in action. Reinforcements. Lieut. R.R.Lee and 2/Lieut.G.R.Wilson.	
Do.	3/5/18.		Artillery fairly active. Increased harassing fire by our Machine Guns. 15,000 rounds fired during the night. 16 guns "C" Coy. relieved 16 guns "D" Company, in the Right Sector. Relief complete by 9-30 p.m. "D" Company went into reserve at BERGUETTE. Casualties. Nil.	
Do.	4/5/18.		Our artillery put down heavy barrage on Right Sector at 3 a.m. Marked decrease in enemy shelling. M.G.barrage altered in accordance with attached appendix1. Position of guns remained the same. 10,750 rounds fired during the night on enemy communications. Enemy plane brought down. Casualties. Nil.	
Do.	5/5/18.		Our artillery moderate. Hostile artillery below normal. Increased harassing fire by our Machine Guns. 16,250 rounds fired. A large number of E.O.Balloons up during the day / but	

Army Form C. 2118.

61 Bn MGCorps

WAR DIARY
or
INTELLIGENCE-SUMMARY.
(Erase heading not required.)

Instructions regarding War Diaries and Intelligence Summaries are contained in F. S. Regs., Part II. and the Staff Manual respectively. Title pages will be prepared in manuscript.

Place	Date	Hour	Summary of Events and Information	Remarks and references to Appendices
ST. VENANT.			but visibility poor. Casualties. Nil. Reinforcements. Lieut.H.M.S.Collinson Jones, Lieut.R.A.Proven, 2/Lieut.R.T.Kirkwood. 2/Lieut.R.Sparshott. 2/Lieut.P.C.Geddes. 2/Lieut.A.McIntosh.	Ref.Map. 36.A. 1/40,000
Do.	6/5/18.		Our artillery fairly active. Enemy artillery active. ISBERGUES Factory shelled from 2-30 p.m. to 6-0 p.m. Our Machine Guns fired 8,250 harassing fire during the night. One E.Plane brought down. Casualties. Nil.	
Do.	7/5/18.		A silent raid was carried out by our infantry on some houses in the vicinity of Q.8.c. Raiding party looked by enemy infantry and withdrew reporting loss of as two officers. Our artillery showed increased activity. Enemy artillery fairly quiet. 7,500 rounds harassing fire expended during the night by our Machine guns, including a concentration shoot by 12 guns on area Q.21.a.88.25. Q.21.a.52.70. Q.15.d.45.00. Q.15.c.92.37. Two white and two red lights were sent up by the enemy followed by artillery fire Casualties Nil. Honours and awards. The Military Medal awarded to the following:- 130634 Pte.J.Price. 19900 Pte.C.Jones. 28630 L/Cpl.S.W.Hill. 134177 Pte.W.E.Philpott.	

61 Bn M.G.Corps

WAR DIARY
or
INTELLIGENCE SUMMARY.
(Erase heading not required.)

Army Form C. 2118.

Place	Date	Hour	Summary of Events and Information	Remarks and references to Appendices
SH. VERANT.	8/5/18.		At 4.30 a.m. heavy drum fire heard to the North. Artillery moderate on both sides during the rest of the day. 7500 rounds harassing fire by our Machine Guns. Increased Aerial activity on both sides. Casualties Nil.	Ref.Map. 36.A. 1/40,000.
Do.	9/5/18.		Our artillery very active all day and night. Enemy artillery normal. 22,000 rounds M.G. harassing fire on roads tracks etc. 2 Machine Guns moved from battery position at Q.19.B.3.4. and took up positions at Q.20.a.65.85. and Q.20.a.32.50. Aerial activity on both sides very marked. Casualties one O.R. killed in action.	
Do.	10/5/18.		Our artillery moderate, enemy artillery below normal. 16,000 rounds harassing fire. Only slight aeroplane activity owing to bad visibility. Casualties Nil.	
Do.	11/5/18.		At 2 a.m. patrols of 5th Gordons and 8th.Argylls reached enemy posts in N.31.d. supported by artillery and Machine gun barrage. No prisoners were taken. Our artillery was very active during the whole period. Enemy artillery below normal. During the night 19,750 rounds harassing fire. A large number of gas shells were fired on our forward system. Casualties Nil. Reinforcements one O.R. The following honours and awards were awarded. 2/Lieut P.Richards. Bar to M.C. 2/Lieut.J.R.Bass M.C. 2/Lieut.E.M.Purdy M.C. 2/Lieut.E.Oliver M.C. Lieut R.A.Moon M.C. 4678 C.S.M.J.Montgomery.D.C.M. 73334 L/Cpl. J.Price D.C.M. 20215 Cbl.G.Patterson M.M.	

/12/5/18.

Army Form C. 2118.

61 Army C Corps

WAR DIARY
or
INTELLIGENCE SUMMARY.
(Erase heading not required.)

Instructions regarding War Diaries and Intelligence Summaries are contained in F. S. Regs., Part II. and the Staff Manual respectively. Title pages will be prepared in manuscript.

Place	Date	Hour	Summary of Events and Information	Remarks and references to Appendices
ST. VENANT.	12/5/18.		Artillery on both sides normal. Our Machine guns fired 8,800 rounds harassing fire. Aerial activity moderate on both sides. "D" Company relieved "B" Company in the Centre Sector. Relief complete 1.a.m.13/5/18. Casualties Nil. Reinforcements One O.R.	Ref.Map 36.A. 1/40,000.
Do.	13/5/18.		Patrol sent out by 2/4th.Oxfords & Bucks L.I. at 11-55 p.m. under cover of artillery and Machine gun barrage. Two prisoners were captured. Machine guns carried out usual harassing fire during the night. 9,000 rounds being fired. Our artillery fairly quiet with exception of raid. Enemy artillery normal.	
Do.	14/5/18.		Artillery on both sides normal. 2/6th.Warwicks supported by artillery raided enemy line at 11-30 p.m. and another raid was carried out by 4th Division on our Right at 2 a.m. 15/5/18. There was only slight retaliation. Usual harassing fire by our machine guns 15,500 rounds being expended. Aircraft active throughout the day owing to good visibility. Casualties Nil.	
Do.	15/5/18.		Intermittent shelling by artillery on both sides during the day. Our artillery active during the night and early morning. Harassing fire carried out during the night 14,000 rounds expended and 500 rounds fired by our M.Gs. on enemy aircraft. Our aircraft very active during the day which prevented much reconnaissance by the enemy.	/16/5/18.

CWB

61 Bn MGCorps

Army Form C. 2118.

WAR DIARY
or
INTELLIGENCE SUMMARY.
(Erase heading not required.)

Instructions regarding War Diaries and Intelligence Summaries are contained in F. S. Regs., Part II. and the Staff Manual respectively. Title pages will be prepared in manuscript.

Place	Date	Hour	Summary of Events and Information	Remarks and references to Appendices
ST. VENANT.	16/5/18.		Artillery quiet during the day, again very active during the night. Our Machine guns fired 10,250 rounds harassing fire. Aerial activity normal. Position of Machine guns and barrage altered in accordance with attached sketch. Appendix II. Reinforcements 5 O.R.	Ref.Map. 36.A. 1/40,000.
Do.	17/5/18.		Position normal. 8 guns under Capt.G.T.Hale detailed for special harassing fire to be known as the "Harassing Force" 4 guns at P.6.b.5.7. and 4 guns at Q.13.a.3.2. Right battery fired 10,000 rounds during the night. The usual was also carried out during the night 11,000 rounds being expended. 200 rounds were fired at enemy aircraft. Enemy bombing machines again very active during the night. Casualties. Nil. Reinforcements. Lieut.C.C.Green.	
Do.	18/5/18.		Artillery normal. Increased back area shelling by enemy. Our Machine guns fired 15,000 rounds harassing fire. Aeroplanes active on both sides. Increased hostile night bombing. Casualties. Nil. The following honours and awards awarded. 139737 L/Cpl. D.Chapman. M.M. 119522 Pte. R.Lang. M.M.	
Do.	19/5/18.		Artillery moderate. back area shelling again marked, and night bombing by enemy machines. Our Machine guns fired 20,500 rounds harassing fire, including 12,000 rounds by Harassing /Force.	

Army Form C. 2118.

61 Bn M G Corps

WAR DIARY
or
INTELLIGENCE SUMMARY.
(Erase heading not required.)

Instructions regarding War Diaries and Intelligence Summaries are contained in F.S. Regs., Part II. and the Staff Manual respectively. Title pages will be prepared in manuscript.

Place	Date	Hour	Summary of Events and Information	Remarks and references to Appendices
ST. VENANT.	20/5/18.		Force. Enemy working party engaged in front of machine gun positions at P.4.b., were dispersed by our M.G.fire. Heavy shelling heard to the North during the early morning. Casualties. One O.R. wounded in action.	Ref. Map 36.A. 1/40,000
Do.	21/5/18.		Our artillery active both day and night. Enemy artillery moderate. Machine guns fired 18,000 rounds harassing fire during the night. Two fires were observed in enemy lines. Casualties. Nil.	
			Artillery normal. Enemy working party at K.32.c.75.21. engaged by our Machine guns and dispersed. 14-500 rounds harassing fire during the night. Our aircraft very active, enemy aircraft very quiet. Enemy machine gun located in house Q.14.c.95.40. and enemy movement at Q.8.d.9.7. 16 of our machine guns relieved the 22 guns of the 59th.Battalion M.G.C. in the AUBOIRES line. The above mentioned 16 guns were composed of 8 guns Harassing Force, 4 guns from Battalion H.G. and 4 guns from "Q" Company. Capt.G.T.Hale in command. On relief the 39 Battalion M.G.C. wnt into Army Reserve. Casualties, Nil. 59535 Sgt. J.Murray awarded the D.C.M.	
Do.	22/5/18.		Artillery normal on both sides. Group of enemy fired on at Q.9.c.8.7. 12,000 rounds were expended during the night on harassing fire. Hostile aircraft was engaged. Casualties. Nil.	

/23/5/18.

Army Form C. 2118.

WAR DIARY
or
INTELLIGENCE SUMMARY.
(Erase heading not required.)

61 Bn M.G.Corps

Instructions regarding War Diaries and Intelligence Summaries are contained in F. S. Regs., Part II. and the Staff Manual respectively. Title pages will be prepared in manuscript.

Place	Date	Hour	Summary of Events and Information	Remarks and references to Appendices
ST.VENANT.	23/5/18.		Artillery normal on both sides. Very little aerial activity owing to bad weather conditions. Left Company fired 1000 round on S.O.S. lines at 2-45 a.m. with satisfactory results. 5,000 round fired during the night harassing. Brigade boundaries altered in accordance with ~~new orders~~. During the night enemy used a large number of Very Lights. Casualties. Nil.	Ref.Map 36.A. 1/40,000
Do.	24/5/18.		Artillery normal. Centre company fired 5,500 rounds S.O.S. test at 3 a.m. Right Company 1500 rounds. Results satisfactory. 150 rounds fired at enemy post opposite M.G. position Q.7.b.20.90. 3000 rounds harassing fire expended during the night. Casualties. Nil.	
Do.	25/5/18.		Our artillery quieter than than usual. Occasional bursts were fired between 3 p.m and 5 p.m. in reply to enemy fire. Enemy targets were engaged during the night by our Machine Guns. About noon a squadron of our planes crossed the enemy's lines but were heavily fired on by Machine and A.A. Guns. Casualties. Nil.	
Do.	26/5/21.		Slight Artillery activity ST.VENANT - ST.FLORIS LOCK - HAVERSKERQUE ROAD were shelled with gas. Enemy Machine guns active against our aircraft during the day, usual activity at night. Our Machine Guns fired 10,000 rounds during the night on Tracks, Dumps and Farms behind /enemy's.	

Army Form C. 2118.

61 Bn MG Corp

WAR DIARY
or
INTELLIGENCE SUMMARY.
(Erase heading not required.)

Instructions regarding War Diaries and Intelligence Summaries are contained in F. S. Regs., Part II. and the Staff Manual respectively. Title pages will be prepared in manuscript.

Place	Date	Hour	Summary of Events and Information	Remarks and references to Appendices
ST, VENANT.	27/5/18		enemy's front line system, also against hostile aircraft. "A" Company relieved "C" Company in the Right Sector and "B" Company relieved "D" Company in the Left Sector.	Ref.Map. 36.A. 1/40,000.
Do.	28/5/18		Hostile artillery and aircraft very active, gas shells on the increase, M.G. position at Q.19.b.30.42. received attention. Back areas were shelled heavily from 11 p.m. to 12-30 a.m. machine Guns fired 9750 rounds intermittently throughout the night on tracks, dumps and enemy's Trench System. At 6-15 p.m. a small enterprise was carried out against enemy's position in Orchard at K.31.d.30.20.. M.Gs.co-operated 2000 rounds fired. No. casualties.	
Do.	29/5/18.		Artillery active both day and night. Several enemy targets were fired on intermittently during the night. Aircraft active, visibility good. At 8 a.m. an aerial fight was in progress, 2 of our Machines brought down in flames. Observation balloons up all day.	
Do.	29/5/18.		Artillery active during the period. Houses in the enemy's front system shelled. Our Machine guns fired on enemy targets 9500 rounds expended. Aircraft very active on both sides. Enemy planes patrolled during absence of our planes but generally kept to their own line. One E. machine crossed our lines and brought down one of our observation balloons. Casualties Nil.	
Do.	30/5/18.		11,000 rounds were expended on enemy targets by our machine guns during the period. Artillery on both sides very active. Aircraft, usual activity, a few bombs dropped during the night. /31/5/18.	

WAR DIARY
or
INTELLIGENCE SUMMARY.
(Erase heading not required.)

61 Bn MGC Army Form C. 2118.

Instructions regarding War Diaries and Intelligence Summaries are contained in F.S. Regs., Part II. and the Staff Manual respectively. Title pages will be prepared in manuscript.

Place	Date	Hour	Summary of Events and Information	Remarks and references to Appendices
ST. VENANT.	31/5/18.		Our artillery fired on enemy back areas, heavies and shrapnel. Enemy artillery active. Our machine guns fired 11000 rounds on various targets. Enemy machine guns fairly active during the night. Enemy plane brought down out of control. Enemy bombing machines active during the night. Six balloons up during the day. Casualties Nil.	Ref. Map. 36.A. 1/40,000

Arthur Bracewell Lieut. MGC
for CO 61st M.G.C.

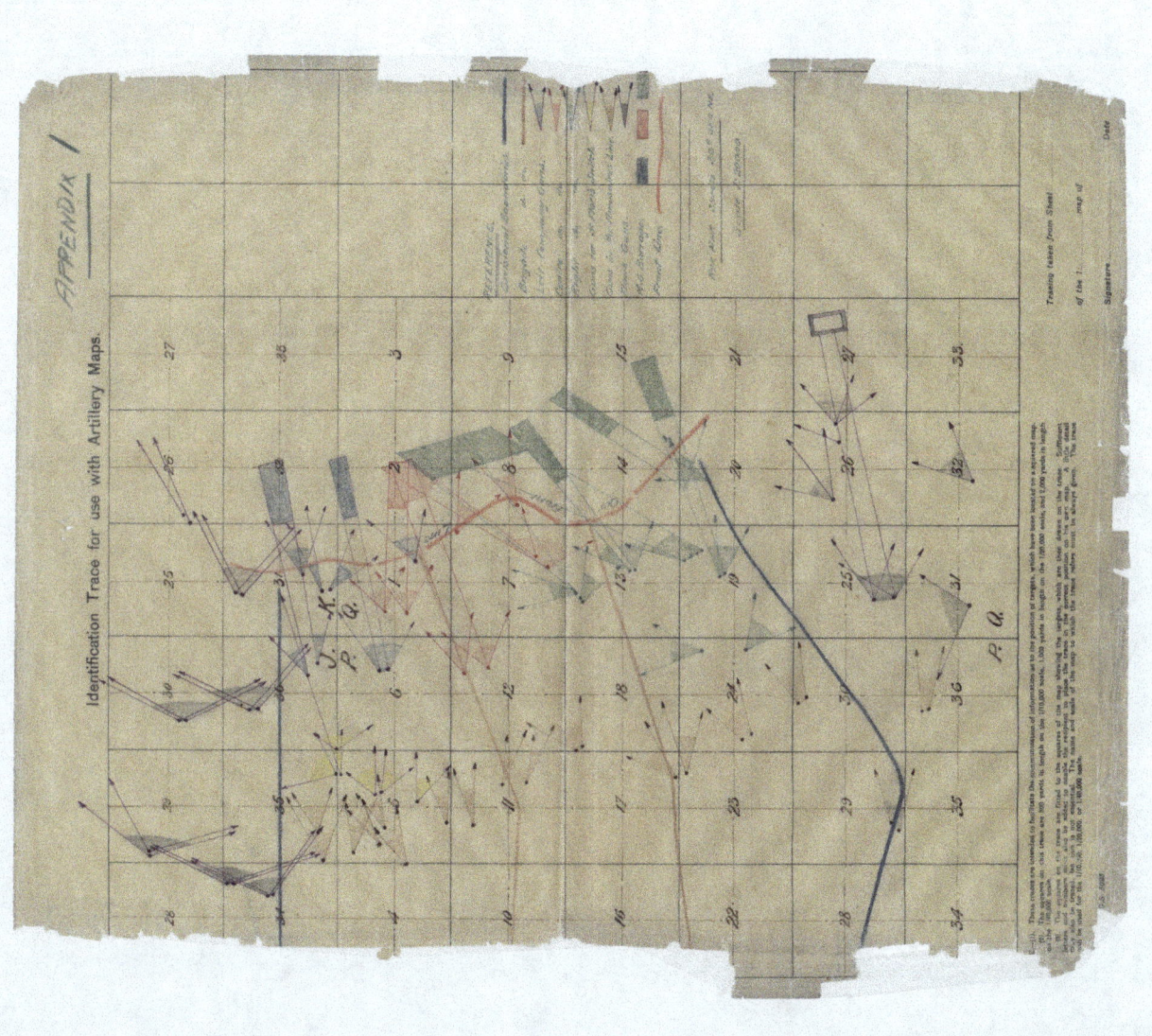

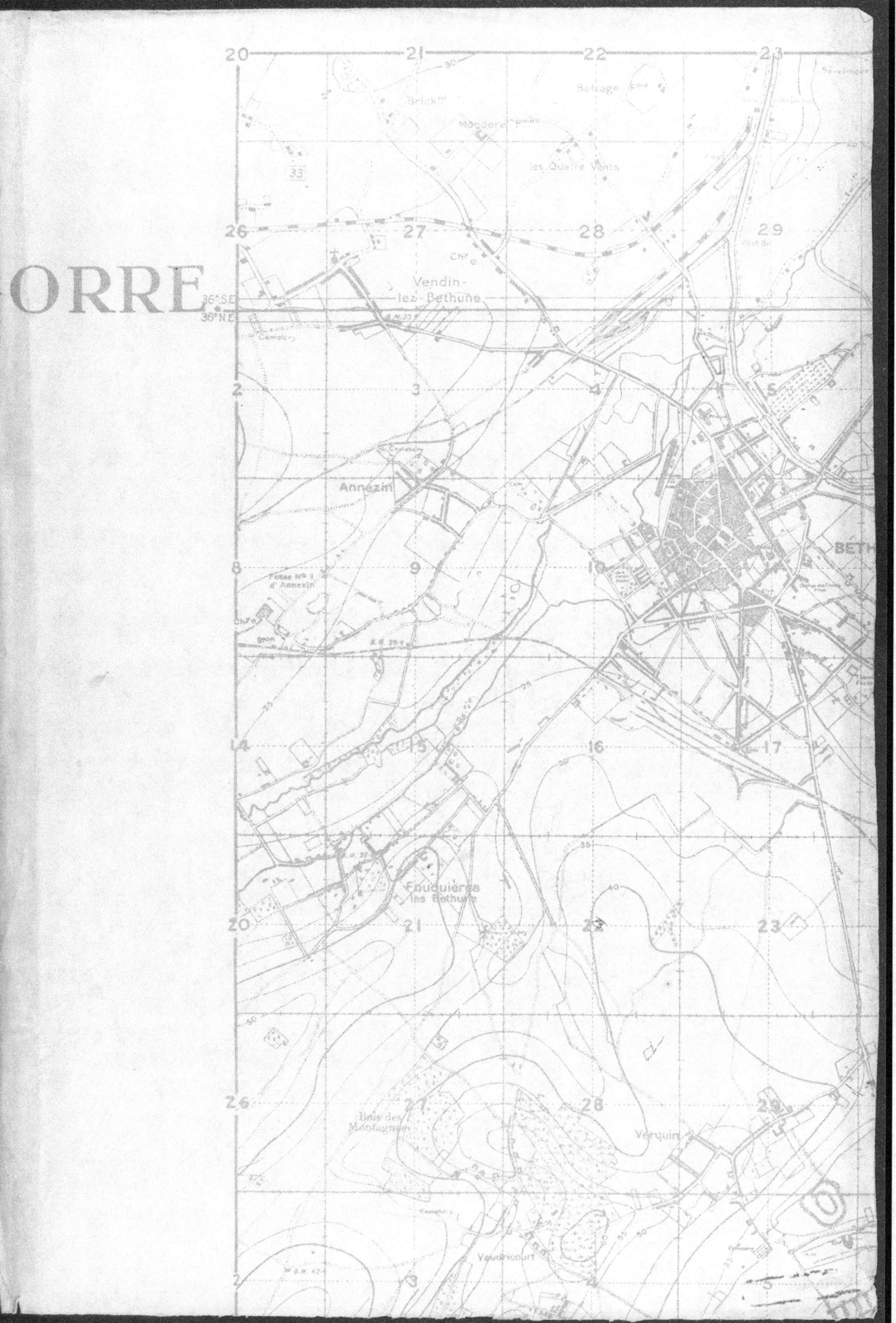

61 Bn MG Corp
Vol 5

War Diary
June 1918.

Army Form C. 2118.

WAR DIARY
or
INTELLIGENCE SUMMARY.
(Erase heading not required.)

61 Bn MGC

Instructions regarding War Diaries and Intelligence Summaries are contained in F.S. Regs., Part II. and the Staff Manual respectively. Title pages will be prepared in manuscript.

Place	Date	Hour	Summary of Events and Information	Remarks and references to Appendices
ST.VENANT	1/6/18.		Our Machine Guns fairly active during the day and night. Many enemy targets were engaged, 11,000 rounds being expended. Enemy Machine Guns active during the night. Training and recreation carried out by reserve company. Casualties. 2 wounded.	Ref.Map 36A. 1/40,000.
Do.	2/6/18.		Many of the targets of the previous day were again engaged, 11,000 rounds fired. During the night enemy swept our parapet in J.36.d. and Q.20.a. Anti-aircraft firing was carried out during the day. Casualties 1 wounded.	
Do.	3/6/18.		"D" Company relieved "B" Company in the left section on night 2nd./3rd.June. Our Machine Guns fired 8,000 rounds on various targets and tracks between rivers CLARENCE and NOC. Enemy Machine Guns swept our positions in Q.7.d. and path Q.13.c. from about Q.8.c.60.60. and post at Q.2.c.00.40. Dumps fired at BERGUETTE. "B" Company took up billets at BERGUETTE. Casualties Nil. Bieut.J.Swaffield awarded the Military Cross.	
Do.	4/6/18.		Our M.Gs. fired 5,500 rounds on Road and tracks Q.2.b. and Q.3.a. and Q.14.d.70.40. Enemy M.Gs. active. Swept tracks from K.31.d.40.30. Training carried out by reserve Coys. Casualties Nil.	/5/6/18.

Army Form C. 2118.

WAR DIARY
or
INTELLIGENCE SUMMARY.
(Erase heading not required.)

61 Bruge

Instructions regarding War Diaries and Intelligence Summaries are contained in F. S. Regs., Part II. and the Staff Manual respectively. Title pages will be prepared in manuscript.

Place	Date	Hour	Summary of Events and Information	Remarks and references to Appendices
ST.VENANT	5/6/18.		Track Q.15.c.70.00 to Q.16.a.50.77, roads and road junctions in Q.9. were fired on by our Machine Guns 9,000 rounds being expended. Enemy machine guns fired intermittently during the night on P.18.d. CALONNE-ROBECQ Road Q.19.c.and d. An explosion, apparently an ammunition dump was observed on a true bearing of 30° from Q.7.d.35.65. Casualties Nil. Honours and Awards. Capt.E.H.Collinson awarded the M.C. 13691 Sgt. Talbot B. awarded the D.C.M.	Ref.Map. 36A. 1/40,000.
Do.	6/6/18.		Various targets were engaged during the 24 hours. 12,000 rounds fired. Enemy machine guns than usual, 4 guns carried out indirect fire from the direction of Q.8.c., Q.8.d., and Q.15.c. occasionally throughout the night. A wide traverse was used but apparently at no particular target. Casualties Nil. Reinforcements 14 O.R.	
Do.	7/6/18.		14,000 rounds were expended during the night on various enemy targets, new trenches, concrete works and ammunition dumps receiving attention. Patrols of the enemy endeavoured to reach our lines in K.31.d. but were engaged by our patrols. Occasional bursts of enemy machine gun fire during the night. A wide traverse was used but apparently at no particular targets. Casualties Nil. Capt.F.J.Goode received the Military Cross.	
Do.	8/6/18.		Roads, tracks, bridges and dumps were engaged, 12,500 rounds fired.	

Army Form C. 2118.

WAR DIARY
or
INTELLIGENCE SUMMARY.
(Erase heading not required.)

Instructions regarding War Diaries and Intelligence Summaries are contained in F.S. Regs., Part II. and the Staff Manual respectively. Title pages will be prepared in manuscript.

Place	Date	Hour	Summary of Events and Information	Remarks and references to Appendices
ST.VENANT.	9/6/18.		Enemy machine guns fired bursts on the CALONNE road and tracks S. of road. Casualties Nil. Training and recreation carried out by the reserve coys.	Ref.Map. 36A. 1/40,000.
Do.	10/6/18.		Many of the targets of the previous night were again engaged 12,500 rounds being expended. Bursts of fire on ground N. of CALONNE-ROBECQ Road, support and reserve lines. M.G. fired from Orchard in Q.14.d. 28522 Sgt.Lee A. awarded Bar to D.C.M. Casualties Nil. "B" Company relieved "D" Company in the Left Group. On relief "D" Company proceeded to billets in BERGUETTE. Road junctions in K.33.a., K.33.c., Q.9.d. and track Q.15.c. Q.16.a. were engaged by our Machine guns 8,000 rounds fired. Enemy Machine guns fired bursts on CALONNE-ROBECQ road and trenches in Q.13. as on previous night. Casualties Nil. Training and recreation commenced by the Company in reserve.	
Do.	11/6/18.		"A" Company relieved "C" Company in the Right Group. On relief "C" Company proceeded to billets in GUARBECQUE. Ammunition dump in Q.15.b.70.30 and Road junction in Q.9.d.30.50. and track Q.15.c.70.00 were fired on by our M.Gs. 6,000 rounds expended. Casualties Nil. Training and recreation commenced by "C" Company.	
Do.	12/6/18.		Dump in Q.15.b. and Q.8.d., Railway Q.2.d. Track Q.8.b. to Q.3.c., Bridge and Road in K.32 central were engaged 9,250 rounds fired. Area Q.13.a. swept with bursts of fire from M.G. in /Q.14.d.	

Army Form C. 2118.

WAR DIARY
or
=INTELLIGENCE SUMMARY=
(Erase heading not required.)

Instructions regarding War Diaries and Intelligence
Summaries are contained in F. S. Regs., Part II.
and the Staff Manual respectively. Title pages
will be prepared in manuscript.

Place	Date	Hour	Summary of Events and Information	Remarks and references to Appendices
ST.VENANT.				Ref.Map. 36A. 1/40,000.
	13/6/18.		in Q.14.d. Casualties Nil. Reinforcements 2 O.R.	
Do.			11,750 rounds were fired during the 24 hours, roads of various references. Enemy Machine Gun at K.31.d.25.25. silenced during the day by our Trench Mortars.	
			Casualties Nil. Reinforcements one O.R.	
Do.	14/6/18.		4,000 rounds harassing fire, Road junction Q.9.a. and 1,500 rounds on Road Q.2.b. to Q.3.c. Enemy machine guns continually searching WOLLOW TREE ROAD.	
			Casualties Nil. Training and recreation carried out by the Companies in reserve.	
Do.	15/6/18.		Many enemy targets were engaged during the period, tracks, roads etc: receiving attention 10,750 rounds fired. Harassing fire by enemy on areas Q.13.a. and Q.19.d. Road Q.19.d.20.80. Q.20.a.60.30.	
			Casualties Nil.	
Do.	16/6/18.		10,250 rounds were expended on various enemy targets in both sections. Enemy Machine guns very quiet except for occasional bursts during the night.	
			Casualties Two O.R. wounded.	
Do.	17/6/18.		Our Machine Guns were active during the night, harassing fire on roads, tracks etc:: A.A. fire was also carried out, 7,550 rounds fired. Enemy M.Gs. very active during the night /sweeping	

Army Form C. 2118.

WAR DIARY
or
INTELLIGENCE SUMMARY.
(Erase heading not required.)

61 Brig E

Place	Date	Hour	Summary of Events and Information	Remarks and references to Appendices
ST.VENANT			sweeping reserve line in Q.13.a. Indirect fire at intervals over ROBECQ CALONNE Road in Q.19.a. and b.and paths in Q.19.c. and d. Also active on A.A. work. Casualties 4 O.R. killed. Reinforcements 3 Officers and 1 O.R. 4678 C.S.M. J.Montgomery awarded the M.S.M.	Ref.Map 36A. 1/40,000.
Do.	18/6/18.		Our Machine Guns not quite so active. 6,000 rounds were fired on K.33.a.25.95.,Q.2.b.25.80. and Level Crossing Q.3.c. Enemy machine guns fired bursts on areas Q.19.a. and Q.15.d. Fire observed in enemy lines in direction of Q.22. Enemy aircraft fired tracer bullets at ground targets about Q.19.a.50.45. Casualties 2 O.R. wounded. Reinforcements 1 O.R. "D" Company relieved "B" Company in the Left Group, any withdrew to billets in BERGUETTE.	
Do.	19/6/18.		10,000 rounds were fired on various enemy targets during the 24 hours, enemy machine gun posts tracks and trenches receiving attention. Enemy M.Gs. fired on Tracks N. and S. of ROBECQ also on our line in Q.7.d. and Q.13.b. "A" Coy. "C" Company relieved "A" Company in the Right Group, and proceeded to billets in GUARBECQUE Casualties Nil.	
Do.	20/6/18.		Enemy posts and tracks were engaged 8,500 rounds being expended. Enemy harassing fire on our lines in Q.7.d. and Q.19.a.. ROBECQ-CALONNE Road swept with occasional bursts of fire /Ammunition dump	

Army Form C. 2118.

WAR DIARY
or
INTELLIGENCE SUMMARY.
(Erase heading not required.)

Instructions regarding War Diaries and Intelligence Summaries are contained in F.S. Regs., Part II. and the Staff Manual respectively. Title pages will be prepared in manuscript.

61Bmcc

Place	Date	Hour	Summary of Events and Information	Remarks and references to Appendices
ST.VENANT.				Ref.Map. 36A. 1/40,000.
	21/6/18.		Ammunition dump exploded in direction of CALONNE (Observation from Q.13.d.90.60.) Many targets were engaged 12,000 rounds expended. Enemy Machine guns active during the night. ROBECQ Road and tracks near Q.19.central were swept with occasional bursts of fire. Casualties Nil. Training and recreation carried out by the companies in reserve.	
Do.	22/6/18.		Enemy posts from Q.14.a.53.90 to Q.8.a.88.65 and tracks from Q.15.d.00.20 to Q.16.a.16.85 were engaged 6,000 rounds fired. Enemy swept ROBECQ-CALONNE Road with bursts of fire at intervals throughout the night. Harassing fire on areas Q.7.d., Q.13.a., Q.19.b.	
Do.	23/6/18.		21,000 rounds were expended on Road junction Q.2.b.30.80., Level Crossing Q.3.c. and Barrage fire in support of a raid carried out by the Infantry on Orchard Q.8.c.60.30. Raid was replied to by active enemy machine gun fire. (SEE MAP ATTACHED)	
Do.	24/6/18.		Various enemy targets were engaged 1,000 rounds on Road Q.2.b.43.51.- Q.2.b.80.50. 2,000 rounds Road junction Q.9.a.70.90. 2,000 rounds Track Q.15.d.00.20 - Q.16.a.60.85. 2,000 rounds on Q.16.a. and 2,000 rounds on Road Junction Q.9.d.28.15. Enemy harassing fire on our front system and tracks in rear. Tactical schemes and recreation carried out by reserve companies.	
Do.	25/6/18.		3,000 rounds fired on Q.9.d. 6,000 rounds on barrage fire in support of a raid on enemy line of posts from Q.1.b.25.00 to Q.1.b.80.60. 4 prisoners taken. Enemy machine guns very active between 10 p.m. and midnight. Gun located firing during from Q.21.c.60.95.	/26/6/18.

Army Form C. 2118.

WAR DIARY
or
INTELLIGENCE-SUMMARY.

(Erase heading not required)

Instructions regarding War Diaries and Intelligence Summaries are contained in F.S. Regs. Part II and the Staff Manual respectively. Title pages will be prepared in manuscript.

6 BN R E

Place	Date	Hour	Summary of Events and Information	Remarks and references to Appendices
ST.VENANT	26/6/18.		6,000 rounds were expended during the night on enemy targets in Q.13.d., Q.16.a. and Railway Q.9.d.38.15. Enemy harassing fire on our front and support systems and on tracks. ROBECQ-CALONNE road swept with occasional bursts of fire	Ref.Map. 36A. 1/40,000.
Do.	27/6/18.		"B" Company relieved "D" Company in the Left Section. Gas was projected by the Division on our right. Offensive operation carried out by Division on our Left. 4,000 rounds were expended on areas Q.8. and Q.9. Enemy carried out harassing fire on the CALONNE-ROBECQ Road, and on tracks in the vicinity of the front line. Casualties Nil.	
Do.	28/6/18.		"A" Company relieved "C" Company in the Right Section. 6,000 rounds were fired on various targets. Brisk harassing fire maintained along our front by the enemy. Training and recreation carried out by the companies in reserve.	
Do.	29/6/18.		Enemy approaches and Q.9. received attention 4,500 rounds being fired. Enemy M.Gs. active against our planes during the day and harassing fire throughout the night.	
Do.	30/6/18.		A.A.fire was carried out by our M.Gs. throughout the day, tracks etc; receiving attention during the night 6,500 rounds fired. Enemy active on area Q.1.a and b. Casualties Nil.	

Strength of Battalion 44 Officers 18/70 OR

Mdiarmid Lieut
Comdg: 6: B.: M.G.C.

REFERENCE:
British Front line
Enemy do. do.
M.G. Barrage

REF. MAP. 36ᴺ S.E.

APPENDIX "A"

SECRET.

61st Battalion Machine Gun Corps Operation Order No.29 dated 4/8/18.

Ref. Map Sheet 36A. (1/40,000.)

1. "A" Company will move to area J.32.d.9.9. commencing at 2.0 p.m.

2. Dismounted personnel will move by Bus or Lorry between 5.0 and 6.0 p.m. tonight.
   Lorries will convey troops to THIENNES, remainder of journey will be completed on foot.

3. Transport will move by march route commencing at 2.0 p.m.
   Route via AIRE - THIENNES - TANNAY.

4. A distance of 25 yards will be maintained between each section of 6 vehicles on march.

5. An Officer will proceed at once to reconnoitre new area.

6. Rations for 5th inst. will be taken up, also cookers and water carts.

7. The Company will be administered by the Battalion.

8. Completion of move will be reported to H.Qrs. 5th Division and to Battalion H.Qrs.

9. ACKNOWLEDGE.

10. Code word for move complete :- "MILLWARD"

                                    Captain & Adjt.,
                                    61st Battalion Machine Gun Corps.
4/8/18.

   Copies to:-
      No. 1. "A" Company.
          2. "B" Company. (for information)
          3. "C" Company.   do.   do.
          4. "D" Company.   do.   do.
          5. 61st Division.
          6. Signalling Officer.
          7. Q.
          8. File.
          9. War Diary. ✓
         10. Intelligence Officer.
         11. 5th Division.

61 Bgy M.G. Corps
Vol 6.

WAR DIARY

VOLUME NO. V

MONTH OF JULY

1918

61 Bn. M.G.C.

Army Form C. 2118.

WAR DIARY
or
INTELLIGENCE SUMMARY.
(Erase heading not required.)

Place	Date	Hour	Summary of Events and Information	Remarks and references to Appendices
ST. VENANT.	1/7/18.		Our Machine Guns fairly active during the day and night. Many enemy targets were engaged, 8,000 rounds being expended. Enemy M.G's active during the night. Casualties :- NIL.	Ref. Map. 36A. 1/40,000.
do.	2/7/18.		Our Machine Guns fired 4,000 rounds on various targets. Enemy M.G's fired on tracks and also traversed our positions in Q.19.d. at intervals. Houses at P.6.c.20.30. and P.6.c.10.60. were set on fire. Two fires in Q.14.b. burned for some time. Casualties :- NIL.	
do.	3/7/18.		Our Machine Guns fired on roads and tracks in Q.15.a.c., 4,000 rounds being expended. Enemy M.G's swept our positions in Q.7.d. and Q.13.a. during the night. Section H.Q. at Q.19.a.60.50. also received attention. Casualties :- NIL.	
do.	4/7/18.		Track in K.33.c. and road in Q.9.a. were fired on by our Machine Guns during the night, 3,000 rounds being expended. Enemy M.G's carried out harassing fire on our front line positions. A large number of GREEN, YELLOW and RED lights were sent up during the night, but no apparent action followed. Training carried out by Reserve Company. Casualties :- NIL. Reinforcements :- 20 O.R's.	

WAR DIARY
or
INTELLIGENCE SUMMARY.
(Erase heading not required.)

Army Form C.

Place	Date	Hour	Summary of Events and Information	Remarks and references to Appendices
St. VENANT.	5/7/18.		Our Machine Guns fired 4,000 rounds on various tracks. Enemy M.G's swept our forward system and tracks during the night. CALONNE and ROBECQ road swept with bursts of fire at intervals. Anti-aircraft firing was carried out during the day. Casualties :- NIL.	Ref. Map 36A. 1/40,000.
do.	6/7/18.		6,000 rounds were fired by our Machine Guns on various roads and tracks during the night. Enemy M.G's traversed our front and support lines also roads and tracks in the vicinity of ROBECQ. Casualties :- NIL.	
do.	7/7/18.		Our Machine Guns active during the night, 14,000 rounds were expended in support of raid by Infantry and also on roads and tracks in Q.15.c. Enemy M.G's fired as per the previous night. E.A. dropped Red Lights over LES AMUSOIRES at 7.15 p.m. no apparent action followed. Casualties :- Killed 1 O.R. Wounded 2 O.R's.	
do.	8/7/18.		"D" Company relieved "B" Company in the Left Section on night 7/8th July. Our Machine Guns fired 8,000 rounds in support of raid by Infantry, also harassing fire on roads and tracks in Q.15.c. Enemy M.G's carried out harassing fire on our Reserve and Support Lines. Casualties :- NIL.	

Army Form C. 2118.

WAR DIARY
or
INTELLIGENCE SUMMARY.
(Erase heading not required.)

Instructions regarding War Diaries and Intelligence Summaries are contained in F. S. Regs., Part II. and the Staff Manual respectively. Title pages will be prepared in manuscript.

Place	Date	Hour	Summary of Events and Information	Remarks and references to Appendices
ST. VENANT.	9/7/18.		"C" Company relieved "A" Company in the Right Section on the night 8/9th July.	Ref. Map. 36A. 1/40,000.
			Roads and tracks in Q.9.a.b., Q.15.a. and Railway running through Q.2.b. were fired on by	
			our Machine Guns, 10,000 rounds being expended. Intermittent bursts from direction of Q.8.	
			central. were fired on our Support Lines in Q.7.d. by enemy M.G's., ROBECQ-CALONNE road	
			swept continuously throughout the night. A considerable number of Very and Parachute Lights	
			were sent up XXX at 11.15 p.m. along BACQUEROLLES-CALONNE Line. No action followed.	
			Casualties :- 1 O.R.	
do.	10/7/18.		Our Machine Guns fired 12,000 rounds on various targets during the night. Enemy M.G's	
			maintained harassing fire throughout the night on our front and support lines, also on	
			tracks in rear. A direct hit was obtained on open emplacements at P.7.d. 00.20.	
			"A" and "B" relieved by 74th Battalion Machine Gun Corps, marched to camp at N.21.a. via	
			MAZINGHAM and ROMBLY.	
			Casualties :- NIL. Reinforcements :- 1 O.R.	
do.	11/7/18.		11,000 rounds were expended by our Machine Guns on orchard in K.32.d. and K.33.c., road	
			junction at Dump Q.15.b. and tracks Q.14.d.-Q.14.c. Enemy M.G's maintained usual	
			harassing fire on our front and support lines also on tracks in rear. House at Q.8.b. on	
			CALONNE road observed to be loop-holed and sandbagged. Casualties :- NIL.	

A0945 Wt: W14142/M1160 350,000 12/16 D. D. & L. Forms/C/2118/14.

WAR DIARY
or
INTELLIGENCE SUMMARY.

(Erase heading not required.)

Army Form C. 2118.

Place	Date	Hour	Summary of Events and Information	Remarks and references to Appendices
ST. VENANT.	12/7/18.		"D" Company relieved by 74th Battalion Machine Gun Corps on night 11/12th July, afterwards marching to camp in N.21.a. via MAZINGHAM and ROMBLY. No firing was done during the night by our Machine Guns on account of reliefs. Enemy M.G's were active during the night, Area Q.19.central. was swept with bursts of fire and our front and support lines were traversed. Bomb was dropped at P.1.d.95.15., Coy. H.Q. of Left group, causing casualties to horses of this Battalion. A large No. of Golden Rain Rockets were sent up between 11.0 and 11.30 p.m. from about Q.8.b.; no apparent action followed. Casualties :- NIL.	Ref. Map. 36A. 1/40,000.
do.	13/7/18.		"J" Company relieved by 74th Battalion Machine Gun Corps on night of 12/13th July, afterwards marching to camp in N.21.a. via MAZINGHAM and ROMBLY. Casualties :- NIL. Reinforcements :- 2nd/Lieut. MILLWARD. B. do. FOLD. E.S.	
ROMBLY.	14/7/18.		Battalion Training.	
do.	15/7/18.		do.	
do.	16/7/18.		do.	

WAR DIARY
or
INTELLIGENCE SUMMARY

(Erase heading not required.)

Army Form C. 2118.

Place	Date	Hour	Summary of Events and Information	Remarks and references to Appendices
ROMBLY.	17/7/18.		Battalion Training. Casualties:- NIL.	Ref. Map. 36A. 1/40,000.
do.	18/7/18.		do. Casualties:- NIL.	
do.	19/7/18.		do. Casualties:- NIL. Reinforcements :- 5 O.R's.	
do.	20/7/18.		do. Casualties:- NIL.	
do.	21/7/18.		do. Casualties:- NIL.	
do.	22/7/18.		Battalion moved to BLARINGHEM. Casualties:- NIL.	
BLARINGHEM.	23/7/18.		Battalion Training. Casualties:- NIL.	Ref. Maps. 36A. & 27. 1/40,000.
do.	24/7/18.		Battalion Training. "B" Company moved to billets at V.17.d.20.10. preparatory to conducting a relief. Casualties:- NIL. Reinforcements:- 1 O.R..	
do.	25/7/18.		Battalion Training. "B" Company relieved "B" Company of 29th Battalion M.G.Corps on night of 24/25th July in the Right Section of the 1st Australian Divisional Sector.	
do.	26/7/18.		Battalion Training. Casualties:- 1 O.R. Reinforcements:- 2nd/Lieut. BARROW.R.T. do. JACKSON.J.G.	Ref. Map. 36A. 1/40,000.

Army Form C. 2118.

WAR DIARY
or
INTELLIGENCE SUMMARY.
(Erase heading not required.)

Place	Date	Hour	Summary of Events and Information	Remarks and references to Appendices
BLARINGHEM.	27/7/18		Battalion Training. Casualties :- 1 O.R.	Ref.Map 36A. 1/40,000.
do	28/7/18		Battalion Training. Casualties :- NIL.	
do	29/7/18		Battalion Training. Casualties :- NIL.	
do	30/7/18		Battalion Training. Casualties :- NIL.	
do	31/7/18		The Battalion (less "B" Company) attached 1st.Australian Division, moved by march route from XV Corps to XI Corps Area. (G.H.Q. Reserve). Casualties :- NIL.	

H. N. L. Collinson-Jones
Lieut.

61 Bde M G Coy
Vol 7

Confidential.

******* W A R D I A R Y. ******
****

MONTH of AUGUST 1918.   VOLUME No. 6.

61 Bn. M.G.C.

Army Form C. 2118.

WAR DIARY
or
INTELLIGENCE SUMMARY.
(Erase heading not required.)

Instructions regarding War Diaries and Intelligence Summaries are contained in F.S. Regs., Part II. and the Staff Manual respectively. Title pages will be prepared in manuscript.

Place	Date	Hour	Summary of Events and Information	Remarks and references to Appendices
WITTERNESSE	1/8/18		Battalion being in G.H.Q.Reserve, a General Programme was carried out. "B" Company rejoined after being attached to the 1st. Australian Division. Casualties :- NIL. Reinforcements :- NIL.	Ref. Map Sheet 36A. (1/40,000.) 61.N.G.
do.	2/8/18		Battalion Training. Casualties :- NIL. Reinforcements :- 2/Lt. BLOXHAM. and 10 Other Ranks.	61.M.G.
do.	3/8/18		Battalion Training. Casualties :- NIL. Reinforcements :- 2/Lt. ANSTEY J. M.M., D.C.M.	61.M.G.
do.	4/8/18		"A" Company relieved one Company of the 5th Battalion M.G.C. as per Operation Order No. 29. Remaining Companies carried out Training Programme. attached as Appendix "A". Casualties :- NIL. Reinforcements :- NIL.	61.M.G.
PECQUEUR	5/8/18		Battalion relieved 5th Battalion Machine Gun Corps as per Operation Order No. 30 attached as Appendix "B". Casualties :- NIL. Reinforcements :- NIL.	61.M.G.
do.	6/8/18		do. do. do. Casualties :- NIL. Reinforcements :- NIL.	61.M.G.
do.	7/8/18		Our M.G's were active firing 3,000 rounds on road M.22.b. to M.23.a.; M.G.Position at K.31.c. and harassing fire on enemys' lines. Enemy M.G's. were fairly quiet throughout the period only occasional bursts being fired into the Forest. An enemy sniper was active during the day firing across road at J.30.a.75.05. "B" Company came under Command of G.O.C. 183rd Infantry Brigade for tactical purposes as per Operation Order No. 31. attached as Appendix "C". Casualties :- 2/Lt BARROTT C.N. (Wounded.) Reinforcements :- NIL.	61.M.G.

WAR DIARY
or
INTELLIGENCE SUMMARY.
(Erase heading not required.)

Army Form C. 2118.

Place	Date	Hour	Summary of Events and Information	Remarks and references to Appendices
PECQUER.	8/8/18.		Our M.G's fired 10,000 rounds on various targets as arranged with Infantry. Enemy's M.G's were observed to be firing from longer ranges, maintaining harassing fire on our lines from 8.30 p.m. to dusk and firing at intervals during the night in areas K.14.b. and K.9.d. Our Infantry captured 2 M.G's. Large numbers of Golden Rain Rockets were sent up between 9.0 and 10.0 p.m. together with RED, GREEN and YELLOW Very Lights from direction of K.11. and K.12. Casualties:- 60 O.R's wounded. 4 O.R's killed. Reinforcements:- NIL.	Ref.Map Sheet 36A (1/40,000) 61.M.C.
do	9/8/18.		Our M.G's fired 6,000 rounds during the night on various targets. Enemy M.G's very quiet during period only slight harassing fire being done from direction of SACHET FARM and VIERHOUCK, on our lines. Factory in K.25.c.30.90. on fire from 9.0 a.m. Casualties:- NIL. Reinforcements:- NIL.	61.M.C.
do	10/8/18.		Our M.G's were active during the night firing 10,000 rounds on various targets. Enemy M.G's Inactive. Occasional bursts of fire on tracks leading to front line. Fires seen N. of MERVILLE between 10.0 and 11.0 p.m. During the same hour 3 dumps went up in the vicinity of K.12. and K.30. Casualties:- NIL. Reinforcements:- 13 O.R's.	61.M.C.
do	11/8/18.		Our M.G's were very active during the period 70,000 rounds were fired at 4.15 a.m. in co-operation with Infantry operations, and in addition 5,000 were fired on ATOM FARM, SACHET FARM and other targets. 700 rounds were also fired at hostile aircraft. Enemy M.G's were quiet during the period. AT 3.0 p.m. our line along Canal Bank was swept from long range and at 4.15 a.m. retaliation with sweeping fire shortly after our barrage commenced. Casualties:- 1 O.R. wounded. Reinforcements:- NIL.	61.M.C.
do	12/8/18.		Our M.G's fired 4,500 rounds on ATOM FARM-SACHET FARM and other targets, also engaging E.A. crossing Divisional Line. Enemy M.G's very quiet during the whole period. During the night "B" Company relieved "A" Company as per Operation Order No.32 attached as Appendix "D". Our artillery fell short on K.10.a. and K.9.b.d. up to 2.0 p.m. Dump blown up in direction of K.17.d. Casualties:- NIL Reinforcements:- NIL.	61.M.C.

WAR DIARY
or
INTELLIGENCE SUMMARY.
(Erase heading not required.)

Army Form C. 2118.

Place	Date	Hour	Summary of Events and Information	Remarks and references to Appendices
PACQUE.	13/8/18.		Our M.G's fairly active during the night, 8,000 rounds being expended on various targets. Enemy M.G's very quiet. Occasional bursts over our Front and support lines, during the night. A few RED lights were observed just after dark. During the night "D" Company relieved "Q" Company as per Operation Order No.32 attached as Appendix "D". Casualties:- NIL. Reinforcements:- 2/Lt.Andrews H.G. and 58 O.R's.	Ref:Map. Sheet 36A (1/40,000) [signature]
do	14/8/18.		Our M.G's quiet during the night, 1,000 rounds expended on BRONCHO FARM and Farm at K.18.b.50.40. Enemy M.G's carried out harassing fire during night, especially on our rear positions from 10.0 p.m. to 12.10 a.m. Silent raid on one of our Right Sector posts on night 13/14th inst. 2 O.R's reported missing and 1 killed. Casualties:- 1 O.R. (Wounded) Reinforcements:- 1 O.R.	[signature]
do	15/8/18.		Our M.G's engaged road in front of BRONCHO FARM and shell hole defences at K.17.c.30.30. and K.12.d.60.70. Enemy M.G's quiet. Occasional bursts during the day from direction of MERVILLE and harassing fire on our lines at odd intervals during the night. Casualties:- NIL. Reinforcements:- NIL.	[signature]
do	16/8/18.		Our M.G's fairly quiet during the period. Targets at K.19.d.0.5. and K.18.a.0.6. being engaged. Enemy M.G's very active. Several of our Left Sector M.G. emplacements were fired on from the direction of MERVILLE during the day, and a continuous harassing fire was kept up by night particularly along the Canal. Casualties:- 2 O.R's (wounded) Reinforcements:- 2/Lt.West L.H. and 32 O.R's.	[signature]
do	17/8/18.		Our M.G's carried out harassing fire during the day and night on ATOM FARM and also on road running through K.18.c. during the night. Number of rounds expended 2,000. Enemy M.G's fired persistently during the night on K.9.b. and K.10.a.&c., also on M.G.Position at K.20.c.20.20. Casualties:- 1 O.R. (wounded) Reinforcements:- 3 O.R's.	[signature]
do	18/8/18.		Our M.G's carried out harassing fire during the day and night on ATOM FARM. and also on Road running through K.18.b. Enemy M.G's were active during the night along our Front and Support lines. Enemy put up a series of RED lights (single and double) along a wide front opposite Right Brigade between 8.30 and 9.30 p.m. No action followed. Dump in direction of K.24.d. on fire between 10.40 p.m. and 11.15 p.m. Casualties :- 2 O.R's (Wounded.) Reinforcements :- NIL.	[signature]

(A9375) Wt W4353/P156 50,000 12/17 D.D. & L. Sch. 52a. Forms/C2118/12

Army Form C. 2118.

WAR DIARY
or
INTELLIGENCE SUMMARY.

(Erase heading not required.)

Instructions regarding War Diaries and Intelligence Summaries are contained in F.S. Regs., Part II. and the Staff Manual respectively. Title pages will be prepared in manuscript.

Place	Date	Hour	Summary of Events and Information	Remarks and references to Appendices
PECQUER.	19/8/18.		No firing was done by our M.G's on account of Infantry Operations and reliefs. Enemy M.G's fired bursts over our lines during the night. An explosion was observed at 11.30 p.m. in MERVILLE. Smoke barrage put up on the front of the Division on our left. Casualties:- 2/Lt. Tait A.J. (Wounded) Reinforcements:- NIL.	Ref.Map Sheet 36A (1/40,000) 6.V.M.G.
do	20/8/18.		Our M.G's were active during the day against hostile aircraft. No firing was done during the night. Enemy M.G's fired occasional bursts during the day and night. Many small balloons were observed during the day. Casualties:- 1 O.R. (Wounded) Reinforcements:- 18 O.R.	6.V.M.G.
do	21/8/18.		No firing was carried out by our M.G's. Enemy M.G's were active across K.10.b. and ARREWAGE during the night. A large fire was observed near MERVILLE CHURCH at 10.15 a.m. which burned all day. Enemy sent up large numbers of RED and GREEN very lights during the night particularly from 8.30 p.m. to 9.0 p.m. These were most noticeable from vicinity of VIERHOUCK and NEUF BERQUIN. Double GREENS and double and single REDS being used. "A" Company relieved "B" Company and "C" Company relieved "D" Company on the morning as per Operation Order No.36 attached as Appendix "F". Casualties:- NIL. Reinforcements:- 1 O.R.	6.V.M.G.
HAVERSKERQUE	22/8/18.		No firing was carried out by our M.Gs during the night. Enemy M.G's very quiet throughout the period. Slight firing from direction of NEUF BERQUIN (long range) at 4.0 p.m. 6 E.O.B's up from midday to 8.0 p.m. Battalion H.Q. "B","C" and "D" Companies moved as per Operation Order No.37 attached as Appendix "G". Casualties:- 4 O.R's (Wounded) Reinforcements:- 1 O.R.	6.V.M.G.
do	23/8/18.		Our M.G's carried out harassing fire during the night on K.26.b.&d.,;L.15.d.,L.9.c&d. and TROMPE BRIDGE, 4,000 rounds being expended. Enemy M.G's swept our forward areas during the night from the direction of L.31.a. Enemy O.B's up during the day. At 10 p.m. a number of Very lights were sent up. Single REDS, double GREENS and single WHITES being used. 7 direct hits were obtained on Building in CARE CROSS. Casualties:- 11 O.R's (Wounded) Reinforcements:- 24 O.R's.	6.V.M.G.

Army Form C. 2118.

WAR DIARY
or
INTELLIGENCE SUMMARY.
(Erase heading not required.)

Instructions regarding War Diaries and Intelligence Summaries are contained in F. S. Regs., Part II. and the Staff Manual respectively. Title pages will be prepared in manuscript.

Place	Date	Hour	Summary of Events and Information	Remarks and references to Appendices
HAVERSKERQUE.	24/8/18.		Harassing fire was carried out by our M.G's during the night on various targets, 4,000 rounds being expended. Enemy M.G's were active from 4.0 p.m. and throughout the night on our forward areas. 2 E.O.B's up during the day. The flash, from what appeared to be an ammunition dump exploding was observed in direction of K.14.b. at 9.0 p.m. Reinforcements:- NIL. Casualties:- 2 O.R's (wounded)	Ref.Map Sheet 36A. (1/40,000) 6.V.M.G. Lt P. RICHARDS. M.C. T. I.O.R.
do	25/8/18.		Our M.G's fired on area L.26.b.&d. and area L.2.c.50.50., L.2.d.90.90., 4,000 rounds being expended. Enemy M.G's were very quiet during the day. Fired along our front lines during the night. 8 E.O.B's were in position along the front during the day. Reinforcements:- NIL. Casualties:- 1 O.R. (wounded)	6.V.M.G. I.O.R.
do	26/8/18.		Our M.G's fairly active during the period, 6,000 rounds being expended on BOWERY COTTAGES, RUE MONTIGNY and area L.26.b.&d. Enemy M.G's were active during the day against our aircraft and swept our forward areas during the night. 2 Heavy bombs were dropped on COCHIN CORNER and HUTTON MILL. Casualties:- NIL. Reinforcements:- NIL.	6.V.M.G. MAJOR. W.G.A.COLDWELL. T. 2. O.R's.
do	27/8/18.		Harassing fire was carried out on BOWERY COTTAGES and RUE MONTIGNY during the night by our M.G's, 5,000 being expended. Enemy M.G's were active during the night searching our forward areas. A large number of RED and GREEN Very lights were sent up about 10.15 p.m. No apparent action followed. Casualties:- 1 O.R. killed. 2 O.R's wounded. Reinforcements:- NIL. 2 O.R's.	6.V.M.G.

WAR DIARY
or
INTELLIGENCE SUMMARY.

(Erase heading not required.)

Army Form C. 2118.

Instructions regarding War Diaries and Intelligence Summaries are contained in F. S. Regs., Part II. and the Staff Manual respectively. Title pages will be prepared in manuscript.

Place	Date	Hour	Summary of Events and Information	Remarks and references to Appendices
HAVERSKERQUE	28/8/18.		Our M.G's fired in conjunction with Infantry Operations. 7,000 rounds being fired on TROMPE BRIDGE—DIRK COTTAGES and RUE MONTIGNY, and 8,000 rounds being fired on DIRK COTTAGES— L.15.b. 70.70.; L.15.d.50.20.; N.9.b.40.70. Enemy M.G's very active during the night firing on our front line. Two large explosions were observed during Bombardment of enemy's line in direction of L.7. central. One E.O.B. observed during the day. "D" Company relieved "A" Company, and "B" Company relieved "C" Company as per Operation Order No.38 attached as Appendix "H". Casualties :- NIL Reinforcements :- NIL	Ref.Map Sheet 36A (1/40,000) C.V.M.E.
do	29/8/18.		Our M.G's were fairly active 3,500 rounds being expended on Enemy forward post and searching Canal bank in L.32. Enemy M.G's were very active during the night. M.G. firing from L.14.b. was engaged and silenced. 3 E.A. crossed our line at 8.0 p.m. During the night two large fires were observed some distance in rear of the enemy's lines. Casualties :- 2/Lt.Andrews H.T. (Wounded) Reinforcements :- 3 O.R's.	C.V.M.E.
do	30/8/18.		Our M.G's supported the Infantry during their advance 10,000 rounds were fired on the right flank at enemy posts and points of resistance. Enemy's M.G's were active during our Bombardment at 1.30 P.M. and occasional bursts were fired during the night. 2 E.A. crossed our lines during the day flying low. 2 E.O.B's observed during the day. A large number of fires observed behind enemy's lines in a N.E.& E.N.E. direction during the night. Casualties :- NIL. Reinforcements :- 22 O.R's.	C.V.M.E.
do	31/8/18.		Our M.G's very quiet. Enemy M.G's were erased by our aircraft during the day. Three E.A's were erased by our aircraft during the day. "D" Company re-inforced 2/4 Royal Berkshire Regiment, and "C" Company moved to area ITCHIN FARM as per Operation Order No.39 attached as appendix "J". Casualties :- 1 O.R. (wounded,accidental) Reinforcements :- NIL.	C.V.M.E.

C.V.M.Evans Lieut.

APPENDIX "B"

SECRET.

Copy No. 10.

61st BATTALION MACHINE GUN CORPS OPERATION ORDER No. 30. dated 5/8/18.

Ref. Map Sheet S/A. (1/40,000.)

1. The Battalion (less "A" Company) will relieve the 5th Battalion M.G.Corps.
   Relief to be completed by 8.0 a.m. on 7th inst.

2. Companies will move as per attached Movement Table.

3. Transport will move by march route and the following intervals will be maintained :-
   (a) 100 yards between Companies and Transport.
   (b) 25 yards between each group of 6 vehicles.

4. All documents relating to Sector, Trench Maps and Aeroplane Photos will be taken over from relieved units.

5. All details of reliefs will be arranged direct between Company Commanders concerned.

6. One Officer per Company will go forward early to reconnoitre camping area for first night.

7. Rations for consumption on day following move will be carried by Companies.

8. Supply arrangements will be notified later. Until further notice Companies will be administered by the Battalion.

9. All moves when complete will be reported at once to Bn. H.Qrs.

10. Map Ref., 5th Battalion M.G.C:-   I.20.c.70.50.

11. ACKNOWLEDGE.

                                        Captain & Adjt.,
                                        61st Battalion Machine Gun Corps.
5/8/18.

Copies to:-
   No. 1. "A" Company.
       2. "B" Company.
       3. "C" Company.
       4. "D" Company.   No. 8. Intelligence Offr.
       5. 61st Division.   9. Q.M.
       6. 5th Division.   10. War Diary.
       7. Signalling Offr.   11. File.

S E C R E T.

MOVEMENT TABLE to accompany 61st Bn. M.G.C. Operation Order No. 30 dated 5/8/18.

Serial No.	Date.	Unit.	From.	To.	Route.	Relieving.	Remarks.
1.	Night 5/6th inst.	"D" Coy.	WITTERNESSE.	Div. Line.	Via AIRE.	1 Coy. 5th Bn. M.G.C.	Dismounted personnel by Lorry. Transport by march route; not to enter AIRE before 7.30 p.m.
2.	6th. inst.	"C" Coy.	WITTERNESSE.	I.20.c.70.30.Via AIRE.		1 Coy. 5th Bn. M.G.C.	Not to enter AIRE before 8.0 a.m. and to be clear by 8.30 a.m.
3.	6th. inst	Bn. H.Qrs.	WITTERNESSE.	I.20.c.70.30.Via AIRE.		H.Q.5th Bn. M.G.C.	Not to enter AIRE before 2.0 p.m. and to be clear by 3.0 p.m.
4.	Night 6/7th inst.	"C" Coy.	I.20.c.70.30.	LINE. (Left Section.)		"B" Coy.5.Bn. M.G.C.	Relief to be completed by daylight on 7th inst.
5.	Night 6/7th inst.	"B" Coy.	WITTERNESSE.	Camp at I.15.a.60.50.	Via AIRE.		Not to enter AIRE before 7.30 p.m.

APPENDIX C

Copy No........

SECRET.

61st Battalion Machine Gun Corps Operation Order No. 51 dated 7/6/18.
REF. MAP NO. 1/4,000.)

1. "B" Company will move at once to SPENNIANO Camp, J.14.D., where they will come under the orders of G.O.C. 183 Inf. Bde.

2. O.C. "B" Company will report at once to the G.O.C. 183 Inf. Bde. at STEENBECQ, for further instructions.

3. Two days preserved rations will be sent up to Coy. O.M's Stores as soon as possible.

4. Exact location of Coy. H.Q., Transport Lines and Coy. Q.M.Stores will be notified to this office on arrival.

5. ACKNOWLEDGE.

7/6/18.

Copies to:-
No. 1. "B" Company.
    2. 183rd Inf. Bde.
    3. C.M.
    4. Signalling Officer.
    5. File.

J. Goode
Captain & Adjt.,
61st Battalion Machine Gun Corps.

Issued at 8.30 P.M.

APPENDIX "D"

SECRET. Copy No. 13

61st BATTALION MACHINE GUN CORPS OPERATION ORDER NO.32   11/8/18.

Ref. Map Sheet 36A.(1/40,000)

1. "B" Company will relieve "A" Company in the Right Section on the night 12/13th August.

2. "D" Company will relieve "C" Company in the Left Section on the night 13/14th August.

3. On completion of relief "A" Company will withdraw to Reserve Billets at THIENNES (I.16.a.)

   "C" Company will take up positions in Div. Line vacated by "D" Coy.

4. All details of relief to be arranged between O.C's concerned.

5. Section Officers and Sergeants will reconnoitre positions and ground beforehand and make themselves fully acquainted with same.

6. All Trench Stores will be handed over and receipted lists forwarded to this office within 24 hours of relief.

7. Company Transport lines will not move until further orders.

8. Relief complete to be reported to this office.

   Code word for para.1 "Two petrol tins."

   Code word for para.2 "Six belt boxes."

9. ACKNOWLEDGE.

Issued at 3.0 p.m.

Captain & Adjt.,
61st Battalion Machine Gun Corps.

Copies to:-
   No. 1. "A" Company.
       2. "B" Company.
       3. "C" Company.
       4. "D" Company.
       5. 61st Division(G)
       6. 182 Inf. Bde.
       7. 183 Inf. Bde.
       8. 184 Inf. Bde.
       9. Quartermaster.
      10. Signalling Officer.
      11. Intelligence Officer.
      12. Lieut. Collinson-Jones.
      13. War Diary.
      14. File.

SECRET.

APPENDIX "F"

Copy No... 13...

61st BATTALION MACHINE GUN CORPS OPERATION ORDER No. 38.

Ref. Map Sheet 36A. (1/40,000.)

1. "A" Company will relieve "B" Company in the Right Section on the morning 21st inst.

2. "C" Company will relieve "D" Company in the Left Section on the morning 21st inst.

3. On relief :-
   (a) "D" Company will withdraw to billets in THIENNES (I.16.a.)
   (b) "B" Company will withdraw to Pill-box Line E. of Wood, vacated by "C" Company.

4. Company Commanders will reconnoitre, and be prepared to relieve at dawn 21st inst. all gun positions forward of the line of retention. Other guns will be relieved in the usual manner during the course of early morning.

5. All details of relief to be arranged between O.C's concerned.

6. Section Officers will reconnoitre beforehand.

7. All Trench Stores will be handed over and receipted lists forwarded to this office within 24 hours of relief.

8. Transport lines will not move.

9. Relief complete to be sent to this office.
   Code word for para 1. "A Muzzle Cup."
   Code word for para 2. "Tout Suit."

10. ACKNOWLEDGE.

J.H. Collinson
Captain for,
Captain & Adjt.,
61st Battalion Machine Gun Corps.

20/8/18.

Copies to :-
No. 1. "A" Company.
    2. "B" Company.
    3. "C" Company.
    4. "D" Company.
    5. 61st Division (G).
    6. 182 Inf. Bde.
    7. 183 Inf. Bde.
    8. 184 Inf. Bde.
    9. Quartermaster.
    10. Signalling Officer.
    11. Intelligence Officer.
    12. 2/Lieut. Vost.
    13. War Diary.
    14. File.

SECRET.

APPENDIX "G"

Copy No. 13

61st BATTALION MACHINE GUN CORPS OPERATION ORDER No. 37.

Ref. Map Sheet 36A. (1/40,000.)

1. On the morning 22nd inst. "C" Company will man the following gun positions in the line of Retention.

   Right Section:-
   - 2 Guns   K.25.d.30.30.   (approx.)
   - 2 Guns   K.26.c.20.70.   do.
   - 2 Guns   K.20.d.70.90.   do.
   - 2 Guns   K.20.b.99.30.   do.

   Left Section. :-
   - 2 Guns   K.15.d.30.40.   (approx.)
   - 2 Guns   K.15.b.20.20.   do.
   - 2 Guns   K.10.a.30.30.   do.   Teams to live in Pill-box gun empt. in trench.
   - 2 Guns   K.4.c.60.70.   do.

2. "C" Company H.Qrs. will move to CORBIE (J.30.d.70.20.) and will come under the orders of the G.O.C. 184 Inf. Bde.

3. This move will be complete by 10.0 a.m. 22nd inst.

4. At 10.30 a.m. 22nd inst "B" and "D" Companies will evacuate all positions and withdraw to :-
   "B" Company to HAVERSKERQUE.
     Guides for billets will be at cross roads at 12.30 p.m.
   "D" Company to DOLL'S HOUSE, where they will wait for their billeting Officer to guide them to billets.
   O.C. "D" will arrange to have dinners at DOLL'S HOUSE.

5. O.C. "B" and "D" Companies will each send one Officer and one N.C.O. to meet Lieut. COLLINSON-JONES at 10.30 a.m. Cross Roads HAVERSKERQUE.

6. Battalion H.Qrs will close at PECQUER at 12 Noon 22nd inst. and re-open at HAVERSKERQUE (J.27.d.50.60.) at that hour.

7. Battalion H.Qrs and Transport will move at 11.0 a.m.
   Lieut. WILSON will move under his own arrangements.

8. A motor lorry will report to the Q.M.Stores at 10.0 a.m.

9. H.Q. Officers kits will be dumped at the Q.M.Stores by 8.30 a.m. Orderly Room will be packed by 10.30 a.m.

10. ACKNOWLEDGE.

S. H. Collinson
Captain &A/Adjt.,
61st Battalion Machine Gun Corps.

21/8/18.

Copies to :-
- No. 1. "A" Company.
- 2. "B" Company.   9. Q.M.
- 3. "C" Company.   10. Signalling Officer.
- 4. "D" Company.   11. Intelligence
- 5. 61st Division. (G)   12. Lieut. Steele.
- 6. 182 Inf. Bde.   13. War Diary.
- 7. 183 Inf. Bde.   14. File.
- 8. 184 Inf. Bde.   15. R.S.M.

SECRET.

APPENDIX "H"

Copy No. 13

61st BATTALION MACHINE GUN CORPS OPERATION ORDER No. 38.

Ref. Map Sheet 36A. (1/40,000.)

1. "D" Company will relieve "A" Company in the Advance Guard Positions on the morning of the 28th inst.

2. "B" Company will relieve "C" Company in the Line of Retention during the morning of the 28th inst.

3. Time for para 1 :- Relief to be complete by dawn.

   Time for para 2.:- Relief to be complete by 10.30 a.m.

4. All details of relief to be arranged between O.C.Companies concerned.

5. Section Officers will recconnoitre beforehand.

6. All Trench Stores will be handed over and receipted lists forwarded to this office within 24 hours of relief.

7. Relief complete to be reported to this office.
   Code Words for para :-
      (1) "Three Balloons."
      (2) "See Bee."

8. ACKNOWLEDGE.

   Issued at 12 noon.

26/8/18.

Captain & Adjt.,
61st Battalion Machine Gun Corps.

Copies to :-
   No. 1. "A" Company.
      2. "B" Company.
      3. "C" Company.
      4. "D" Company.
      5. 61st Division. (G).
      6. 182 Inf. Bde.
      7. 183 Inf. Bde.
      8. 184 Inf. Bde.
      9. Quartermaster.
      10. Signalling Officer.
      11. Intelligence Officer.
      12. War Diary.
      13. do.
      14. File.

APPENDIX "U"

S E C R E T. Copy No. 13

61st. BATTALION MACHINE GUN CORPS OPERATION ORDER NO. 39.

Ref. Map Sheet 36A (1/40,000)

1. "D" Company will reinforce 2/4 Royal Berkshire Regiment as laid down in 184th. Inf. Bde. Order No. 215.

2. "C" Company will move to the area ITCHIN FARM today 31st. August as laid down in 184th. Inf. Bde. Order No. 215 and G.347/A dated 31/8/18.

3. Move will be completed by 10.0 a.m. today 31st. inst., from which hour "C" Company will come under the orders of the G.O.C. Advanced Guard Brigade.

4. Rations will be drawn from the Quartermaster by 7.0a.m. for consumption on the 1st September, and will be carried by Company concerned.

5. Completion of move will be reported to this Office and to H.Q. 184th. Inf. Bde. by the code word;

    "JAMB"

6. ACKNOWLEDGE.

                                    A.W. Collinson
                                    Captain & Adjt.
31/8/18.   61st. Battalion Machine Gun Corps.

Copies to:-
No. 1. "D" Company.
    2. "C" Company.
    3. "A" Company.
    4. "B" Company.
    5. 61st. Division (G).
    6. 182 Inf. Bde.
    7. 183 Inf. Bde.
    8. 184 Inf. Bde.
    9. Quartermaster.
    10. Signalling Officer.
    11. Intelligence Officer.
    12.- 13 War Diary.
    14. File.

61 Bn M.G Corps
V.8

CONFIDENTIAL.

- WAR DIARY -

FOR THE MONTH

OF

SEPTEMBER

VOLUME NO. VII.

(6392) Wt. W6192/P875 1,500,000 4/18 McA & W Ltd (E 2815) Forms W3091/4.   Army Form W.3091.

Cover for Documents.

Nature of Enclosures.

Notes, or Letters written.

Army Form C. 2118.

WAR DIARY
or
INTELLIGENCE SUMMARY.
(Erase heading not required.)

Instructions regarding War Diaries and Intelligence Summaries are contained in F.S. Regs., Part II. and the Staff Manual respectively. Title pages will be prepared in manuscript.

Place	Date	Hour	Summary of Events and Information	Remarks and references to Appendices
HAVERSKERQUE.	1/9/18.		Our M.G's did not fire owing to forward movement. Enemy M.G's very quiet. E.A. active during the day flying low. Enemy Aircraft were active at night bombing back areas. 6 bombs were dropped on area J.21.a. Casualties :- NIL. Reinforcements :- NIL.	Ref. Maps Sheets 36A & 36. (1/40,000.)
do.	2/9/18.		Our M.G's were very active throughout the period and assisted Infantry to advance successfully across a stream. "D" Company successfully engaged an enemy M.G. killing 2 men of the team, causing the remainder to run away and capturing the M.G. Four other enemy M.G's were put out of action. Enemy M.G's were very active, especially during attack by our Infantry. "D" Coy. moved forward during the night to new positions. E.A. active during the day. Many large fires observed behind the enemy's lines. Casualties :- NIL. Reinforcements :- NIL.	
do.	3/9/18.		Our M.G's quiet owing to relief. Enemy M.G's fairly quiet, occasional bursts being fired during the night. One E.O.B. observed during the day. "A" Company relieved "B" Company in the Line of Retention and "B" Company relieved "D" Company in the Advanced Guard as per Operation Order No. 40. (Attached as appendix "A".) Casualties :- Killed: 1 O.R. Wounded: 1 O.R. Reinforcements :- NIL.	

Army Form C. 2118.

WAR DIARY
or
INTELLIGENCE SUMMARY.
(Erase heading not required.)

Place	Date	Hour	Summary of Events and Information	Remarks and references to Appendices
HAVERSKERQUE.	4/9/18.		Our M.G's were inactive throughout the period owing to forward movement to take up new positions. Enemy M.G's very quiet throughout period. Many large fires and explosions observed behind the enemy's lines. E.A. active throughout the day. 2 E.O.B's observed during the day. Casualties :- 2 O.R's Wounded. Reinforcements :- NIL.	Ref. Maps Sheets 36A & 36. (1/40,000.)
LA GORGUE.	5/9/18.		Both our M.G's and enemy M.G's were very quiet during the day. Usual harassing fire during the night. Enemy M.G's fired occasional bursts on roads and tracks during the night. E.A. very active during the day. 3 Planes observed flying over LA GORGUE and ESTAIRES about 5.0 p.m. During the day Battalion H.Qrs. and "D" Company moved from HAVERSKERQUE to LA GORGUE as per Operation Order No. 41. (Attached as appendix "B".) Casualties :- NIL. Reinforcements :- NIL.	
do.	6/9/18.		Our M.G's very active throughout the night, 5,000 rounds being expended on enemy posts and tracks leading to posts. Enemy M.G's fired occasional bursts during the night along out front posts. "C" Company moved forward and took up positions in BAC-ST-MAUR and N. of LAVENTIE. Casualties :- 6 O.R's Wounded. Reinforcements :- Lieut. J.YEO & 2/Lieut.V.R.WINTLE. 10 O.R's.	

Army Form C. 2118.

WAR DIARY
or
INTELLIGENCE SUMMARY.
(Erase heading not required.)

Instructions regarding War Diaries and Intelligence Summaries are contained in F.S. Regs., Part II. and the Staff Manual respectively. Title pages will be prepared in manuscript.

Place	Date	Hour	Summary of Events and Information	Remarks and references to Appendices
LA GORGUE.	7/9/18.		M.G's were very active and assisted the Infantry in an Offensive Operation. The local operation consisted of the taking of RUE BATAILLE and establishing a line at junction of ROAD - RAILWAY at H.14.a.70.40. The guns of 1 Section of "B" Company, were pushed up to the RAILWAY and gave covering fire whilst the Infantry made good up to S.W. corner of RUE BATAILLE POST. The covering fire drove the enemy out and he came under the fire of our machine guns in the open. One gun was then rushed up the RAILWAY almost to LEVEL CROSSING and firing from both sides of a hedge inflicted several casualties. Those of the enemy that got away took cover under a bank at H.14.a.70.45. A gun was quickly brought to fire on these and 15 of them surrendered to the Section Officer. The Enemy M.G's were very quiet during the operation but heavy artillery and M.G. fire was opened for 2 hours after the attack. CASUALTIES:- 1 O.R. killed 6 O.R's wounded. REINFORCEMENTS:- NIL.	
do	8/9/18.		Our M.G's were very active throughout the night 2,500 rounds being expended on roads and tracks behind the enemy line. Enemy M.G's active throughout the night. CASUALTIES:- 3 O.R's wounded. REINFORCEMENTS :- NIL.	
do	9/9/18.		Usual harassing fire by our M.G's during the night. 3,500 rounds fired on PORTeCLOUS FARM and ORCHARD in H.15.c. during attack by our Infantry on enemy posts. Enemy M.G's were very active during the night with harassing fire and fire enfilading BAC ST MAUR. Enemy snipers	

Army Form C. 2118.

WAR DIARY
of
INTELLIGENCE SUMMARY.

(Erase heading not required.)

Instructions regarding War Diaries and Intelligence
Summaries are contained in F. S. Regs., Part II.
and the Staff Manual respectively. Title pages
will be prepared in manuscript.

Place	Date	Hour	Summary of Events and Information	Remarks and references to Appendices
LA GORGUE	9/9/18.		were also active. One E.A. observed over our lines at 7.0 p.m. was heavily engaged by A.A. and M.G. fire. "A" Company relieved guns of "B" and "C" Companies and "D" Company relieved guns of "B" and "C" Companies as per Operation Order No.42 attached as appendix "G". Casualties :- NIL Reinforcements :- 2/Lt.W.T. Pledger. 2/Lt.G.Malthouse.	Ref Maps Sheets 36A & 36 (1/40,000)
do	10/9/18.		Our M.G's were active throughout period and fired on enemy movement observed in H.15.a. Usual night harassing fire was carried out 2,500 rounds being expended on Road in H.33.c.& a. - H.27.c. Enemy M.G's were fairly active throughout the night occasional bursts being fired on roads and tracks behind our front line. Enemy aircraft fairly quiet, only 3 planes being observed at 7.0 a.m. One E.O.B. seen during the day. Casualties:- NIL. Reinforcements:- NIL.	
do	11/9/18.		Our M.G's co-operated with our Infantry in an offensive operation at 5.30 a.m. 15,000 rounds were fired on BARLETTE FARM. 5,000 on ROAD running N.&S. through H.33.c. 11,250 rounds on areas H.20.c. H.20.d. H.21.a.& b. Total ammunition expended 31,250 rounds. Enemy M.G's were very active throughout the night on roads and tracks near our front line. Heavy fire opened during our attack at 5.30 a.m. Enemy Trench mortars were active during the day and bombarded our M.G. positions in H.31.d.15.25. Enemy aircraft were active patrolling over our lines. Casualties :- 1 O.R. (wounded) Reinforcements:- NIL.	

Army Form C. 2118.

WAR DIARY
or
INTELLIGENCE SUMMARY.

(Erase heading not required.)

Instructions regarding War Diaries and Intelligence Summaries are contained in F. S. Regs., Part II. and the Staff Manual respectively. Title pages will be prepared in manuscript.

Place	Date	Hour	Summary of Events and Information	Remarks and references to Appendices
LA GORGUE	12/9/18.		Our M.G's were inactive owing to the Infantry Patrol activity. Enemy M.G's quieter than usual occasional bursts on roads and tracks during the night. Owing to weather conditions aircraft activity less than usual. One E.A. observed over our lines at 4.30 and 5.30 p.m. which was heavily engaged by A.A. fire. Casualties:- 2 O.R's (wounded) Reinforcements:- 1 O.R.	Ref.Maps Sheets 36A&36 (1/40,000)
do	13/9/18.		Our M.G's carried out a special shoot at 12 midnight and 5.0 a.m. in co-operation with our Artillery. 36,000 rounds being expended on the following targets. CROSS ROADS and ENCLOSURES in H.33.a. and ROADS and ENCLOSURES running from H.30.b.80.00. to H.27.a.80.90. Enemy M.G's were very active during the night sweeping ground round our M.G. positions especially during shoot at midnight. One enemy M.G. was engaged by Lewis Gun fire and silenced. 2 E.A. came over our lines about 6.0 p.m. and were heavily engaged by A.A. fire. Casualties :- 1 O.R. killed. 4 O.R's wounded. Reinforcements :- LT.BUTLER J.E. 2/LT.CLANCY H.G.	
do	14/9/			
do	14/9/18.		Our M.G's were very active during the night 8,000 rounds being fired on CROSS ROADS in H.33.c. ROAD running N.& S. through H.27.b. FLEURBAIX. Enemy M.G's were active on forward areas during the night. M.G. located firing from approximately H.26.a.40.45. Several E.A. crossed our lines during the afternoon but were heavily engaged by our A.A. and M.G. fire. A large mine exploded at CROSS ROADS in G.29.d. about 7.45 p.m. Casualties:- NIL. Reinforcements;:- NIL.	

Army Form C. 2118.

WAR DIARY
or
INTELLIGENCE SUMMARY.
(Erase heading not required.)

Instructions regarding War Diaries and Intelligence Summaries are contained in F. S. Regs., Part II. and the Staff Manual respectively. Title pages will be prepared in manuscript.

Place	Date	Hour	Summary of Events and Information	Remarks and references to Appendices
LA GORGUE.	15/9/18.		Our M.G's active throughout period. 9,000 rounds being fired on BARTLETT FARM (H.26.a.) and approaches to FLEURBAIX. 4,500 rounds on CROSS ROADS and ENCLOSURES in H.20.d. and H.21.a. 6,500 on ROAD running N.& S. through H.27.b. and 1,500 on N.2.d.20.36. (suspected M.G position). Total number rounds expended 21,500. Hostile T.M's fired a few rounds from H.26.d. Enemy M.G's were very active between 8.0 and 9.0 p.m. on ROADS and TRACKS in forward areas. M.G's located firing from H.32.b.50.60. and JUNCTION POST. E.A. were more active than usual many planes flying over our lines during the day. One E.A. flying low fired into our forward trenches. One E.O.B. observed in position from 11.0 a.m. to 4.0 p.m. Casualties :- 1 O.R. (wounded) Reinforcements :- NIL.	Ref.Maps. Sheets 36A & 36 (1/40,000)
do	16/9/18.		Our M.G's were inactive during period. Enemy M.G's were active at intervals during the night on tracks &c., in the forward area. E.A. were fairly active throughout period. No.3 Section "A" Company obtained an enemy light M.G. from a forward post. Four mines exploded in SAILLY-SUR-LA-LYS during the day. Company reliefs as per 0.0.43 attached as Appendix "D". Manning of Corps Line by nucleus garrisons of Infantry and M.G's as per O.O.44 attached as Appendix "E". Casualties :- 6.O.R. (wounded) 2/Lt.MALTHOUSE G. Reinforcements :- NIL.	
do	17/9/18.		Harassing fire was carried out by our M.G's throughout the day and night. 17,800 rounds were expended on the following targets :- ROAD H.21.a.75.30 to H.21.d.50.40. FLEURBAIX. Railway H.10.c.00.50. to H.21.d.50.40. ROAD H.33.c.30.80. to H.33.c.40.41. Enemy M.G. at H.15.c.80.80.	

Army Form C. 2118.

WAR DIARY
INTELLIGENCE SUMMARY.
(Erase heading not required.)

Instructions regarding War Diaries and Intelligence Summaries are contained in F.S. Regs., Part II. and the Staff Manual respectively. Title pages will be prepared in manuscript.

Place	Date	Hour	Summary of Events and Information	Remarks and references to Appendices
LA GORGUE	17/9/18.		ROAD H.26.c.10.18. to H.32.b.70.70. The Enemy M.G's were active during the night firing on our forward positions. E.A. were only slightly active no E.A. having crossed our lines. There was an explosion in House at H.17.c.10.80. at 9.45.a.m. 16th.inst. Casualties :- 4 O.R. (wounded) LT.BUTLER J.E. (wounded) Reinforcements :- NIL.	Ref.Maps Sheets 36& & 36 (1/40,000) C1&2
do	18/9/18.		Our M.G's were exceeding active 30,000 rounds being expended on H.15.c.40.30. H.11.c.50.60. FLEURBAIX. Tracks and roads in H.21.a. and H.10.d. H.33.c.30.50. to H.33.c.30.80. H.33.a.30.00. to H.33.c.50.35. H.33.a.60.65. PLANTATIONS on RUE QUESNOY H.26.d.47.70. to H.26.b.95.13. CROSS ROADS at LA CROIX LESCORNEX (H.26.d.10.18.) Enemy M.G's were active during the night and in retaliation to our M.G. fire. Enemy T.M's fired a few rounds on G.31.d.50.60. during the morning. E.A. activity was slight one plane crossed our lines flying low but was driven off by our scouts. One E.O.B. observed at 3.0 p.m. Explosion in a house G.17.c.95.95. at 5.0 p.m. Casualties :- 1 O.R. (wounded) Reinforcements :- 21 O.R's.	C1&2
do	19/9/18.		Our M.G's were very active throughout the day and night 37,000 rounds being expended on the following targets:- H.4.d.30.50 to H.5.c.30.50. FLEURBAIX. ROADS and TRACKS in H.16.d. H.11.c. and H.22.a. & c. CROSS ROADS H.26.d.10.15. and Trenches H.26.d.50.40. TRACK H.32.d.60.50. Enemy M.G's fairly active on our forward positions. Casualties :- NIL. Reinforcements :- NIL.	C1&2

Army Form C. 2118.

WAR DIARY
or
INTELLIGENCE SUMMARY.
(Erase heading not required.)

Instructions regarding War Diaries and Intelligence Summaries are contained in F.S. Regs., Part II. and the Staff Manual respectively. Title pages will be prepared in manuscript.

Place	Date	Hour	Summary of Events and Information	Remarks and references to Appendices
LA GORGUE.	20/9/18.		Our M.G's active throughout the period firing 18,000 rounds on the following targets. Cross Roads H.26.d. Roads and tracks H.32.a. & H.20.d. Trench in H.26.d. & Roads and tracks in H.33.c. & H.22.a. & C. - H.16.d. - H.11.c.- H.21.d. Enemy M.G's were active during the night, carrying out long range fire on G.36.c.& D. E.A. were inactive, one crossing our lines at 7.0 p.m. 3 E.O.B's observed during the day. At 11.30 a.m. Factory G.22.b.50.60. demolished by a mine also Cross roads at SAILLY at 5.10 p.m. Unusual number of lights sent up by enemy during the night. A German Carrier pigeon shot down by No.3 Section "B" Company and message found sent in to JUBE. Casualties :- 3 O.R's. Reinforcements :- NIL.	Ref.Maps Sheets 36A & 36 (1/40,000)
do	21/9/18.		Our M.G's carried out harassing fire on Roads and tracks in FLEUR BAIX and tracks and roads in H.32.d., H.32.b. H.26.d. and Trenches in H.27.c., 12,000 rounds being expended . Enemy M.G's were very active all night retaliating to our M.G.fire. One E.A. over our lines at 6.30 p.m. House in G.17.central demolished by a mine at 8.45 p.m., also crossing at G.29.b.30.48. A large fire was observed behind enemy lines in direction of ERQUINGHEM at 6.0 p.m. Casualties :- 2 O.R's. Reinforcements :- NIL.	
do	22/9/18.		Harassing fire was done by our M.G's on roads and tracks in H.20.b.,H.21.a.,H.32.d.& H.20.b. 13,000 rounds being expended. Enemy M.G's were active during the night on Roads and tracks in forward area. 2 E.A. were over our lines during the morning. Casualties:-NIL Reinforcements :- NIL.	

Army Form C. 2118.

WAR DIARY
of
INTELLIGENCE SUMMARY.
(Erase heading not required.)

Instructions regarding War Diaries and Intelligence Summaries are contained in F. S. Regs., Part II. and the Staff Manual respectively. Title pages will be prepared in manuscript.

Place	Date	Hour	Summary of Events and Information	Remarks and references to Appendices
LA GORGUE	23/9/18.		Our M.G's very active throughout the period firing 28,000 rounds on roads and tracks and suspected M.G.emplacements. Enemy M.G's were very active replying vigorously to our M.G.fire. Area in H.24.b. was swept at intervals during the night. E.O.B. observed during the day. E.A's were active. Casualties:- 5 O.R's. Reinforcements:- NIL.	Ref.Maps Sheets 36A & 36 (1/40,000)
do	24/9/18.		Our M.G's were active during the night firing 12,500 rounds on various targets. Enemy M.G's were very active continually harassing our patrols. One E.A. over our Lines during the day. 3 E.O.B's were observed. Casualties :- 1 O.R. Reinforcements:- 10 O.R's.	
do	25/9/18.		Our M.G's were very active during the period firing 40,000 rounds on various targets and in co-operation with Infantry.attacks. Enemy M.G's were very active from 10 - 11.30 p.m. in the right subsector. All attempts by E.A's to cross our lines were stopped by A.A. fire. 11 E.O.B's were observed during the day. Inter-Company relief as per O.O.45 attached as Appendix "F". Casualties :- 1 O.R. Reinforcements:- NIL.	
do	26/9/18.		Our M.G's very active throughout period firing 40,000 rounds on the following targets:- Roads and enclosures in H.32.d.; H.26.d.; H.27.a. H.33.a. H.20.b.& d. Enemy M.G's were fairly	

Army Form C. 2118.

WAR DIARY
or
INTELLIGENCE SUMMARY.

(*Erase heading not required.*)

Instructions regarding War Diaries and Intelligence Summaries are contained in F. S. Regs., Part II. and the Staff Manual respectively. Title pages will be prepared in manuscript.

Place	Date	Hour	Summary of Events and Information	Remarks and references to Appendices
	26/9/18.		active throughout the night. E.A's were active at intervals being heavily engaged by A.A. fire. Fires were observed in the direction of FLEURBAIX at 10.p.m. Casualties:- 3 O.R's. Reinforcements :- NIL.	Ref.Maps 36A 36 1/40,000)
LA GORGUE.	27/9/18.		Our M.G's fired 8,500 rounds on roads in H.33.c. and H.26.d. to H.27.a. Enemy M.G's fired at intervals throughout the night. E.A. were inactive. 8 E.O.B's were observed from 2.p.m. to 4.p.m. Enemy used Golden Rain and Red Lights at intervals. Big explosion in enemy's lines about 4.30 a.m, Casualties:- NIL Reinforcements :- NIL.	
do	28/9/18.		Our M.G's active throughout the night firing 8,000 rounds on roads in H.21.d.05.15.-H.27.d.10.90. and H.32.b.85.30. - H.33.e.15.85. Enemy M.G's were active firing on roads in G.30 and G.36. also along front line and the BAC ST MAUR road throughout the night. E.A. were active being over our lines at 3.0., 5.15 .nd 6.0 .p.m. A smoke cloud was seen blowing towards ARMENTIERES from a northernly direction from 2.30 p.m. to 5.0 p.m. 2 E.O.B's observed. Casualties :- NIL Reinforcements :- NIL.	
do	29/9/18.		Our M.G's fired 41,000 rounds in conjunction with Infantry Operations. Enemy M.G's were fairly active during the night. Very few lights were fired by the enemy during our attack and enemy	

Army Form C. 2118.

WAR DIARY
or
INTELLIGENCE SUMMARY.
(Erase heading not required.)

Instructions regarding War Diaries and Intelligence Summaries are contained in F.S. Regs., Part II. and the Staff Manual respectively. Title pages will be prepared in manuscript.

Place	Date	Hour	Summary of Events and Information	Remarks and references to Appendices
LA GORGUE	29/9/18.		artillery fire was weak for the first ten minutes. Casualties :- NIL. Reinforcements :- NIL.	Ref Maps. Sheets 36A 36 NW.E (1/40,000)
do	30/9/18.		Our M.G.s were active throughout the period 6,000 rounds being expended on Roads and enclosures in H.26.d.40.60. - H.27.a.20.40. Forward Guns "A" Company engaged enemy M.G's from 6.30 a.m. to 7.0 a.m. (35,000 rounds) in the vicinity of BARTLETTE Farm. Enemy M.G's were active throughout the night, from Vicinity of BARTLETTE Farm. E.A's were inactive, one E.A. flew low over JUNCTION POST at 3.0 p.m. but was driven off by Machine Gunners with a Lewis Gun. See O.O. 47 attached as appendix "G". Casualties:- 5 O.R's. Reinforcements :- NIL.	

SECRET
Appendix "A"   Copy No. 12

61st. BATTALION MACHINE GUN CORPS OPERATION ORDER NO.40.

Ref. Maps Sheet 36A (1/40,000)
     do   36 N.W. (1/20,000)

1. "A" Company will relieve "B" Company in the Line of Retention on the morning 3rd.inst.

2. On relief "B" Company will relieve "D" Company in the Advanced Guard during the afternoon and evening 3rd.inst.

3. Relief of "B" Company to be complete by 10.0 a.m.

4. On relief "D" Company will withdraw to Billets in HAVERSKERQUE and will be in Divisional Reserve.

5. "C" Company will remain as at present.

6. All details of relief to be arranged between O.C's concerned.

7. All Trench Stores will be handed over and receipted lists forwarded to this Office within 24 hours of relief.

8. Relief complete to be reported to this Office.
   Code word for para(1) "Bachelor of Arts"
        do   do para(2) "Bring Deputy"

9. ACKNOWLEDGE.

S. H. Collinson
Captain & Adjt.
61st. Battalion Machine Gun Corps.

2/9/18.

Copies to :-
No. 1. "A" Company.
    2. "B" Company.
    3. "C" Company.
    4. "D" Company.
    5. 61st.Division (G).
    6. 182 Inf.Bde.
    7. 183 Inf.Bde.
    8. 184 Inf.Bde.
    9. Quartermaster.
    10. Signalling Officer.
    11. Intelligence Officer.
    12. War Diary.
    13.   do
    14. File.

SECRET.   *Appendix "B."*

Copy No......15......

61st BATTALION MACHINE GUN CORPS OPERATION ORDER No. 41.

Ref. Map Sheet 36A (1/40,000.)

1. Battalion H.Qrs. and "D" Company will move from HAVERSKERQUE Area to LA GORGUE Area on 5th inst.

2. "D" Company. will move under own arrangements on the morning 5th inst.

3. Battalion H.Qrs will close at HAVERSKERQUE at 3.0 p.m. and re-open at L.34.d.20.90. at the same hour.

4. Transport Officer will detail 1 G.S.Wagon and 1 Limber to report to Battalion H.Qrs. at 1.0 p.m.
   2 G.S.Wagons to report to Q.M. at 11.0 a.m.

5. Q.M. will arrange to have Store at about L.28.c.50.50.

6. Signalling Officer will move under own arrangements.

7. All transport will move to L.34.d.50.80. and dump at this point. Transport Officer will arrange lines at approximately L.28.c.

8. Lieut. EVANS C.V.H. M.C., will move at 8.0 a.m. with H.Qrs. details to be detailed by R.S.M.to prepare billet.

9. ACKNOWLEDGE.

Issued at 6.45 p.m.

4/9/18.

P H Collinson
Captain & Adjt.,
61st Battalion Machine Gun Corps.

Copies to :-
No. 1. "A" Company.
2. "B" Company.
3. "C" Company.
4. "D" Company.
5. 61st Division (G).
6. 182 Inf. Bde.
7. 183 Inf. Bde.
8. 184 Inf. Bde.
9. Quartermaster.
10. Signalling Officer.
11. Intelligence Officer.
12. R.S.M.
13. 25th Battalion M.G.C.
14. 104th Battalion M.G.C.
15-16. War Diary.
17. File.

Appendix. "C"

SECRET.   Copy No. 14

61st. BATTALION MACHINE GUN CORPS OPERATION ORDER NO.42.

Ref. Map. Sheet 36. & 36A.
1/40,000

1. The following relief will take place on night 9th. inst.

2. "D" Company will relieve guns of "B" and "C" Company in
(a) the right sector of the advanced guard Brigade.
(b) "A" Company will relieve guns of "B" and "C" Company in
the left sector of the advanced guard Brigade.

3. Company Commanders will meet at "B" Company Headquarters at 8 a.m. (G.27.d.55.60) on 9th. inst to make all arrangements.

4. All Trench Stores will be handed over and receipted lists forwarded to this Office within 24 hours of relief.

5. Relief complete to be forwarded to this Office under the following Code Words:-
For (a) "BREAK DOWN"
"   (b) "COMING ACROSS"

6. ACKNOWLEDGE.

Issued at 7 p.m.

P. H. Collen
Capt. & Adjt,
61st. Battalion M.G.C.

Copies To:-
No. 1. "A" Company.
2. "B" "
3. "C" "
4. "D" "
5. 61st. Division "G"
6. 182. Bde.
7. 183 "
8. 184 "
9. Quartermaster.
10. Signalling Officer.
11. Intelligence Officer.
12. 25th. Battalion M.G.C.
13. 104 Battalion M.G.C.
14/15 War Diary.
16. File.

ADDENDUM TO 61st BATTALION OPERATION ORDER NO.42.

1. On relief "B" Company will withdraw to billets at LA GORGUE and become Company ready for "Line of Retention" under 184 Infantry Brigade.

2. On relief "C" Company will withdraw to billets vacated by "A" Company and become Company ready for "Line of Retention" under 182 Infantry Brigade.

ACKNOWLEDGE.

8/9/18.

C H Collins
Capt. & Adjt,
61st. Battalion MGC.

Copies To:-
All recipients of Operation Order No.42.

SECRET.   Appendix "D"

                                      Copy No. 14

61st BATTALION MACHINE GUN CORPS OPERATION ORDER NO. 43.

                              Ref. Maps. Sheets 36 & 36A.
                                   (1/40,000.)

1. The following reliefs will take place during the afternoon and evening of the 15th inst.

(a) "C" Company will relieve "A" Company in the Left Section of the Advance Guard Brigade.

(b) "B" Company will relieve "D" Company in the Right Section of the Advance Guard Brigade.

2. On completion of relief "A" Company will withdraw to billets at L.6.a.30.30.

    On completion of relief "D" Company will withdraw to billets in LA GORGUE.

3. All details of relief to be arranged between O's C concerned.

4. Transport lines will not move.

5. All Trench Stores will be handed over and receipted lists forwarded to this office within 24 hours of relief.

6. Relief complete will be reported to this office by the following Code words :-

        For (a) "Count Aeroplanes".
         " (b) "Brought Down".

7. ACKNOWLEDGE.

        Issued at 10.0 a.m.
                                          P.H. Collinson
14/9/18.   Captain & Adjt.,
                                  61st Battalion Machine Gun Corps.

        Copies to:-
            No. 1. "A" Company.
                2. "B" Company.
                3. "C" Company.
                4. "D" Company.
                5. 61st Division (G).
                6. 182 Inf. Bde.
                7. 183 Inf. Bde.
                8. 184 Inf. Bde.
                9. Quartermaster.
               10. Signalling Officer.
               11. Intelligence Officer.
               12. 25th Battalion M.G.C.
               13. 104th Battalion M.G.C.
               14/15. War Diary.
               16.   File.

SECRET

AMENDMENT NO.1 TO OPERATION ORDER No.43 dated 14/9/18.

Reference para 2.

1. (a) On completion on relief "A" Company will occupy the six Gun positions in the Corps Line vacated by "C" Company.

    (b) "D" Company will occupy the six Gun positions vacated b- "B" Company in the Corps Line.

2. These positions are to be reconnoitred before hand.

3. ACKNOWLEDGE.

                                            [signature]
                                          Captain & Adjt.
                                  51st. Battalion Machine Gun Corps.

14/9/18.

Appendix "E"

SECRET   Copy No. 12

61st. BATTALION MACHINE GUN CORPS OPERATION ORDER NO.44

Ref.Map Sheets 36 and 36A (1/40,000)

1. It is the intention of the Corps to man the Corps Battle line with a nucleus garrison composed of Infantry and Machine Guns. The following points will be covered by this garrison :-

    (i) HUDDY LANE POST (G.33.c.1.5. & G.35.c.1.7.) mixed platoon of 61st and 59th Divisions.
    (ii) NOUVEAU MONDE (G.27.c.7.2.) 2 ROADS.
    (iii) G.27.c.4.5. Road Bridge.
    (iv) High ground immediately E. of Canal at G.21.d.7.0. this post to be responsible for footbridge at G.27.a.9.3. and Road bridge at G.21.d.5.2. (PONT DE LA JUSTICE)
    (v) G.21.d.8.8. - 2 Road bridges - Post also to be responsible for foot bridges at G.21.d.7.6. and G.21.b.95.60. respectively. Mixed platoon of Right & Left Brigades.
    (vi) G.16.c.8.8. (PT.TOURNANT) road bridge.
    (vii) G.10.d.75.45. road bridge - post also to be responsible for footbridge at G.16.b.35.35. and for road bridge at G.16.b.85.85.
    (viii) G.10.d.75.45. - road bridge - post also to be responsible for footbridge at G.10.d.85.15.
    (ix) House G.10.b.0.1. Mixed platoon of 61st.& 40th Divisions.

2. Officers Commanding the Reserve Companies will therefore detail guns to occupy the following positions :-

    SOUTHERN (Right Brigade) SECTOR.

        G.35.a.20.30.   (2 guns)
        G.27.a.70.35.   (do)
        G.21.d.15.25.   (1 Gun)
        G.21.b.70.10.   (do)

    NORTHERN (Left Brigade) SECTOR.

        G.15.d.75.25.   (2 Guns)
        G.16.a.75.75.   (do)
        G.10.b.10.30.   (1 Gun)
        G.10.a.80.10.   (do)

    The position of these guns ensures the points mentioned in para 1. being covered.

3. O.C. Companies will man these positions with as few men as possible - observing the usual rules with regard to sentries in the Main Line of Resistance.
    2 Guns in each Sector will be mounted for anti-aircraft work.
    Sections in the line will be relieved at frequent intervals in order to allow full use to be made of training.
    Positions for Guns will be dug and shelters etc. made for the teams. Positions trench stores will be handed over on the relief.

4. Move to be complete by 12 noon 15/9/18.
    Code word :-
        "C" Company "GOOD"
        "D" Company "LORD"

5. ACKNOWLEDGE.

                                W.G.A. Coldwell
                                            Major.
14/9/18.   O/C. 61st. Battalion Machine Gun Corps.

Copies to :-
No. 1. "A" Company.
2. "B" Company.
3. "C" Company.
4. "D" Company.
5. 61st Division (G)
6. 182 Inf.Bde.
7. 183 Inf.Bde.
8. 184 Inf.Bde.
9. Quartermaster.
10. Signalling Officer
11. Intelligence Officer.
12. War Diary ✓
13.   do
14. File.

SECRET.   Appendix "F"

                                              Copy No. 14

61st BATTALION MACHINE GUN CORPS OPERATION ORDER NO. 45.

Ref. Maps Sheet 36 (1/40,000.)
          36A   do.
---

1. "D" Company will relieve "B" Company in the Right Sub-sector during evening and night of 25/26th September.

2. "A" Company will relieve "C" Company in the Left Sub-sector during evening and night of 25/26th September.

3. On relief "B" Company will take over the 6 gun positions vacated by "D" Company in the C.B.L.
   "C" Company will take over the 6 gun positions vacated by "A" Company in the C.B.L.

4. All details of relief to be arranged between O.C's concerned.

5. All Trench Stores will be handed over and receipted lists forwarded to this office within 24 hours of relief.

6. Relief complete will be reported to this office by the following code words :-

   Code word for para 1. "Bridge Down".

   Code word for para 2. "Corn Account".

7. ACKNOWLEDGE.

                                              P. K. Collins
25/9/18.   Captain & Adjt.,
                                      61st Battalion Machine Gun Corps.

   Copies to :-
      No. 1. "A" Company.
          2. "B" Company.
          3. "C" Company.
          4. "D" Company.
          5. 61st Division (G)
          6. 182 Inf. Bde.
          7. 183 Inf. Bde.
          8. 184 Inf. Bde.
          9. Quartermaster.
         10. Signalling Officer.
         11. Intelligence Officer.
         12. 25th Bn. M.G.C.
         13. 39th Bn. M.G.C.
      14-15 War Diary.
         16. File.

SECRET.   Appendix "G"   Copy No. 8

61st BATTALION MACHINE GUN CORPS OPERATION ORDER No. 47.

Ref. Map Sheet 36 N.W.
Ed. 9.a. (1/20,000.)

1. Reference operation directed against JUNCTION POST. 8 Guns of "A" Company from the vicinity of H.19.a. will place a standing barrage from H.26.d.70.95 to H.27.c.60.50. from ZERO plus 5 to ZERO plus 20 min., rate of fire 1 belt per 2 mins. - and will then cease fire - there will be no S.O.S. Barrage.

2. 6 Guns of "D" Company will take up the following approximate positions in co-operation with the Infantry Attack:-
    2 Guns in the vicinity of Cross Roads H.31.d.05.15.
    2 Guns in the vicinity of H.32.b.85.70.
    2 Guns in the vicinity of JUNCTION POST.
Arrangements for advance of M.G's to be made by O.C."D" Coy. with 2/5 GLOUCESTERSHIRE REGT.
The 2 Guns at approx. H.31.d.50.55. may be moved slightly E. or W. in order to avoid Enemy barrage but will be responsible for guarding the Right Flank.

3. O.C."D" Company will be responsible for obtaining ZERO Hour and communicating it to O.C."A" Company and for mutual synchronisation of Watches.

4. Harassing fire will be carried out vigorously by "A" and "D" Companies between the hours of 4.0 and 5.30 a.m. in the direction of H.33.c. in order to cover the noise made by 2/5 Gloucestershire Regt. in forming up for the attack.

5. ACKNOWLEDGE.

Captain & Adjt.,
Lieut. Col.,
29/9/18.   Cmdg. 61st Battalion Machine Gun Corps.

Copies to :-
    No.1. "A" Company.
    2. "D" Company.
    3. 182nd Inf. Bde.
    4. 183rd Inf. Bde.
    5. 184th Inf. Bde.
    6. 2/5th Gloucestershire Regt.
    7-8. War Diary.
    9. File.

WAR DIARY

FOR THE MONTH

OF OCTOBER

1918.

(6392) Wt. W6192/P875 1,500,000 4/18 McA & W Ltd (E 2815) Forms W3091/4.	Army Form W.3091.

Cover for Documents.

Nature of Enclosures.

Notes, or Letters written.

Army Form C. 2118.

WAR DIARY
or
INTELLIGENCE SUMMARY.
(Erase heading not required.)

Instructions regarding War Diaries and Intelligence Summaries are contained in F. S. Regs., Part II. and the Staff Manual respectively. Title pages will be prepared in manuscript.

Place	Date	Hour	Summary of Events and Information	Remarks and references to Appendices
LA GORGUE	1/10/18.		Our M.G's active throughout period. 6,000 rounds were expended on Road and Enclosures H.26.a. 40.60. - H.27.a.20.40. Enemy M.G's active throughout period from direction of BARTLETTE FARM. Enemy aircraft showed slight activity. Casualties :- NIL Reinforcements :- NIL	Ref. Maps. Sheets 36A.36 (1/40,000)
do	2/10/18.		Our M.G's very active firing 58,000 rounds in conjunction with Infantry attack in the vicinity of BARTLETTE FARM as per Warning Order attached as Appendix "A". Enemy M.G's active throughout the night on our forward system. Enemy aircraft slightly active. 1 E.A. flying low over our lines at 1700 hrs. driven off by M.G. and Rifle fire. Casualties :- NIL Reinforcements :- NIL	
do	3/10/18.		"A" and "B" Companies advanced in close support of the Infantry following up the enemy retirement. "C" and "D" Companies were relieved in the Reserve area by two Companies of the 200th.M.G.Battalion and moved with Battalion Headquarters to the FONTES - MAZINGHEM area. During the night "A" and "B" Companies were relieved by two Companies of 200th.Batt.M.G.C. in the line, as per Operation Order O.49 and March Table attached as Appendix "B" Casualties:- Capt. RICHARDS P. MC (killed) 2/Lt.ASPLAND S.R. (killed) 1 O.R. (killed) 6 O.R's (wounded). Reinforcements :- 2/Lt.DAVIES W.D.M. Lieut.GRAY G.S., 10 O.R's.	
do	4/10/18.		"A" and "B" Companies moved to the FONTES - MAZINGHEM area. Casualties :- NIL. Reinforcements :- Major BROOKS W.H.	
MANQUEVILLE	5/10/18.		Battalion Training as per Detailed Training Programme. Casualties :- NIL. Reinforcements :- NIL.	LENS 1/100,000.
do	6/10/18.		Battalion moved to DOULLENS area by rail as per Administrative Instructions attached as appendix "C". Casualties :- NIL. Reinforcements :- Lieut.WHEATLEY L.A. 2/Lt.DEW C.C.	
T ERRAMESNIL	7/10/18		Battalion Training. Casualties :- NIL. Reinforcements :- NIL.	

Army Form C. 2118.

WAR DIARY
or
INTELLIGENCE SUMMARY.

(Erase heading not required.)

Instructions regarding War Diaries and Intelligence Summaries are contained in F. S. Regs., Part II. and the Staff Manual respectively. Title pages will be prepared in manuscript.

Place	Date	Hour	Summary of Events and Information	Remarks and references to Appendices
TERRAMESNIL.	8/10/18.		Battalion Training. Casualties :- NIL Reinforcements :- NIL.	Ref.Map.LENS. 1/100,000
do	9/10/18.		The Battalion moved to MOEUVRES area by rail as per Entraining Table attached as Appendix "D". Casualties :- NIL. Reinforcements :- NIL.	57B. 1/40,000
MOEUVRES	10/10/18.		"B&"D" Companies with Battn.H.Qrs moved to GRAINCOURT. "C" Company with 182 Inf.Brigade to ANNEUX. "A" Company moved to CANTAING with 183rd.Inf.Brigade. Casualties:- NIL. Reinforcements :- Major DEMPSTER R.T.	
GRAINCOURT	11/10/18.		Battalion Training. Casualties :- NIL Reinforcements :- 2/Lt.MITCHELL C.H. 2/Lt.ROBERTSON C.S. 20 O.R's.	
do	12/10/18.		Battalion Training as per Detailed Training Programme. Casualties :- NIL. Reinforcements :- NIL.	
do	13/10/18.		Battalion Training. Casualties :- NIL. Reinforcements :- NIL.	
do	14/10/18		Battalion Training. Casualties :- NIL. Reinforcements :- 5 O.R's.	
do	15/10/18.		Battalion Training. Casualties :- NIL. Reinforcements :- NIL.	
do	16/10/18.		Battalion Training. Casualties :- NIL. Reinforcements :- Lieut.CLAY W.A. Lieut.WOODGER A.C.	
RIEUX	17/10/18.		The Battalion moved by road to RIEUX and was attached to the 19th.Division., as per Operation order No.51 attached as appendix "E". Casualties :- NIL. Reinforcements :- 10 O.R's.	Ref.Map. Sheet 57C 1/40,000.

A6945 Wt. W14422/M160 350,000 12/16 D. D. &L. Forms/C/2118/14.

Army Form C. 2118.

WAR DIARY
or
INTELLIGENCE SUMMARY.
(Erase heading not required.)

Instructions regarding War Diaries and Intelligence Summaries are contained in F. S. Regs., Part II. and the Staff Manual respectively. Title pages will be prepared in manuscript.

Place	Date	Hour	Summary of Events and Information	Remarks and references to Appendices
RIEUX	18/10/18.		Battalion Training. Casualties :- NIL. Reinforcements :- NIL.	Ref.Map. 57.C. 1/40,000.
do	19/10/18.		All Companies moved into the Line to co-operate in attack by 19th.Division on High ground East of the River SELLE., as per Battalion Operation order No.52 attached as appendix "F". Casualties :- NIL. Reinforcements :- NIL.	
do	20/10/18.		Our M.G's fired 200,000 rounds on Barrage lines in support of attack by 19th.Division. "A", "C" and "D" Companies were withdrawn to RIEUX. "B" Company remained in line. Casualties :- NIL. Reinforcements :- NIL.	
do	21/10/18.		"B" Company was withdrawn from the line to RIEUX. Casualties :- 1 O.R. (wounded). Reinforcements :- NIL.	
do	22/10/18.		Battalion Training. Casualties :- NIL. Reinforcements :- NIL.	
do	23/10/18.		The Battalion less "C" and "D" Companies moved to ST AUBERT as per O.O.53 attached as appendix "G". "C" Company with 183 Inf.Brigade., and "D" Company with 182 Inf.Brigade moved into the Line. "A" and "B" Companies moved by night into barrage positions in the line. Casualties :- NIL. Reinforcements :- NIL.	
ST.AUBERT	24/10/18.		Owing to Enemy withdrawal "A" and "B" Companies did not barrage. The Division attacked at 0400 hours and captured BERMERAIN and SOMMAING. "C" and "D" Companies in close support of the attack successfully engaged Enemy M.G's and Infantry with direct fire. Heavy resistance was encountered at VENDEGIES from enemy M.G's. One section of "A" Company which got over the River ECAILLON at Q.20.b. inflicted heavy casualties during enemy counter attack. "B" Company moved into close support positions in Q.19.a. "A" Company moved forward following enemy retirement with 184 Inf.Brigade, and took up positions on high ground through Q.4. and Q.11. O.O.54 attached as appendix "H". Casualties :- 2/Lt.BOYCE C.W.(killed) Major GOODE F.J. (wounded) 5 O.R's(killed) 32 O.R's (wounded Reinforcements :- NIL.	Ref.Map Sheet. 51A. 1/40,000.

Army Form C. 2118.

WAR DIARY
or
INTELLIGENCE SUMMARY.
(Erase heading not required.)

Instructions regarding War Diaries and Intelligence Summaries are contained in F. S. Regs., Part II. and the Staff Manual respectively. Title pages will be prepared in manuscript.

Place	Date	Hour	Summary of Events and Information	Remarks and references to Appendices
VENDEGIES.	25/10/18.		Battalion H.Qrs. moved to VENDEGIES. "B" Company moved into VENDEGIES into Billets and were in reserve. Enemy M.G's were very active firing on crossings of River RHONELLE in K.29.d. "C" and "D" Companies remained in their old positions and were in support. Casualties :- 5 O.R's (wounded) Reinforcements :- NIL.	Ref.Map. 51A.1/40,000
do	26/10/18.		"C" Coy moved to positions on high ground Q.11. and Q.18. "A" Company moved two sections forward to K.35.& L.31. and carried out harassing fire on ground north of river RHONELLE. Casualties :- 2 O.R's (wounded). Reinforcements :- NIL.	
do	27/10/18.		"B" Company relieved "A" Company in the forward positions. "A" Company relieved "D" Company in support. "D" Company went into reserve in Billets at VENDEGIES. "B" & "C" Companies carried out harassing fire on Northern outskirts of MARESCHES, firing 32,000 rounds on roads and enclosures, as per 0.0.55 attached as appendix "I". Casualties :- 10 O.R's (wounded). Reinforcements :- NIL.	
do	28/10/18.		"B" & "C" Companies fired 30,000 rounds on harassing fire targets in conjunction with the Artillery. Enemy aircraft fairly active over our lines. One E.A. flew over VENDEGIES and brought down one of our O.B's. Casualties :- 4 O.R's.(wounded) 1 O.R. (Killed) Reinforcements :- NIL.	
do	29/10/18.		"A" Company relieved "C" Company in the Right Sector. "C" Company went into Billets in BERMERAIN. 30,000 rounds were fired on harassing fire targets. Enemy M.G's were active firing on our forward positions. 0.0.56 attached as appendix "J". Casualties :-XXII O.R. (killed) 3 O.R's (wounded). Reinforcements :- NIL.	
do	30/10/18.		Harassing fire was continued by night in conjunction with the artillery. Targets were engaged in K.30.s.and b. and L.25.d. Enemy aircraft slightly active during morning. One E.A. was broughtdown at L.26.central by M.G. and A.A. fire. Casualties :- NIL. Reinforcements :- NIL.	
do	31/10/18.		Our M.G's engaged targets in L.22.a.&d. and L.25.b. Good direct targets were successfully engaged by Guns of "A" Company from positions in L.32.c. Enemy M.G's were active during the	

Army Form C. 2118.

WAR DIARY
or
INTELLIGENCE SUMMARY.
(Erase heading not required.)

Instructions regarding War Diaries and Intelligence Summaries are contained in F. S. Regs., Part II. and the Staff Manual respectively. Title pages will be prepared in manuscript.

Place	Date	Hour	Summary of Events and Information	Remarks and references to Appendices
			night firing on our forward positions from emplacements in MARESCHES and Northern outskirts. Casualties :- 1 O.R. (killed) Reinforcements :- NIL.	

SECRET.   APPENDIX "A"   Copy No. 6

WARNING ORDER

M.G.103.

1. The 182nd Brigade has been ordered to capture and consolidate CLOVE Farm and enclosures at H.12.b.20.15. - Time and date to be notified later.

2. The M.G.Company of the Northern Sector of the Advanced Guard (A Coy) and the Reserve M.G. Company of the Northern Sector of the Corps Battle line (C Coy) will assist this operation - supplying 10 guns and 8 guns respectively.

3. Attached tracing shows proposed M.G. Barrage. RED shows barrage to be employed from Zero to the time objectives are taken. BROWN shows S.O.S. barrage to be put up in case of the S.O.S. signal going up after capture of objectives.

4. Barrages marked "A" will be arranged for by the M.G. Company manning the Northern Sector of the Corps Battle line ("C" Coy). Barrage marked "B" will be arranged for by the M.G. Company manning the Northern Sector of Advance Guard ("A" Coy).

5. The barrage in H.20.a. & b. will be supplied by the 2 guns located approximately at H.14.c.00.30. with direct fire.

6. All further details will be issued later.

7. ACKNOWLEDGE.

W Coldwell
Major., for
Cmdg. 21st. Battalion Machine Gun Corps.

1/10/18.

Copies to :-

No. 1. "A" Company.
2. "B" Company.
3. "C" Company.
4. "D" Company.
5. 182nd. Inf. Brigade.
6. War Diary.
7. do
8. File.

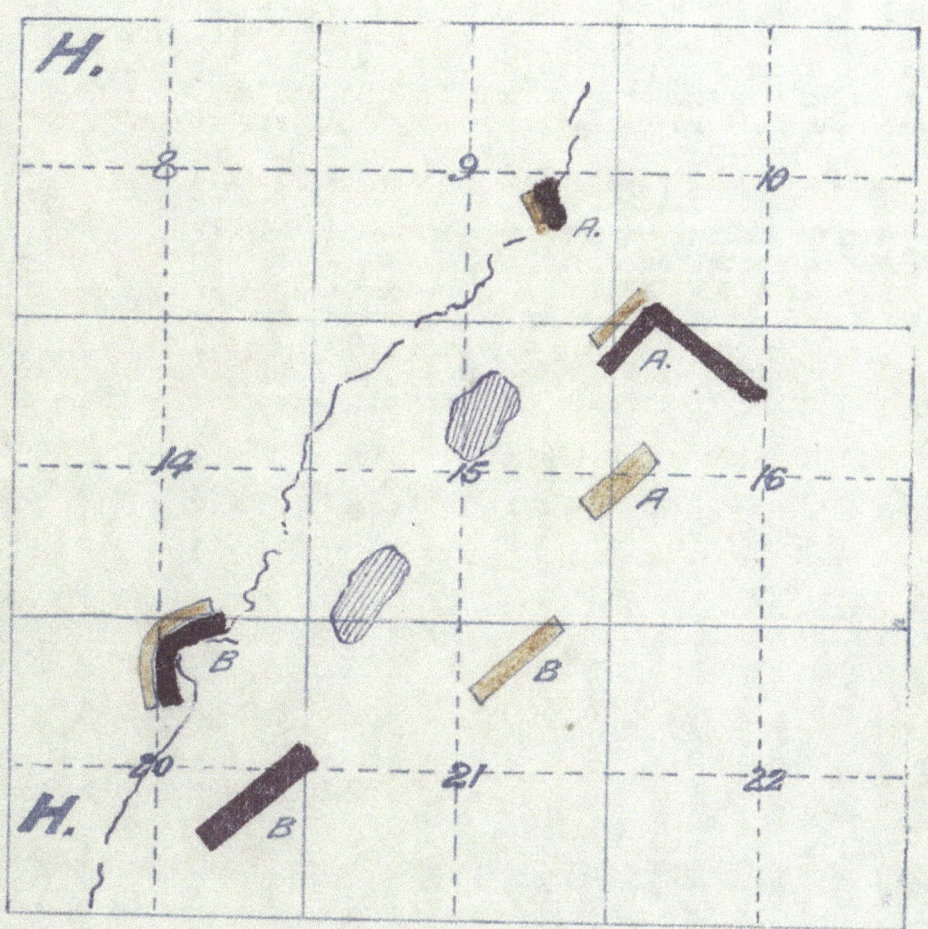

TO ACCOMPANY M.G. 106.

Reference:
Objectives thus :-
Enemy Front Line :-
M.G. Barrage :-
S.O.S. Barrage Lines after objective has been taken :-

Ref. Map. Sheet 36 N.W.   Scale 1:20,000.

SECRET.   APPENDIX "B"   Copy No. 15

61st BATTALION MACHINE GUN CORPS OPERATION ORDER No. 49.

1. The 59th Division will relieve the 61st Division during 3rd/4th and 4th/5th. inst.
   The 200th Machine Gun Battalion will relieve the 61st Machine Gun Battalion during the period as per attached march table.

2. All documents relating to the area, Trench maps, Defence Scheme and Instructions, Aeroplane Photos and current Intelligence Summaries will be handed over and receipts obtained.

3. Command will pass on completion of relief.

4. The following personnel will be left in the line with the 200th Battalion M.G.C. :-
   1 Officer per Company.
   1 N.C.O. per Section.
   1 O.R. per Gun.

5. All other details to be arranged between C.O's concerned.

6. All details as to train destinations etc., will be issued later.

7. Relief orders will be issued in detail later.

8. ACKNOWLEDGE.

A. H. Collinson
Captain & Adjt.,
61st Battalion Machine Gun Corps.

2/10/18.

Copies to:-
No. 1. "A" Company.
   2. "B" Company.
   3. "C" Company.
   4. "D" Company.
   5. 61st Division (G).
   6. 182nd Inf. Bde.
   7. 183rd Inf. Bde.
   8. 184th Inf. Bde.
   9. 25th Battalion M.G.C.
   10. 59th Battalion M.G.C.
   11. Quartermaster.
   12. Intelligence Officer.
   13. Signalling Officer.
   14. R.S.M.
   15-16. War Diary. ✓
   17. File.

SECRET   Copy No...17...

ADDENDUM TO OPERATION ORDER NO.49 dated 2/10/18.

1. (a) "C" Company 200th.Battalion M.G.C. will relieve "A"
        Company 61st.Battalion M.G.C. during night 3/4th. inst.

    (b) "D" Company 200th.Battalion M.G.C. will relieve "B"
        Company 61st.Battalion M.G.C. during night 4/5th.inst.

2. (a) On relief "A" Company will move back under orders which
        will be issued later.

    (b) "B" Company will move as per orders contained in the
        March Table attached to O.O.49.

3. (a) "A" Company 200th.Battalion M.G.C. will relieve "C"
        Company 61st.Battalion M.G.C. during 3rd.inst.

    (b) "B" Company 200th.Battalion M.G.C. will relieve "D"
        Company 61st.Battalion M.G.C. during 3rd.inst.

4. These Companies will move under orders to be issued later.

5. All details of relief to be arranged between O.C's concerned.

6. ACKNOWLEDGE.

                                                Captain & Adjt.
2/10/18.   61st. Battalion Machine Gun Corps.

        Copies to all recipients of O.O.49.

        "A" Company 200th.Battalion M.G.C.)
        "B"   do   do   do   )Copies.
        "C"   do   do   do   )
        "D"   do   do   do   )

March Table to accompany 61st Battalion Machine Gun Corps Operation Order No. 49.

Serial.	Date.	Unit.	From.	To.	Route.	Relieved by	Remarks.
1.	3rd.	H.Qrs. 61st Bn. M.G.C.	LA GORGUE.	Notified later.		H.Qrs. 200th Bn. M.G.C.	
2.	3rd.	"C" & "D" Companies 61st Bn. M.G.C.	Reserve Area.	do.	do.	2 Companies. 200th Bn. M.G.C.	Details will be issued later.
3.	Night 3rd/4th.	"A" Company. 61st Bn. M.G.C.	Left Front.	do.	do.	1 Company. 200th Bn. M.G.C.	To be completed by 0400 4th inst.
4.	Night 4th/5th.	"B" Company. 61st Bn. M.G.C.	Right Front.	FORTES - AZINCAEL Area.	S. VENANT - GUARBECQUE.	1 Company. 200th Bn. M.G.C.	To be completed by 0400 5th inst.

H.Q.
6'
MACHINE GUN BATTN.
AR 2445

APPENDIX "C"

Copy No. 10

61st. BATTALION MACHINE GUN CORPS ADMINISTRATIVE INSTRUCTIONS FOR MOVE BY RAIL 6/10/18.

1. The Battalion complete with transport will move by rail from its present location to DOULLENS on the 6th. inst.

2. **TRAIN ARRANGEMENTS.**
   "A" & "B" Coys. will proceed by train No.13 leaving BERGEUTTE Station at 0930 Hours on 6th. inst.
   Battalion Headquarters, "C" and "D" Coys. will proceed on train No.16 leaving BERGEUTTE STATION at 1230 Hours on 6th. inst.

3. **ENTRAINING.**
   Details as to exact time Companies should be at the Station will be issued later.

4. **LOADING.**
   Loading Parties are being provided.

5. **RATIONS.**
   Rations for consumption 5th. & 6th.inst. will be issued to Companies. Rations for consumption 7th. inst. will be drawn at the entraining station. Details will be issued later.

6. **BILLETING.**
   Lieut. HNS. Collinson-Jones will proceed in advance with 4 O.Rs. on train No.4 leaving BERGEUTTE STATION at 0030 hours 6th.inst.
   On arrival at DOULLENS he will report to D.A.A.G. 61st. Div. at the Town Major's Office.

7. **SURPLUS KITS.**
   On arrival in the new area, Companies will at once sort out all kit with a view to dumping any that they may now not require for active operations.
   Detailed orders as to the dump will be issued later.

8. **ACKNOWLEDGE.**

Capt. & Adjt,
61st. Battalion M.G.C.

Copies To:-
No. 1. "A"Coy.
2. "B" "
3. "C" "
4. "D" "
5. Quartermaster.
6. Signalling Officer.
7. Lieut. HNS.Collinson-Jones.
8. R.S.M.
9. File.
10/11 War Diary.

SECRET. APPENDIX "D" Copy No. 14

61st. BATTALION MACHINE GUN CORPS ORDERS FOR MOVE BY RAIL on 9/9/18.

1. The 61st. Division (Less Transport) is moving by rail on 9/10/18 to the HOEUVRES-GRAINCOURT Area.

2. In addition to personnel trains No.1, 5, & 9 will carry 4 limbers, 16 animals, ans 3 Chargers of "A" "B" & "C" Coys. All the Transport of "D" Company will move by March Route on the 8th. inst.

3. Personnel of M.G.Companies will act as loading and unloading Parties, and will be at the entraining station 3 hours before the time of departure.

4. Lorries will carry Battalion Headquarters Q.M.Stores to entraining Station.
   Assistance will be given to Companies to carry their Mess Kit that they require for the 9th. inst; but this must be reduced to a minimum.

5. ACKNOWLEDGE.

(Signed) E H Collinson
Capt. & Adjt,
61st. Battalion M.G.C.

Copies To:-
  No. 1. O.C. "A" Company.
      2.   "   "B"   "
      3.   "   "C"   "
      4.   "   "D"   "
      5. Quartermaster.
      6. Signalling Officer.
      7. R.S.M.
      8. File.
      9. War Diary.
  10/14 Spare.

ENTRAINING TABLE.

Train. No.	Coy.	Entraining Station.	Time of Loading.	Time of Departure.	Nature of Train.	Detraining Station.
1.	"A"	MONDECOURT	0200 hrs.	0306 Hrs.	Transport etc.	FREMICOURT.
5.	"D"	DOULLENS	2930 Hrs.	1936 Hrs.	do	do
7.	Batt:n H.Q.	MONDECOURT	1400 Hrs.	1506 "	Personnel.	HERMIES.
8.	"B"	DOULLENS	1430 Hrs.	1523 "	Personnel.	HERMIES.
9.	"C"	DOULLENS	1530 Hrs.	1632 "	Transport etc.	FREMICOURT.

NOTE:- Train No.1 will carry in addition 1 Cooker & Water Cart of "A" Company,
Train No.9 one Cooker of "C" Company.

HERMIES STATION is on the Canal Bank due South of HERMIES.

ENTRAINING TABLE.

Train. No.	Coy.	Entraining Station.	Time of Loading.	Time of Departure.	Nature of Train.	Detraining Station.
1.	"A"	LONDESCOURT	0800 hrs.	0806 Hrs.	Transport etc.	FREMICOURT.
5.	"D"	DOULLENS	0930 Hrs.	1036 Hrs.	do	do
7.	Battn. H.Q.	LONDESCOURT	1400 Hrs.	1406 "	Personnel.	ERVILLERS.
8.	"B"	DOULLENS	1430 Hrs.	1436 "	Personnel.	HERMIES.
9.	"C"	DOULLENS	1330 Hrs.	1336 "	Transport etc.	FREMICOURT.

NOTE:- Train No.1 will carry in addition 1 Cooker & Water Cart of "A" Company, Train No.9 one Cooker of "C" Company.

HERMIES STATION is on the Canal Bank due South of HERMIES.

APPENDIX
"E"

SECRET
Copy No. 7...

61st. BN. MACHINE GUN CORPS OPERATION ORDER No. 8.

Ref: 1:100,000. Valenciennes 12.
1:20,000. Valenciennes 12.

1/10/18.

1. The 61st. Battalion Machine Gun Corps is placed at the disposal of the 19th. Division and will march to RUESNES today 17th. inst.

2. The Battalion will march as per table attached.

3. Dress will be Full Marching Order. Blankets to be carried on the Limbers.

4. Battalion Headquarters will close at present location at 1100 hours and re-open at RUESNES at 1700 hours; location to be notified later.

5. ACKNOWLEDGE.

Copies To:—
No. 1/4. All Coys.
5. Quartermaster.
6. Signalling Officer.
7. R.S.M.
8. File.
9. War Diary.

[signature]
Captain & Adjt.
61st Battalion M.G.C.

H.Q.
61ST BATTALION,
MACHINE GUN CORPS.

No: ....
Date: ....

MARCH TABLE ISSUED IN CONNECTION WITH OPERATION ORDER No.51. 17/10/18.

Company.	STARTING POINT.
Battn. HQ.	To move from present Headquarters at 1115 Hours.
"B" Coy.	To Pass Sugur Factory at 1130 Hours.
"D" "	To pass Sugur Factory at 1145 Hours.
"A" "	To pass Cross Roads F.19.c.10.90 at 1215 Hours.
"C" "	To Pass Cross Roads at F.15.d.10.40 at 1230 Hours.

SECRET.　　　　　　　　　APPENDIX "F"　　　　　　　Copy No.........

AMENDMENT NO.1　　to
61st. BATTALION MACHINE GUN CORPS OPERATION ORDER No.52. 19/10/18.

1. Lieut. WILSON will remain at Headquarters 19th. Battn. M.G. Corps as liaison Officer, and will forward all reports to Advanced Battn. Headquarters.

2. 61st. Battn. M.G. Corps Advanced Headquarters will be at the present Headquarters of 61st. Div. T.M. at AVESNES at U.28.a.00.40.

3. Company Transports will return to RIEUX not to AVESNES as arranged.

4. Companies will be prepared to remain in their positions for the day 20th. inst. and should make the necessary arrangements for rations.

5. Forward Guns must be prepared to bring direct fire onto the Country E. of River SELLE.

6. In the event of any Guns having to move forward "A" Company will be prepared to do this.

7. 50 Boxes of S.A.A. will be drawn from Battalion Headquarters and sent up by 0700 hours 20th. inst. to Battle Positions.

8. ACKNOWLEDGE.

　　　　　　　　　　　　　　　　　　　　　　　　　S. H. Collinson
　　　　　　　　　　　　　　　　　　　　　　　　　Captain & Adjt.
19/10/18.　　　　　　　　　　　　　　　　　61st. Battalion Machine Gun Corps.

Copies to all recipients of Operation Order No.52.

SECRET   Copy No......

61st. BATTALION MACHINE GUN CORPS OPERATION ORDER NO.52.

1.   On the Morning of the 20th.inst. the 19th.Division will attack and capture High ground east of the River SELLE. The attack will be carried out by the 57th. and 58th.Inf.Brigades.

2.   Objectives.
     The capture of the ridge running from MAISON BLANCHE through MAISON BLEUE to P.23.central.

3.   61st.Battalion Machine Gun Corps with two Companies of 19th. Battalion Machine Gun Corps will form a frontal creeping barrage extending across the front with special concentrations as indicated on chart.

- - - - - - - - - - - - - - - -

SPECIAL ORDERS.

1.   Forward Move.
     Companies will arrange to have their Gun teams and Transport in suitable positions E.of AUBERT by daylight ready to move forward at dusk to their prepared Battery Positions.

2.   Transport.
     After unloading Guns all limbers will return to AVESNES and report to 61st.Battn.M.G.C. Advanced Headquarters. They will remain there until sent forward to fetch back guns.

3.   Personnel.
     Each Gun team will consist of 1.N.C.O. and 4.O.R's.

4.   Grouping.
     Each Company will furnish two Batteries known as Right and Left Batteries. Companies will be known as "A" Group "B" Group etc. Each Gun will have 10,000 rounds of ammunition with it.

5.   COMMUNICATIONS.
     A Battalion Report Centre under Lieut.YEO will be established at V.S.c.80.10. this will also form a Runner Relay Post.
     4 Runners will be kept here permanently for communication with 19th.Battalion M.G.Corps Headquarters at ST.AUBERT.
     Companies will supply runners from this Report Centre to their Group Headquarters.

6.   Signals.
     A Signal Station will be established at V.S.d.40.10. and will connect by Lamp with each Group Headquarters. A Line will be laid from this Station to the Report Centre from which place messages will be transmitted by Runner to 19th.Battn.M.G.Corps Headquarters who will repeat by phone to 61st.Battn.M.G.Corps Advanced Headquarters.

7.   Infantry Advanced Headquarters.
     These will be notified later.

8.   Dress.
     Battle Order, Jerkins to be worn, Great coats to be carried on limbers.

9.   Rations.
     Haversack Rations for 20th.inst. will be carried on the man.

10. Chorlide of Lime.
     For anti-gas purposes will be taken by each Battery.

11. Medical.
     There is an R.A.P. at V.13.b.

12. Zero Hour.
     Will be at 0200 hours morning 20th.October.

(2)

13. **Synchronisation of Watches.**
Each Company will send an Officer to Battalion Advanced Headquarters at AVENUE at 1630 hours on the 19th.inst. to sychronise Watches.

14. **Secrecy.**
Regarding above Operation is essential. Any Information given to troops should be the minnum compatible with their carrying out the task.

15. The exact Location of Battalion Advanced Headquarters will be notified as soon as possible.

16. ACKNOWLEDGE.

A. H. Collinson

Captain & Adjt.
61st. Battalion Machine Gun Corps.

19/10/18.

Copies to:-
    No.1 "A" Company.
       2. "B" Company.
       3. "C" Company.
       4. "D" Company.
       5. 61st.Division.
       6. Intelligence Officer.
       7. Signalling Officer.
       8. Quartermaster.
       9. 19th.Battn.M.G.C.
     10. File.
     11. War Diary.
     12.   do
     13 Spare.

SECRET.

APPENDIX "G"

Copy No. 7

61st. BATTALION MACHINE GUN CORPS OPERATION ORDER NO.53.

Ref. Maps, Sheet.
51A & 57B (1/40,000)

1. The Battalion less two Companies ("C" & "D") will move to ST.AUBERT tomorrow 23rd.inst., as per attached March Table.

2. Lieut. YEO with an Officer and 4 O.R's from each of those Companies ("C"&"D") will be at the Town Major's Office ST.AUBERT at 0900 hours.
A and B

3. "C" and "D" Companies are attached to 183 and 182 Inf. Brigades respectively and will move under orders of those Brigades.

4. Headquarters will close at RIEUX at 0900 hours and reopen at ST.AUBERT at a place to be notified later at the same hour.
A messenger will be at 19th. Battalion Machine Gun Corps Headquarters to collect any messages until the new Headquarters is established.

5. All dismounted troops will march off the roads as far as possible.

6. Accommodation forward will be limited.

7. Completion of Moves and location of Headquarters will be sent to those Headquarters as soon as possible.

8. ACKNOWLEDGE.

Captain & Adjt.,
61st. Battalion Machine Gun Corps.

22/10/18.

Copies to:-
No. 1. "A" Company.
2. "B" Company.
3. "C" Company.
4. "D" Company.
5. 61st. Division "G".
6. Quartermaster.
7. Signalling Officer.

8. Intelligence Officer.
9. 19th. Battn. M.G. Corps.
10. File.
11. War Diary.
12. do.

MARCH TABLE, to accompany Operation Order No.53 dated 22/10/18.

UNIT	PLACE	TO	ROUTE	TIME	REMARKS.
91st.Battn.M.G. Headquarters.	RIEUX	ST.AUBERT.	AVESNES LEZ AUBERT.	0900 Hours.	To move on Road running through U.20.c.50.90. U.20.d.60.80. U.21.central.
"A" Company.	do	do	do	0910	
"B" Company.	do	do	do	0920	Thence on Road side from AVESNES to ST.AUBERT.

APPENDIX "H"

SECRET.   Copy No.........

61st. BATTALION MACHINE GUN CORPS OPERATION ORDER NO.54.

Ref. Maps, Sheets
51A.&57B 1/40,000.

1. The 61st. Division will attack and capture the high Ground E. of the River ECAILLON on the 24th. October. The 2nd. Division (6th. Corps) and the 4th. Division (22nd. Corps) will be attacking at the same time on the Right and Left respectively.

2. Objectives and Boundaries.
The attack will consist of two phrases.
"A" The crossing of the Rivers HARPIES and ECAILLON, and the capture of the villages ST. MARTIN and BERLAIN, VENDEGIES and SOMAINGE.
"B" The Capture of the High ground to NE. of the ECAILLON from LA FOLIE (Q.25.a.) to L'EPINE (Q.3.a.). The Boundaries and Objectives will be as shown on the attached map.

3. The attack will be carried out by the 183rd. Inf. Brigade on the Right and 182nd. on the Left. "C" Company will be allotted to 183rd. Brigade and "D" Company to 182nd. Inf. Brigade. 184th. Inf. Brigade will be in Divisional Reserve. "A" Company on the extreme Right and "B" Company on the extreme Left with 2 Companies of the 19th. M.G. Corps in the centre on a line running from Q.35.a. to P.24.a. will support the Infantry advance by concentrated fire on selected areas.

4. The attacking Brigades will move forward during the night 23rd-24th. October and will form up along tape line behind the advanced Post of the 19th. Division. At Zero Hour the attacking Troops will advance in conformity with a creeping Artillery Barrage. The General Direction of the advance being a magnetic compass bearing of 58 degrees. As the attacking Brigades form up troops of the 19th. Division in rear will be withdrawn should it be necessary to withdraw the advanced posts of the 19th. Division before zero hour, the troops on the forming up line will protect their own front without posts. Arrangements to be made in this respect and the hour at which commands will pass to G.O.C.61st. Division will be notified to all concerned.

5. Artillery Arrangements.
The attack will be carried out under a creeping barrage on Field Artillery and Machine gun fire. The attack will be supported by.

Right Group.
4 Brigades R.F.A.

Left Group.
5 Brigades R.F.A.   17th. Corps Heavy Artillery will
co-operate.
The barrage will commence to move forward at the rate of 100 yards in three minutes up to the first protective barrage. It will lift off this line and will advance at the rate of 100 yards in six minutes up to the second protective barrage, with the exception of Batteries firing west of the road Q.7.d.3.5. XX Q.2.c.3.3., which will lift in accordance with Barrage map. It will lift off the second protective barrage line at Zero plus 130 and will move forward at a rate of 100 yards in four minutes up to the third and final protective barrage line. The final protective barrage will remain for 15 minutes and then cease. Thermite at an increased range of 20 yards will be fired at each lift to mark the flanks of Battalions and Brigades throughout the advance. A salvo of thermite will also be fired when each protective barrage is reached.

continued:-

1 Section of 18pdrs on each Infantry Brigade front will be detailed to accompany the advancing Infantry and will be pushed well forward on reaching the final objective for the purpose of engaging hostile tanks.

6   Machine Gun Arrangements.

In continuation of para.3 "C" and "D" Companies will each detail two Sections as forward Guns and 2 Sections as rear Guns to co-operate with 185 Inf.Brigade and 182nd.Inf.Brigade respectively. "A" and "B" Companies plus 2 Companies of 19th.Battn..G.C will be located as under and each Company will be divided into two Batteries of 8 Guns., Numbering from right to left.
"A" Company Q.33.a.   No.1 Battery.
    do   Q.32.b.   No.2 Battery.
1 Company 19th.Battn..G.C. Q.25.d.   MAISON   BLEUE.No.3 Battery.
    do   do   Q.25.c.   No.4 Battery.
  2 Company do   P.30.b.   No.5 Battery.
    do   do   P.24.d.   No.6 Battery.
"B" Company 61st.Battn. P.24.a.   No.7 Battery.
    do   do   P.24.a.   No.8 Battery.

Tasks.
No.1 Battery.   (A) 0 to 0 plus 30 Road Q.23.b.9.9.80. to Q.23.d.00.30.
    (B) Zero plus 30 to 0 plus 64 Road Q.22.b.80.40. to Q.23.a.70.00.
No.2 Battery.   (A) 0.to 0 plus 40. Triangle formed by three following points Q.22.c.30.90., Q.21.b.70.00., Q.22.a.30.70.
(B) 0. plus 40 to 0 plus 64 Gardens west of Road in Q.22.a. and Q.16.c.
No.3 Battery.   0 to 0 plus 40 Road Junction and area in Q.14.a.80.30
No.4 Battery. 0. to 0 plus 40 Road 1.21.b.50.00. to Q.21.a.70.40.
No.5 Battery. 0 to 0 plus 20 search and traverse Cross Roads at P.14.d. and Quarry in Q.15.c.
No.6 Battery.   0 to 0 plus 58 Road triangle formed by points P.7.d.30.50. Q.7.d.70.40. Q.7.b.99.60.
No.7 Battery.   (A) 0 to 0 plus 18 Road and enclosures at Q.13.a.70.70.   (B) 0 plus 18 to 0 plus 58 Chappel Road in Q.7.c.90.70. to Q.7.b.10.70.
No.8 Battery.   (A) 0 to 0 plus 18 Wood east of Road in Q.13.d.
(B) 0 plus 18 to 0 plus 46 Cross Roads and Gardens in Q.14.a.20.30. searching Road to Q.8.c.80.80.

7.   Reserve Guns.
(A) "A" and "B" Companies on completion of tasks in Para 6 will be regrouped into Divisional Reserve and will move forward to suitable positions west of River ECAILLON so as to cover the E. & N. approaches of BERMERAIN in the case of "A" Company, and the W.& N. approaches of SOMMAING in the case of "B" Company.
(B) The two Companies of the 19th.Battn..G.C. will remain in their Battery Positions until ordered to withdraw by O.C. 61st.Battalion.

8.   (A) 10 foot Bridges will be placed in position over Rivers and will be marked by cross shaped white sign boards.
    (B) Field Artillery Bridges will be constructed at Q.7.d.20.30, and Q.28.a.7.9.
    (C) Heavy Bridges at:-
    Q.14.b.40.00.   Q.20.a.30.60.   Q.20.a.90.80.   Q.21.d.80.60.

(3)

Continuation.

9. It is of special importance that the enemy be denied the Village line in event of counter attack. A proportion of M.G's will be detailed to sweep all approaches.

10. Light Signals.
   Para (A). White Very Lights will be used by the most advanced Troops to denote their positions.
   (B) Red flares will be lit by the most advanced troops on or near the final objective.
   (C) The S.O.S. SIgnal is a Rifle Grenade bursting into RED over GREEN over RED.

11. Co-operation with R.A.F..
   Contact Aeroplanes will call for flares at 0 plus 3½ hrs. 0 plus 5 hrs. 0 plus 7 hrs
   A Counter attack machine will be in the air continuously from daylight.

12. Reserve Brigade.
   184th.Inf.Brigade will move from ST.AUBERT at daybreak at 24th.inst. across the SELLE river to about the square V.5., to occupy the high ground to the west of the River, with Brigade Headquarters at the SANDPITS (V.5.a.)

13. Reports.
   Advanced Divisional Headquarters, will close at ST.AUBERT at Zero on 24th.Inst. and will open at MONTRECOURT at the same hour.
   Headquarters of attacking Brigades will be as follows:-
   183rd.Inf.Brigade V.5.c.50.10.
   182nd.Inf.Brigade V.5.a. (SANDPITS).
   Advanced Battalion Headquarters will be at HAUSSY location to be notified later.

14. "A" and "B" Companies will sychronise at rear Battalion Headquarters at ST.AUBERT at 1830 hours on 23rd.inst.

15. Liaison.
   Companies will use intelligent men to locate positions of Machine Gun Units of Div. on our Flanks.

16. Ammunition Dumps will be notified later.

17. Zero Hour will be at 0400 hours early morning of 24th.inst.

18. ACKNOWLEDGE.

P.H. Collinson

Captain & Adjt.,
61st. Battalion Machine Gun Corps.

23/10/18.

Copies to:-
No.1. "A" Company
2. "B" Company.
3. "C" Company.
4. "D" Company.
5. 61st.Division.
6. 19th.Division "G".
7. 19th.Battn.M.G.Corps.
8. 183rd.Inf.Brigade.
9. 184th.Brigade.
10. 182nd.Inf.Brigade.
11. Intelligence Officer
12 Quartermaster. 13.File. 14 & 15 War Diary.

SECRET   APPENDIX "I"   Copy No. 13

61st. BATTALION MACHINE GUN CORPS OPERATION ORDER NO 55.

Ref. Map. Special Sheet, part 51A (1/40,000).

1. The 61st. Battalion Machine Gun Corps in conjunction with the 61st. Divisional Artillery will harass the Village and outskirts of MARESCHES with intense fire as per map attached.

2. The Artillery Programme will be as follows :-

FROM	TO
1915 Hours	1930 Hours.
2000 do	2010
2050	2055
2120	2130
0010 → 0100	0015 → 0110
0410 → 0145	0415 → 0150
0500	0510
0605	0615

3. During those times the Artillery and Machine Guns will fire intensely, ordinary harassing fire being carried out during the remaining periods.

4. A silent period will be observed from 2200 hours to 2359 and from 0200 hours to 0400 hours. Machine Guns and Artillery will not fire during those periods.

5. ACKNOWLEDGE.

           [signature]

           Captain & Adjt.,
27/10/18.   61st. Battalion Machine Gun Corps.

```
Copy No. 1   "A" Company.
         2   "B" Company.
         3   "C" Company.
         4   "D" Company.
         5   61st. Division "G"
         6   182nd. Inf. Brigade.
         7   183rd. Inf. Brigade.
         8   184th. Inf. Brigade.
         9   C.R.A.
        10   Intelligence Officer.
        11   Quartermaster.
        12   File.
        13   War Diary. ✓
        14      do
        15   Spare.
```

SECRET.   Copy No. 12

APPENDIX "J"

61st. BATTALION MACHINE GUN CORPS OPERATION ORDER NO.56.

Ref. Map 51A.
(1/40,000).

1. "A" Company will relieve "C" Company in the Right Battery Sector during the evening of 29th.inst.

2. On relief "C" Company will withdraw into Billets in BERMERAIN.

3. All details of relief to be arranged between O.C's concerned.

4. Relief to be complete before dark.

5. All calculations for harassing fire to be handed over.

6. Relief complete to be sent to this Office by Code word "CABBAGES".

7. ACKNOWLEDGE.

(Signed) E H Colleman
Captain & Adjt.
61st. Battalion Machine Gun Corps.

29/10/18.

Copy to:-

No. 1 "A" Company.
2 "B" Company.
3 "C" Company.
4 "D" Company.
5 61st. Division "G".
6. 182nd. Inf. Brigade.
7 183rd. Inf. Brigade.
8. 184th Inf. Brigade.
9 Quartermaster.
10 Intelligence Officer.
11 File.
12 War Diary.
13   do
14 Spare.

6.1 Bn Tank Corps
No 10

WAR DIARY

FOR

THE MONTH

OF

NOVEMBER 1918

(6392) Wt. W6192/Ps75 1,500,000 4/18 McA & W Ltd (E 2815) Forms W3091/4. Army Form W.3091.

Cover for Documents.

Nature of Enclosures.

Notes, or Letters written.

Army Form C. 2118.

WAR DIARY
or
INTELLIGENCE SUMMARY.
(Erase heading not required.)

Instructions regarding War Diaries and Intelligence Summaries are contained in F. S. Regs., Part II. and the Staff Manual respectively. Title pages will be prepared in manuscript.

Place	Date	Hour	Summary of Events and Information	Remarks and references to Appendices
VENDEGIES-SUR-ECAILLON	1/11/18.		"B" Company attacked in close support with 182nd.Inf.Brigade at 0515 hours with objective MARESCHES and high ground East of it. All Objectives gained. "A" Company on the right supported the attack by barrage fire from Battery positions in R.2.a.&b. "D" Company on the left supported by barrage fire from Battery positions in K.35.d. and K.36.c. "C" Company moved up from Billets in BERMERAIN into reserve at L'ROGNEAU in Q.9.d. At 1000 hours enemy counter-attacked with Tanks and our line was forced back to the western outskirts of MARESCHES. The guns of "B" Company inflicted very heavy losses on the enemy by direct fire during this withdrawal. A Battery of opportunity of "A" Company suitated at K.31.c. also engaged some good targets during the counter-attack. At 1930 hours "C" Company with 184th.Inf.Brigade attacked and regained Objective. Casualties :- 2/Lt.MITCHELL W.H. (Killed) 1 O.R. (wounded). Reinforcements:- NIL.	Ref.Map Sheet 51A 1/40,000.
do	2/11/18..		The Division was relieved in the line by the 19th. and 24th.Divisions. "A" Company were relieved by a Company of the 24th.Division. "B" Company withdrew. "C" Company were relieved by a Company of the 19th.Division. "D" Company were relieved by a Company of the 19th.Division. "A" & "B" Companies moved into Billets at VENDEGIES sur ECAILLON. "C" Company moved into Billets at BERMERAIN. "D" Company moved into Billets at SOMMAING. CASUALTIES:- Lt.WOODGER A.C. (wounded) 2 O.R's (Wounded) 2 O.R's (missing). Reinforcements:- NIL.	
AVESNES LEZ AUBERT.	3/11/18.		The Battalion moved into Billets at AVESNES-LEZ-AUBERT,asPer 0.0.60 attached as Appendix "A". Casualties:- NIL. Reinforcements :- NIL.	
do	4/11/18.		"D" Company with 182nd.Inf.Brigade Group moved to HAUSSY, as per O.O.61 attached as Appendix "B". Battalion Training as per Detailed Training Programme. Casualties :- NIL. Reinforcements:- Major BLOOMFIELD A. Lt.STOYLE A. 2/Lt.HARDEN H.E.	

Army Form C. 2118.

WAR DIARY
or
INTELLIGENCE SUMMARY.
(Erase heading not required.)

Instructions regarding War Diaries and Intelligence Summaries are contained in F. S. Regs., Part II. and the Staff Manual respectively. Title pages will be prepared in manuscript.

Place	Date	Hour	Summary of Events and Information	Remarks and references to Appendices
AVESNES LEZ AUBERT.	5/11/18.		"C" Company with 184th.Inf.Brigade Group moved to BERMERAIN. Battalion Training as per detailed Training Programme. Reinforcements :- 31 O.R's. Casualties :- NIL.	
do	6/11/18.		Battalion Training. Casualties :- NIL. Reinforcements :- NIL.	
do	7/11/18.		do do Casualties :- NIL. Reinforcements :- NIL.	
do	8/11/18.		"A" & "B" Companies moved to Billets in ST.MARTIN., as per O.O.63 attached as Appendix "C". "C" Company moved to Billets in MARESCHES. "D" Company moved to Billets in VENDEGIES-sur-ECALLION. Reinforcements:- NIL. Casualties :- NIL.	
ST.MARTIN.	9/11/18.		Battalion Training. Casualties :- NIL. Reinforcements:- 2/Lt. TURK C.E.	
do	10/11/18.		do do Casualties :- NIL. Reinforcements:- NIL.	
do	11/11/18.		do do Casualties :- NIL. Reinforcements:- NIL.	
do	12/11/18.		do do Casualties :- NIL. Reinforcements:- NIL.	
do	13/11/18.		Battalion moved to Billets in ST.AUBERT, as per O.O.64 attached as Appendix "D". Reinforcements:- 20 O.R's. Casualties :- NIL.	
ST.AUBERT.	14/11/18.		Battalion moved to CAMBRAI, as per O.O.65 attached as Appendix "E". Reinforcements:- 49 O.R's. Casualties :- NIL.	

Army Form C. 2118.

WAR DIARY
or
INTELLIGENCE SUMMARY.
(Erase heading not required.)

Instructions regarding War Diaries and Intelligence Summaries are contained in F. S. Regs., Part II. and the Staff Manual respectively. Title pages will be prepared in manuscript.

Place	Date	Hour	Summary of Events and Information	Remarks and references to Appendices
CAMBRAI.	15/11/18.		Battalion Training as per detailed Training Programme. Reinforcements :- NIL. Casualties :- NIL.	Ref. Map 57B 1/40,000
do	16/11/18.		Battalion Training. Reinforcements :- 49 O.R's. Casualties :- NIL.	
do	17/11/18.		Battalion Training. Reinforcements:- NIL. Casualties :- NIL.	
do	18/11/18.		Battalion Training. Reinforcements :- NIL. Casualties :- NIL.	
do	19/11/18.		Battalion Training. Reinforcements:- NIL. Casualties :- NIL.	
do	20/11/18.		Battalion Training. Reinforcements:- 5 O.R's. Casualties :- NIL.	
do	21/11/18.		Battalion Training. Reinforcements:- NIL. Casualties :- NIL.	
do	22/11/18.		Battalion Training. Reinforcements :- 2/Lt.COOPER S.J. Casualties :- NIL.	
do	23/11/18.		Transport moved to BERNAVILLE area as per O.O.66 attached as Appendix "F". Reinforcements:- 22 O.R's. Casualties :- NIL.	
BERNEUIL.	24/11/18.		"A" Company moved by Rail to Billets in BERNEUIL. Reinforcements:- NIL. Casualties :- NIL.	
do	25/11/18.		"B" Company moved by Rail to Billets in BERNEUIL. Reinforcements :- NIL. Casualties :- NIL.	

Army Form C. 2118.

WAR DIARY
or
INTELLIGENCE SUMMARY.

(Erase heading not required.)

Instructions regarding War Diaries and Intelligence Summaries are contained in F.S. Regs., Part II. and the Staff Manual respectively. Title pages will be prepared in manuscript.

Place	Date	Hour	Summary of Events and Information	Remarks and references to Appendices
BERNEUIL	26/11/18.		Battalion Headquarters moved by rail to Billets BERNEUIL. Reinforcements :- NIL. Casualties :- NIL.	Ref. Map LENS 11. 1/100,000.
do	27/11/18.		"C" and "D" Companies moved by rail to Billets in BERNEUIL. Administrative Instructions Reinforcements :- 7 O.R's. attached as Appendix "G". Casualties :- NIL.	
do	28/11/18.		Battalion Training. Reinforcements :- NIL. Casualties :- NIL.	
do	29/11/18.		Battalion Training. Reinforcements :- NIL. Casualties :- NIL.	
do	30/11/18.		Battalion Training. Reinforcements :- NIL. Casualties :- NIL.	

APPENDIX "A"

Copy No. ...

61st. BATTALION MACHINE GUN CORPS OPERATION ORDER No.00. 2/11/18.

Ref. Map. 51A(1/40,000)

1. The Battalion will move by March Route from its present location to the area AVESNES-LES-AUBERT tomorrow 3rd.inst., as per March Table attached.

2. The starting point will be the Cross Roads at P.24.d.10.20. The route will be CHAUSSEE BRUNEHAUT - MONTRECOURT - S. AUBERT to AVESNES LES AUBERT.

3. Lieut. HEO accompanied by one Officer and 1 O.R. from each Company will proceed on Bicycles to Billet the Battalion, leaving Battalion Headquarters VENDEGIES at 0830 hours.

4. Two Motor lorries will be at the Church SOMMAING at 1100 hours to convey the Quartermaster Stores to the new Camp. Q.M. will arrange for two guides to meet them and guid them to his Store.

5. Strict attention will be paid to March Discipline and intervals between Companies and Transports.

6. Dinners will be cooked on route and consumed on arrival at new Camp.

7. ACKNOWLEDGE.

Major., for
Lieut.Colonel Cmdg.61st.Battn.M.G.Corps.

2/11/18.

Copies to:-
No.1 "A" Company.
 2 "B" Company.
 3 "C" Company.
 4 "D" Company.
 5 61st.Division "G"
 6 182nd.Inf.Bde.
 7 183rd.Inf.Bde.
 8 184th.Inf.Bde.
 9 Quartermaster.
10 File.
11-12 War Diary. ✓

MARCH TABLE.

DATE	COLUMN	FROM	TO	TIME AT WHICH TO PASS STARTING POINT	REMARKS.
2nd.	H.Q. Coy.	SOMALIA	AMERICAN LEG. AREA	0900 HOURS	
3rd.	"B" Company.	PROGRESS	do	0830 HOURS	Any Coyto may be taken to the Starting Point. Great care must be taken to arrive punctually so as not to dislocate traffic.
3rd.	"A" Company.	do	do	0815 HOURS	
3rd.	"C" Company.	ECHELNALN	do	0820 HOURS.	
3rd.	"D" Company.	SOMALIA	do	0825 HOURS.	

SECRET.   APPENDIX "B"   Copy No. 12

61st. BATTALION MACHINE GUN CORPS OPERATION ORDER NO.61. 3/11/18.

Ref.Map 51A (1/40,000)

1. The following moves will take place tomorrow 4th.inst.
"C" Company 61st.Battalion Machine Gun Corps with 184th.Brigade Group to BERMERAIN. Route as per today.
"D" Company 61st.Battalion Machine Gun Corps with 182nd.Brigade to HAUSSY.

2. Orders as to time of marching will be issued later on receipt of Brigade time table but Companies will be prepared to move by 0800 hours.

3. Rations for 5th.inst. will be delivered to the respective Companies.

4. "D" Company will send Billeting party of 1 Officer and 1 O.R., with Strength Statement to meet STAFF CAPTAIN 182nd.Brigade at Church HAUSSY at 0750 hours tomorrow 4th.inst.
"C" Company will send 1 Officer and 1 O.R. mounted, to proceed in advance to BERMERAIN and will obtain Billets from Town Major. They should be at the Town Major's Office at 0930 hours.

5. ACKNOWLEDGE.

C.V.M. Evans Lieut
for Major.,
Cmdg.61st.Battalion Machine Gun Corps.

3/11/18.

Copies to:-

No.1 "A" Company.
No.2 "B" Company.
3 "C" Company.
4 "D" Company.
5 61st.Division."G".
6 182nd.Inf.Bde.
7 183rd.Inf.Bde.
8 184th.Inf.Bde.
9 Quartermaster.
10 O.M.G.O.
11 File.
12 War Diary.
13 War Diary.
14 Spare.

SECRET　　　　　　　　APPENDIX "C"　　　　Copy No. 13

　　　　　　　　　　　　　　　　　　　　　　　　　　　Ref. Map.
61st. BATTALION MACHINE GUN CORPS OPERATION ORDER No.63.　51A.
　　　　　　　　　　　　　　　　　　　　　　　　　　　1/40,000

1. The Battalion will proceed to BERMERAIN area by March Route today the 8th.inst. in accordance with attached March Table.

2. To avoid congestion dismounted Troops will march across Country or on side of the Road whenever possible.
　Usual distances and halts will be maintained.

3. Companies will forward at once Billeting Party of 1 Officer and 1 O.R. mounted, to meet 2/Lt.Barton at CHURCH, BERMERAIN at 1130 hours.

4. Billets will be thoroughly cleared before moving off and a certificate to this effect rendered to Battalion Headquarters by 1130 hours.

5. Battalion Headquarters will close at AVESNES LES AUBERT at 1200 hours and open at BERMERAIN on arrival.

6. ACKNOWLEDGE.

　　　　　　　　　　　　　　　　　　　　　　[signature]
　　　　　　　　　　　　　　　　　　　　　　　　　　　Major.,
8/11/18.　　　　　　　　　　　　Comdg.61st. Battalion M.G. Corps.

　Copies to:-
　　　　No.1　"A" Company.
　　　　　 2　"B" Company.
　　　　　 3　"C" Company.
　　　　　 4　"D" Company.
　　　　　 5　61st. Division. "G"
　　　　　 6　182nd. Inf. Bde.
　　　　　 7　183rd. Inf. Bde.
　　　　　 8　184th. Inf. Bde.
　　　　　 9　Quartermaster.
　　　　　10　Intelligence Officer.
　　　　　11　O.C.G.O.
　　　　　12　File.
　　　　　13　War Diary.
　　　　　14　War Diary.
　　　　　15　Spare.

MARCH TABLE

TO ACCO?NY 51st.B?TN..?.G. O?ERATIO O?D?R No.?. 8/11/18.

UNIT	STARTING POINT	HRS. TO PASS	ROUTE	R?M?RKS
?.?S.	BA?I? ?.?. ??S.	1305	ST. ?UL?EN-HAUC?T - X ROADS ?.1.d. - X ROADS G.31.b.?.?.	Troops and Transport will move straight to billets on arrival.
?A? CO?.	do	1308	do	do
??" CO?.	do	1312	do	do

APPENDIX "D"

Copy No. ....

61st. BATTALION MACHINE GUN CORPS OPERATION ORDER No.64. 13/11/18.

Ref.No:- G.1A (1/10.009)

1. The Battalion (less "B"&"C" Companies) will move tomorrow the 14th.inst.to ST.AUBERT.

2. Battalion Headquarters will close at ST.MARTIN at 1000 hours and reopen at ST.AUBERT upon arrival.

3. Order of march:-
"HQ", "D" Company "A" Company.
Head of column will be in position on road at CHURCH ST.MARTIN by 1040 hours.
"D" and "A" Companies will parade on Company parade ground and will keep clear of the main ST.MARTIN-ESCAUDIN Road.

4. The usual distances will be maintained.

5. Billeting Party of 1 Officer and 2 O.R's (mounted) per Company will report to R/Lt.DAWSON at Battalion Headquarters at 0900 hours 14th.inst.

6. Billets and Horse Lines will be thoroughly cleaned before moving off and a certificate rendered to Battalion Headquarters by 0930 hours.

7. ACKNOWLEDGE.

C. V. M. Evans.
Captain & Adjt.,
61st. Battalion Machine Gun Corps.

13/11/18.

Copies to :-
No.1 "A" Company.
2 "D" Company.
3 183rd.Inf.Bde.
4 61st. Division.
5 Quartermaster.
6 Intelligence Officer.
7 M.O.
8 File.
9 War Diary.

APPENDIX "E"   Copy No......

61st. BATTALION MACHINE GUN CORPS OPERATION ORDER No.

1. The Battalion will march to SENEKAL (?) tomorrow 14th. inst.

2. Order of March as follows:-
   "H.Q.", "A", "B", "C", "D" Companies.
   Head of column will pass starting point, Crossroads V.15c.9.0.
   at 1150 hours.

3. Route
   A.SHEDD - CHARO ROAD C.6.b.6.d. - SOMEROUT - VASTERI Road.

4. Dismounted troops will march across country or a set of roads.
   The usual distances will be maintained by Companies and transport.
   on the line of march.

5. Companies will detail Billeting Party of 1 Officer and 1 N.C.O.
   (mounted) to meet 2/Lt. SMITH at Battalion Headquarters at 0720 hours
   tomorrow 14th. inst.

6. Guides will be stationed at main SOMEROUT Road at Railway crossing
   at A.11.b.9.5. to meet Companies upon arrival.

7. ACKNOWLEDGE.

                                                C.P.M. Evans.
                                                Captain & Adjt.
                                             61st. Battalion Machine Gun Corps.
13/11/18.

Copies to:-
   No.1 "A" Company.
   2 "B" Company.
   3 "C" Company.
   4 "D" Company.
   5 61st. Division "Q".
   6 Quartermaster.
   7 Intelligence Officer.
   8 R.S.M.
   9 O.R.Q.M.S.
   10 File.
   11-12 War Diary.

SECRET.   APPENDIX "F"   Copy No. 10

61st. BATTALION MACHINE GUN CORPS OPERATION ORDER No.88.   22/11/18
───

                                                   Ref.Map.LENS
                                                   VALENCIENNES 1/100,000.

1.   The Battalion including portion of Transport detailed below
will proceed by Tactical Train to the BERSAILLE area on the
24th. and 25th.inst., in accordance with Instructions to be
issued later.

2.   The Battalion Transport less :-

        1 Cooker "A","B" and "D" Companies.
        1 Limber per Company
        1 Limber between "A" and "B" Companies.)   To be arranged
        1 Limber between "C" and "D" Companies.)   between O.C's
        1 Mess Cart.   Concerned.
        2 Limbers Battalion Headquarters
  P.   1 Water Cart of "C" Company.
        2 Chargers per Company.
        3 Chargers per Headquarters.

will move under orders of 183 Inf.Brigade Group tomorrow 23rd.inst.
to the vicinity of BAPAUME.   Time of starting will be notified
later.   Lieut.SEPHTON "C" Company will be in charge of
Battalion Transport.

3.   Blankets and steel Helmets will be dumped at Q.M.Stores at
a time to be notified later, and carried on the train.

4.   ACKNOWLEDGE.

                                          C V M Evans
                                             Captain & Adjt.,
22/11/18.   61st. Battalion Machine Gun Corps.

        Copies to:-

            No.1 "A" Company.
               2 "B" Company.
               3 "C" Company.
               4 "D" Company.
               5 61st. Division. "G".
               6 Quartermaster.
               7 Intelligence Officer.
               8 File.
               9 War Diary.
              10 War Diary. ✓

SECRET   Copy No.....

                                                                M.G.27L.

In continuation of O.O.66 dated 22/11/18.

1.   Lieut. JONES will go forward tomorrow to reconnoitre Starting
     Point. All precautions will be taken to prevent causing a
     block in the Traffic.

2.   A Field Officer detailed by 182 Inf.Brigade will be in charge
     of the whole Divisional Transport Column, and will be
     responsible for arranging halting places for watering, and
     for allotting areas at each staging point.

3.   2/Lt. PLEDGER ("A" Company) will report at 183rd.Inf.Brigade
     Headquarters at 0700 hours 23rd.inst. for the purpose of
     synchronizing watches.

4.   ACKNOWLEDGE.

                                                    [signature]
                                                    Captain & Adjt.,
                                                    61st. Battalion Machine Gun Corps.

22/11/18.

        Copies to:-

             No.1 "A" Company.
                2 "B" Company.
                3 "C" Company.
                4 "D" Company.
                5 File.
                6 War Diary.
                7 War Diary.

SECRET. APPENDIX "G" Copy No....

ADMINISTRATIVE INSTRUCTIONS ISSUED IN CONNECTION WITH

61st. BN. MACHINE GUN CORPS OPERATION ORDER NO.66 22/11/18.

1. The Battalion less portion moving by March Route will entrain as per Table "A" attached.

2. DRESS.

Men will wear Greatcoats and will carry Blankets in packs. Steel helmets (in bundles of 12) will be dumped at Battalion Quartermaster Stores at 1630 hours today 23rd.inst.

3. LORRIES.

(a) For Entrainment.

One lorry will be outside Main entrance to CAMBRAI VILLE Station at 1400 hours 24th.inst. to do two journeys to No.4 Train. The Q.M. will arrange a guide to meet lorry at Rendezvous and a sufficient number of men to accompany lorry to act as unloading party and Guard over Stores while dumped at Station.

(b) For Detrainment.

Lorries to take Stores from Detraining Station to Billeting area will meet Train No.4. CONTEVILLE at approximately 0400 hours 25th.inst.

4. SUPPLIES.

Rations for the whole Battalion for 25th.and 26th.inst. will be drawn at Refilling point CAMBRAI VILLE Station at 0700 hours on the 24th.inst. Each Company will take its rations on the Train on which it travels.

5. "A" "B" and "C" Companies will be at Entraining Station 3 hours before time of departure of their respective trains, and will act as loading party for the Brigade Group. They will also act as unloading Party on detrainment.

6. "C" Company will arrange that the Water cart is filled.

7. ACKNOWLEDGE.

Captain & Adjt.,
23/11/18. 61st. Battalion Machine Gun Corps.

Copies to:-
No. 1 "A" Company.
2 "B" Company.
3 "C" Company.
4 "D" Company.
5 61st. Division "G"
6 183rd.Inf.Brigade.
7 Quartermaster.
8 Signalling Officer.
9 Intelligence Officer.
10 R.S.M.
11 File.
12 War Diary.
13 War Diary.
14 C.M.G.O. (XVII Corps.)
15 Spare.

TABLE "A".

Entraining Table issued in connection with ADMINISTRATIVE INSTRUCTIONS of 23/11/18.

TRAIN NO.	DATE	PERSONNEL	TRANSPORT.	CHARGERS	ENTRAINING STATION.	TIME FOR ARRIVAL at STATION.	TIME of DEPARTURE.	DETRAINING STATION.	TYPE OF TRAIN.
1.	24th.Nov.	"A" Coy.	1 Cooker "A"Coy. 1 limber "A" do 1 limber"A"&"B" Coys. 1 limber "B" Coy.	2"A" Coy. 2B"B"Coy.	CAMBRAI VILLE	0930 Hrs.	1229 Hrs.	AUXI-LE-CHATEAU.	Transport.
4.	25th.Nov.	"B" Coy.	1 Cooker"B" Coy. 1 Mess Cart(Bn.H.Q) 2 Limbers BN.H.Q. Bn.Q.M.Stores.	3 Bn.H.Q. 2 "C" Coy.	do	2130 Hrs (24th.inst.)	0929 Hrs. (25th.inst)	CONTEVILLE.	TRansport.
6.	25th.Nov.	Bn.H.Qrs.	-----	-----	do	0730 Hrs.	0829 Hrs.	do	Personnel.
7.	25th.Nov.	"C" Coy.	1 Limber "C" Coy. 1 Limber "C""D" Coy. 1 limber "D" Coy. 1 Cooker"D" Coy. 1 Water Cart."C" Coy.	2 "D" Coy.	do	0930 Hrs.	1229 Hrs.	do	Transport.
9.	25th.Nov.	"D" Coy.	-----	-----	do	1930 Hrs.	2020 Hrs.	do	Personnel.

Strict attention will be paid to General Rules laid down for "Transport by Rail".

TABLE "B"

This Table cancels Table "A" issued with Administrative Instructions dated 23/11/18.

TRAIN No.	DATE	PERSONNEL.	TRANSPORT.	CHARGERS.	ENTRAINING STATION.	TIME FOR ARRIVAL at STATION.	TIME of DEPARTURE.	DETRAINING STATION.	TYPE of TRAIN.
5.	25th.Nov.	"B" Coy.	1 Cooker "B" Coy. 1 Mess Cart.(Bn.H.Q.) 2 limbers Bn.H.Qrs. Bn.Q.M.Stores.	3 Bn.H.Q. 1 "B" Coy. 2 "C" Coy.	CAMBRAI VILLE.	0130Hrs.	0429 Hrs.	CONTEVILLE.	Transport.
6.	25th.	Bn.H.Qrs.	-----	-----	do	0730 Hrs.	0829 Hrs.	do	Personnel.
7.	25th.	"C" Coy.	-----	-----	do	0930 Hrs.	1229 Hrs.	do	Personnel.
9.	25th.	"D" Coy.	1 Limber "C" Coy. 1 limber "C" & "D" Coys. 1 limber "D" Coy. 1 Cooker "D" Coy. 1 Water Cart "C" Coy.	2 "D" Coy.	do	1730 Hrs.	2029 Hrs.	do	Transport.

Strict attention will be paid to General Rules laid down for "Transport by Rail".

61 Bn M.G.Corps
1918

CONFIDENTIAL.

WAR DIARY FOR MONTH DECEMBER 1918.

VOLUME No. X.

(6339) Wt. W160/M3016 1,500,000 10/17 McA & W Ltd (E 1898) Forms W3091.   Army Form W.3091.

Cover for Documents.

Nature of Enclosures.

Notes, or Letters written.

MARCH TABLE
to
[illegible] OPERATION ORDER No.37. 9/12/18.

DATE.	COMPANY.	FROM.	TO.	ROUTE.	STARTING POINT.	HOURS TO PASS.	REMARKS.
9/12/18.	Hd.Q.Qrs.	[illegible]	[illegible]	[illegible] - X Rds. S.E. of [illegible] - [illegible].	[illegible].12.80.	1000 Hours.	
9/12/18.	"A" Coy.	do	do	do	do	1005 Hours.	
9/12/18.	"B" Coy.	do	do	do	do	1007 Hours.	
9/12/18.	"C" Coy.	do	do	do	do	1011 Hours.	
9/12/18.	"D" Coy.	[illegible]	do	[illegible] - X Rds. [illegible] of [illegible] - [illegible].	[illegible].23.34.	1009 Hours.	To join Column in rear of "[illegible]" Company at X Roads [illegible].

Army Form C. 2118.

WAR DIARY
or
INTELLIGENCE SUMMARY.
(Erase heading not required.)

Instructions regarding War Diaries and Intelligence Summaries are contained in F. S. Regs., Part II. and the Staff Manual respectively. Title pages will be prepared in manuscript.

Place	Date	Hour	Summary of Events and Information	Remarks and references to Appendices
BERNEUIL.	1/12/18.		Battalion Training. Casualties :- NIL. Reinforcements :- NIL.	Ref. Map. LENS 11. 1/100,000.
do.	2/12/18.		Battalion Training. Casualties :- NIL. Reinforcements :- NIL.	
do.	3/12/18.		Battalion Training. Casualties :- NIL. Reinforcements :- NIX. 2 O.R's.	
do.	4/12/18.		Battalion Training. Casualties :- NIL. Reinforcements :- NIL.	
do.	5/12/18.		Battalion Training. Casualties :- NIL. Reinforcements :- NIL.	
do.	6/12/18.		Battalion Training. Casualties :- NIL. Reinforcements :- NIL.	
do.	7/12/18.		Battalion Training. Casualties :- NIL. Reinforcements :- NIL.	
BERNAVILLE.	8/12/18.		The Battalion moved by march route from BERNEUIL to the BERNAVILLE Area, as per O.O.67. (attached as Appendix "A"). Reinforcements:- NIL. Casualties :- NIL.	
do.	9/12/18.		Battalion Training. Casualties :- NIL. Reinforcements :- NIL.	
do.	10/12/18.		Battalion Training. Casualties :- NIL. Reinforcements :- NIL.	
do.	11/12/18.		Battalion Training. Casualties :- NIL. Reinforcements :- NIL.	

Army Form C. 2118.

WAR DIARY
or
INTELLIGENCE SUMMARY.
(Erase heading not required.)

Instructions regarding War Diaries and Intelligence Summaries are contained in F. S. Regs., Part II. and the Staff Manual respectively. Title pages will be prepared in manuscript.

Place	Date	Hour	Summary of Events and Information	Remarks and references to Appendices
BERNAVILLE.	12/12/18.		Battalion Training. Casualties :- NIL. Reinforcements :- NIL.	Ref. Map. LENS 11. 1/100,000.
do.	13/12/18.		Battalion Training. Casualties :- NIL. Reinforcements :- 2/Lieut. MORRIS H. 2/Lieut. KNEE C.A. 2/Lieut. LAWFORD H.H.	
do.	14/12/18.		Battalion Training. Casualties :- NIL. Reinforcements :- NIL.	
do.	15/12/18.		Battalion Training. Casualties :- NIL. Reinforcements :- NIL.	
do.	16/12/18.		Battalion Training. Casualties :- NIL. Reinforcements :- NIL.	
do.	17/12/18.		Battalion Training. Casualties :- NIL. Reinforcements :- NIL.	
do.	18/12/18.		Battalion Training. Casualties :- NIL. Reinforcements :- 2 O.R's.	
do.	19/12/18.		Battalion Training. Casualties :- NIL. Reinforcements :- NIL.	
do.	20/12/18.		Battalion Training. Casualties :- NIL. Reinforcements :- NIL.	
do.	21/12/18.		Battalion Training. Casualties :- NIL. Reinforcements :- 1 O.R.	
do.	22/12/18.		Battalion Training. Casualties :- NIL. Reinforcements :- NIL.	

Army Form C. 2118.

WAR DIARY
or
INTELLIGENCE SUMMARY.
(Erase heading not required.)

Instructions regarding War Diaries and Intelligence Summaries are contained in F. S. Regs., Part II. and the Staff Manual respectively. Title pages will be prepared in manuscript.

Place	Date	Hour	Summary of Events and Information	Remarks and references to Appendices
BERNAVILLE.	23/12/18.		Battalion Training. Casualties :- NIL. Reinforcements :- NIL.	Ref. Map. LENS 11. 1/100,000.
do.	24/12/18.		Battalion Training. Casualties :- NIL. Reinforcements :- NIL.	
do.	25/12/18.		CHRISTMAS DAY. Casualties :- NIL. Reinforcements :- NIL.	
do.	26/12/18.		Battalion Training and Sports. Casualties :- NIL. Reinforcements :- NIL.	
do.	27/12/18.		Battalion Training. Casualties :- NIL. Reinforcements :- NIL.	
do.	28/12/18.		Battalion Training. Casualties :- NIL. Reinforcements :- NIL.	
do.	29/12/18.		Battalion Training. Casualties :- NIL. Reinforcements :- NIL.	
do.	30/12/18.		Battalion Training. Casualties :- NIL. Reinforcements :- NIL.	
do.	31/12/18.		Battalion Training. Casualties :- NIL. Reinforcements :- NIL.	

APPENDIX "A"

21st BATTALION M.G.C. ORDERS (OPERATIONAL) ORDER No. 27. 6/12/18.

Ref. MAP LILLE
1/100,000.

1. The Battalion will move to RONCHIN in accordance with March Table attached.

2. The usual distances and strict march discipline will be maintained on the line of march.

3. Companies will detail billeting party of 1 Officer and 1 O.R. to report to Captain FINCH at Battalion Headquarters at 1000 hrs. 7th.inst. to proceed to RONCHIN to arrange accommodation.

4. Billets will be thoroughly clean before moving off and a certificate to this effect will be rendered to Battalion Headquarters by O.C.s Coys 7th.inst.

5. ACKNOWLEDGE.

C.V.M Evans
Captain & Adjt.,
21st. Battalion Machine Gun Corps.

6/12/18.

Copies to:-
No.1 "A" Company.
2 "B" Company.
3 "C" Company.
4 "D" Company.
5 51st.Division."G"
6 Quartermaster.
7 Signalling Officer.
8 Intelligence Officer.
9 G.S.O.I. (XVII Corps).
10 File.
11-13 Sundry.

61st. BATTALION MACHINE GUN CORPS.

WAR DIARY.

1st. JANUARY 1919   to   31st. JANUARY 1919

(VOLUME No. 21)

(6392) Wt. W6192/P875 1,500,000 4/18 McA & W Ltd (E 2815) Forms W3091/4. Army Form W.3091.

Cover for Documents.

Nature of Enclosures.

Notes, or Letters written.

Army Form C. 2118.

WAR DIARY
or
INTELLIGENCE SUMMARY.
(Erase heading not required.)

Instructions regarding War Diaries and Intelligence Summaries are contained in F. S. Regs., Part II. and the Staff Manual respectively. Title pages will be prepared in manuscript.

Place	Date	Hour	Summary of Events and Information	Remarks and references to Appendices
Bernaville	1/1/19.		Battalion Training.	Ref. Map Long. 11. 4/100,000.
			Casualties:- NIL.	
			Reinforcements:- NIL.	
do.	2/1/19.		Battalion Training.	
			Casualties:- NIL.	
			Reinforcements:- NIL.	
do.	3/1/19.		Battalion Training.	
			Casualties:- NIL.	
			Reinforcements:- NIL.	
do.	4/1/19.		Battalion Training.	
			Casualties:- NIL.	
			Reinforcements:- 2/Lieut.EVANS R.F. 2/Lieut.GARNER G.C. from Base Depot.	
do.	5/1/19.		Battalion Training.	
			Casualties:- NIL.	
			Reinforcements:- NIL.	
do.	6/1/19.		Battalion Training.	
			Casualties:- NIL.	
			Reinforcements:- NIL.	
do.	7/1/19.		Battalion Training.	
			Casualties:- NIL.	
			Reinforcements:- NIL.	
do.	8/1/19.		Battalion Training.	
			Casualties:- NIL.	
			Reinforcements:- NIL.	
do.	9/1/19.		Battalion Training.	
			Casualties:- NIL.	
			Reinforcements:- NIL.	
do.	10/1/19.		Battalion Training.	
			Casualties:- NIL.	
			Reinforcements:- NIL.	
do.	11/1/19.		Battalion Training.	
			Casualties:- NIL.	
			Reinforcements:- NIL.	

Army Form C. 2118.

WAR DIARY
or
INTELLIGENCE SUMMARY.
(Erase heading not required.)

Instructions regarding War Diaries and Intelligence Summaries are contained in F. S. Regs. Part II. and the Staff Manual respectively. Title pages will be prepared in manuscript.

Place	Date	Hour	Summary of Events and Information	Remarks and references to Appendices
Bernaville.	12/1/19.		Battalion Training. Casualties:- NIL. Reinforcements:- Lieut. JONES H.V. from Base Depot.	Ref. Map Lens 11. 1/100,000.
do.	13/1/19.		Battalion Training. Casualties:- NIL. Reinforcements:- 2 O.R's from Base Depot.	
do.	14/1/19.		Battalion Training. Casualties:- NIL. Reinforcements:- 2 O.R's from Base Depot.	
do.	15/1/19.		Battalion Training. Casualties:- NIL. Reinforcements:- NIL.	
do.	16/1/19.		Battalion Training. Casualties:- NIL. Reinforcements:- 1 O.R. from Base Depot.	
do.	17/1/19.		Battalion Training. Casualties:- NIL. Reinforcements:- 1 O.R. from Base Depot.	
do.	18/1/19.		Battalion Training. Casualties:- NIL. Reinforcements:- NIL.	
do.	19/1/19.		Battalion Training. Casualties:- NIL. Reinforcements:- NIL.	
do.	20/1/19.		Battalion Training. Casualties:- NIL. Reinforcements:- NIL.	
do.	21/1/19.		Battalion Training. Casualties:- NIL. Reinforcements:- NIL.	

Headquarters,
ABBEVILLE AREA.

D.A.G.
3rd. Echelon.

Herewith War Diary for the month of February 1919.

(VOLUME NO. 12)

2/Lt. & A/Adjt.
61st. Battalion Machine Gun Corps.

1/3/19.

Army Form C. 2118.

WAR DIARY
or
INTELLIGENCE SUMMARY.
(Erase heading not required.)

Instructions regarding War Diaries and Intelligence Summaries are contained in F. S. Regs., Part II. and the Staff Manual respectively. Title pages will be prepared in manuscript.

Place	Date	Hour	Summary of Events and Information	Remarks and references to Appendices
BERNAVILLE.	22/1/19.		Battalion Training. Casualties:- NIL. Reinforcements:- NIL.	Ref.Map Lens 11. 1/100,000.
do.	23/1/19.		Battalion Training. Casualties:- NIL. Reinforcements:- NIL.	
do.	24/1/19.		Battalion Training. Casualties:- NIL. Reinforcements:- NIL.	
do.	25/1/19.		Battalion Training. Casualties:- NIL. Reinforcements:- NIL.	
do.	26/1/19.		Battalion Training. Casualties:- NIL. Reinforcements:- 2 O.R's from Base Depot.	
do.	27/1/19.		Battalion Training. Casualties:- NIL. Reinforcements:- NIL.	
do.	28/1/19.		Battalion Training. Casualties:- NIL. Reinforcements:- NIL.	
do.	29/1/19.		Battalion Training. Casualties:- NIL. Reinforcements:- NIL.	
do.	30/1/19.		Battalion Training. Casualties:- NIL. Reinforcements:- NIL.	
do.	31/1/19.		Battalion Training. Casualties:- NIL. Reinforcements:- XXX 3 O.R's from Base Depot.	

WAR DIARY.

61ST. BATTALION MACHINE GUN CORPS.

1st. FEBRUARY 1919 to 28th. FEBRUARY 1919.

(Volume No. 12)

(6392) Wt. W6192/P875 1,500,000 4/18 McA & W Ltd (E 2815) Forms W3091/4.   Army Form W.3091.

Cover for Documents.

Nature of Enclosures.

Notes, or Letters written.

Army Form W.3091.

Army Form C. 2118.

WAR DIARY
or
INTELLIGENCE SUMMARY.
(Erase heading not required.)

Instructions regarding War Diaries and Intelligence Summaries are contained in F. S. Regs., Part II. and the Staff Manual respectively. Title pages will be prepared in manuscript.

Place	Date	Hour	Summary of Events and Information	Remarks and references to Appendices
BERNAVILLE	1/2/19		Battalion Training. Casualties:- NIL. Reinforcements:- NIL.	Ref. Map. 1/100,000
do.	2/2/19		Battalion Training. Casualties:- NIL. Reinforcements:- NIL.	
do.	3/2/19		Battalion Training. Casualties:- NIL. Reinforcements:- NIL.	
do.	4/2/19		Battalion Training. Casualties:- NIL. Reinforcements:- 2 O.R's. from Base Depot.	
do.	5/2/19		Battalion Training. Casualties:- NIL. Reinforcements:- NIL.	
do.	6/2/19		Battalion Training. Casualties:- NIL. Reinforcements:- NIL.	
do	7/2/19		Battalion Training. Casualties:- NIL. Reinforcements:- NIL.	
do	8/2/19		Battalion Training. Casualties:- NIL. Reinforcements:- NIL.	
do	9/2/19		Battalion Training. Casualties:- NIL. Reinforcements:- NIL.	
DRUCAT	10/2/19		The Battalion moved by march route from BERNAVILLE to DRUCAT (ABBEVILLE area) as per 61st.Div.instruction Reinforcements:- NIL.	

Army Form C. 2118.

WAR DIARY
or
INTELLIGENCE SUMMARY.
(Erase heading not required.)

Instructions regarding War Diaries and Intelligence Summaries are contained in F.S. Regs., Part II. and the Staff Manual respectively. Title pages will be prepared in manuscript.

Place	Date	Hour	Summary of Events and Information	Remarks and references to Appendices
DRUCAT	11/2/19		Battalion Training. Casualties:- NIL. Reinforcements:- NIL.	
	12/2/19		Battalion Training. Casualties:- NIL. Reinforcements:- NIL.	
	13/2/19		Battalion Training. Casualties:- NIL. Reinforcements:- NIL.	
	14/2/19		Battalion Training. Casualties:- NIL. Reinforcements:- NIL.	
	15/2/19		Battalion Training. Casualties:- NIL. Reinforcements:- NIL.	
	16/2/19		Battalion Training. Casualties:- NIL. Reinforcements:- NIL.	
	17/2/19		Battalion Training. Casualties:- NIL. Reinforcements:- NIL.	
	18/2/19		Battalion Training. Casualties:- NIL. Reinforcements:- NIL.	
	19/2/19		Battalion Training. Casualties:- NIL. Reinforcements:- NIL.	
	20/2/19		Battalion Training. Casualties:- NIL. Reinforcements:- NIL.	
	21/2/19		Battalion Training. Casualties:- NIL. Reinforcements:- NIL.	
	22/2/19		Battalion Training. Casualties:- NIL. Reinforcements:- NIL. Lieut-Colonel N.G.Burnand D.S.O. on Leave. Major W.H.Brooks assumes Command.	
	23/2/19		Battalion Training. Casualties:- NIL. Reinforcements:- NIL.	
	24/2/19		Battalion Training. Casualties:- NIL. Reinforcements:- NIL.	

Army Form C. 2118.

WAR DIARY
or
INTELLIGENCE SUMMARY.

(Erase heading not required.)

Instructions regarding War Diaries and Intelligence Summaries are contained in F. S. Regs., Part II. and the Staff Manual respectively. Title pages will be prepared in manuscript.

Place	Date	Hour	Summary of Events and Information	Remarks and references to Appendices
DRUCAT	25/2/19		Battalion Training. Casualties:- NIL. Reinforcements:- NIL.	
	26/2/19		Battalion Training. Casualties:- NIL. Reinforcements:- NIL.	
	27/2/19		Battalion Training. Casualties:- NIL. Reinforcements:- NIL.	
	28/2/19		Battalion Training. Casualties:- NIL. Reinforcements:- NIL.	

61st. BATTALION MACHINE GUN CORPS.

WAR DIARY.

1st. March 1919 to 31st. March 1919.

(VOLUME NO. 13)

(6339) Wt. W160/M3016 1,500,000 10/17 McA & W Ltd (E 1898) Forms W3091. Army Form W.3091.

Cover for Documents.

Nature of Enclosures.

Notes, or Letters written.

Army Form C. 2118.

WAR DIARY
or
INTELLIGENCE SUMMARY.
(Erase heading not required.)

Instructions regarding War Diaries and Intelligence Summaries are contained in F. S. Regs., Part II. and the Staff Manual respectively. Title pages will be prepared in manuscript.

Place	Date	Hour	Summary of Events and Information	Remarks and references to Appendices
DRUCAT	1/3/19		Reinforcements:- NIL.	Ref. Map ABBEVILLE 1⁴ 1/100,000
do	2/3/19		Reinforcements:- NIL.	
do	3/3/19		Reinforcements:- NIL.	
do	4/3/19		Reinforcements:- NIL.	
do	5/3/19		Reinforcements:- NIL.	
do	6/3/19		Reinforcements:- NIL.	
do	7/3/19		Reinforcements:- NIL.	
do	8/3/19		Reinforcements:- NIL.	
do	9/3/19		Reinforcements:- NIL.	
do	10/3/19		Reinforcements:- NIL. Lieut-Colonel N.G.Burnand D.S.O. assumes Command on return from Leave to U.K.	
do	11/3/19		Reinforcements:- NIL.	
do	12/3/19		Reinforcements:- NIL.	
do	13/3/19		Reinforcements:- NIL.	
do	14/3/19		Reinforcements:- NIL.	
do	15/3/19		Reinforcements:- NIL.	
do	16/3/19		Reinforcements:- NIL.	
do	17/3/19		Reinforcements:- NIL.	

Army Form C. 2118.

WAR DIARY
or
INTELLIGENCE SUMMARY.
(Erase heading not required.)

Instructions regarding War Diaries and Intelligence Summaries are contained in F. S. Regs., Part II. and the Staff Manual respectively. Title pages will be prepared in manuscript.

Place	Date	Hour	Summary of Events and Information	Remarks and references to Appendices
DRUCAT	18/3/19		Reinforcements:- NIL.	Ref. Map ABBEVILLE 14 1/100,000
do	19/3/19		Reinforcements:- NIL.	
do	20/3/19		Reinforcements:- NIL.	
do	21/3/19		Reinforcements:- NIL.	
do	22/3/19		Reinforcements:- NIL.	
do	23/3/19		Reinforcements:- NIL.	
do	24/3/19		Reinforcements:- NIL.	
do	25/3/19		Reinforcements:- NIL.	
do	26/3/19		Reinforcements:- NIL.	
do	27/3/19		Reinforcements:- Capt. BOSWELL J. ⎫ Lieut. MATTHEWS T. ⎬ from 21st. Battalion M.G.C. " BURKE J.R. ⎪ 2/Lt. WILLIAMS C.R. ⎪ " SLAYMAKER S.C. ⎭ Lieut. JENRICK P.H. ⎫ from 38th. Battalion M.G.C. " WHEELOCK H.J. ⎭ 4 O.Rs. From 21st. Battalion M.G.C. 1 O.R. " 39th. do (from Leave) to U.K.)	
do	28/3/19		Reinforcements:- 1 O.R. From 39th. Battalion M.G.C. (from Leave to U.K.)	

Army Form C. 2118.

WAR DIARY
or
INTELLIGENCE SUMMARY.
(Erase heading not required.)

Instructions regarding War Diaries and Intelligence Summaries are contained in F. S. Regs., Part II. and the Staff Manual respectively. Title pages will be prepared in manuscript.

Place	Date	Hour	Summary of Events and Information	Remarks and references to Appendices
DRUCAT.	29/3/19		Reinforcements:- Major GILBERT E. ⎫ Lieut. BURNS F.J. ⎬ 2/Lt. PRATT G.W. ⎬ from 39th. Battalion M.G.C. " BURNETT H.E. ⎬ " RUTTER G.A. ⎬ " BELL F. ⎭ 99 O.Rs. from 21st. Battalion M.G.C. do (from Leave to U.K.) 1 O.R. from 39th.	Ref.Map ABBEVILLE 14 1/100,000
do	30/3/19		Reinforcements:- Major HOWARD C.M.⎫ from 21st. Battalion Machine Gun Corps. 2/Lieut NEILL G. ⎬ do do Lieut. FAIRHURST H. ⎭ do do 2 O.Rs from 21st. Battalion M.G.C.	
do	31/3/19		Reinforcements:- 2 O.Rs. from 39th. Battalion M.G.C. (from Leave to U.K.)	

Headquarters,
    61st. Division.

                                    PA 399/11

        Herewith War Diary for the Month of APRIL 1919.

        (Volume No. 14).

                            [signature]
                                                Lieut-Colonel,
1/5/19.   Cmdg. 61st. Battalion Machine Gun Corps.

> 61st BATTALION,
> MACHINE GUN
>   CORPS.
>
> No..............
> Date............

61st. BATTALION MACHINE GUN CORPS.

WAR DIARY.

1st. APRIL 1919 TO 30th. APRIL 1919.

(Volume No. 14.)

61ST BATTALION,
MACHINE GUN
CORPS

(6392) Wt. W6192/P875 1,500,000 4/18 McA & W Ltd (E 2815) Forms W3091/4.   Army Form W.3091.

Cover for Documents.

Nature of Enclosures.

Notes, or Letters written.

Army Form C. 2118.

WAR DIARY
or
INTELLIGENCE SUMMARY.
(Erase heading not required.)

Place	Date	Hour	Summary of Events and Information	Remarks and references to Appendices
DRUCAT	1/4/19		Reinforcements:- Major W.L.Adamson MC From 38th. Bn. M.G.C. 2/Lieut. C.Niel : 21st. : : : : Lieut. P.McGrath : 39th. : On expiration of leave. 2/Lieut. J.L.F.Devereux From 38th. Bn. M.G.C. : : H.Makin : 39th. : : : Lieut. B.R.Edwards : 38th. : : : Lieut. E.G.Horne : : : : : Q.O.R. From 21st. Bn. M.G.C. On expiration of leave. 33 O.Rs. : 38th. : : : : : 125 : : 39th. : : : : :	Ref. Map ABBEVILLE 14 1/100,000
do	2/4/19		Reinforcements:- Q.O.R. From 21st. Bn. M.G.C.	
do	3/4/19		Reinforcements:- NIL.	
do	4/4/19		Reinforcements:- NIL.	
do	5/4/19		Reinforcements:- Lieut. J.Howells From 38th. Bn. M.G.C. On expiration of leave. Lieut. G.Cruse : : : : On expiration of leave to U.K. 2 O.Rs. From 21st. Bn .M.G.C. : : : : : PARIS. 2 O.Rs. : : : : : : : : :	
do	6/4/19		Reinforcements:- 1 O.R. From 21st Bn. M.G.C. On expiration of leave to U.K.	
do	7/4/19		Reinforcements:- Lieut. W.G.Coutts From 38th. Bn. M.G.C. On expiration of leave to U.K. F.G.Ritchie : : : : : : : : :	
do	8/4/19		Reinforcements:- 1 O.R. From 21st. Bn. M.G.C. On expiration of leave to U.K. 1 : : No. 5 Military Prison & ETAPLES G.B.D.	
do	9/4/19		Reinforcements:- 1 O.R. From Hospital Whilst on leave to U.K. Capt. R.W.Goldsborough From 38th. Bn. M.G.C.	
do	10/4/19		Reinforcements:- Lieut. & Qmr. F.J.Cosgreve From Cmmdt. CALAIS.	
do	11/4/19		Reinforcements:- 1 O.R. From 39th. Bn. M.G.C. On expiration of leave to U.K. 1 : : : 21st. : : : : : : :	

Army Form C. 2118.

WAR DIARY
or
INTELLIGENCE SUMMARY.
(Erase heading not required).

Instructions regarding War Diaries and Intelligence Summaries are contained in F.S. Regs., Part II. and the Staff Manual respectively. Title pages will be prepared in manuscript.

Place	Date	Hour	Summary of Events and Information	Remarks and references to Appendices
DRUCAT.	12/4/19.		Reinforcements:- 111 O.Rs. From 58th. Bn.M.G.C.	Ref. Map ABBEVILLE 14 1/100,000
do	13/4/19		Reinforcements:- 1 O.R. From 39th.Bn.M.G.C. & ETAPLES G.B.D. 58 O.Rs. From 63rd. Bn.M.G.C.	
do	14/4/19		Reinforcements:- NIL.	
do	15/4/19		Reinforcements:- 57 O.Rs. From 31st. Bn.M.G.C. 1 O.R. " 21st. " . On expiration of leave to U.K.	
do	16/4/19		Reinforcements:- 1 O.R. From 63rd. Bn. M.G.C. On expiration of leave to U.K.	
do	17/4/19		Reinforcements:- 1 O.R. From 31st Bn. M.G.C. On expiration of Leave to U.K. 58 O.Rs. From 38th. Bn. M.G.C.	
ABBEVILLE	18/4/19		Battalion Headquarters moved from DRUCAT to ABBEVILLE 18/4/19.	Ref. Map ABBEVILLE 14 1/100,000
do	:		Reinforcements:- 1 O.R. From 63rd Bn.M.G.C. On expiration of leave to U.K. 1 O.R. " 31st. " : : . 1 " " 39th. " : : . From 5th. Army Conc. Camp. 2 O.Rs. " 31st. " : : & ETAPLES G.B.D. On expiration of leave to U.K.	
do	19/4/19		Reinforcements:- NIL.	
do	20/4/19		Reinforcements:- 2/Lieut. P.Philbin From 39th. Bn. M.G.C.	
do	21/4/19		Reinforcements:- 1 O.R. From 102 Bn. M.G.C. & ETAPLES G.B.D. 2 O.Rs. From 38th. Bn. M.G.C. On expiration of leave to U.K.	
do	22/4/19		Reinforcements:- NIL. Two and a Half Companies proceeded to Main Cage P.O.W.Camp, ABBEVILLE for duty as Guards and Escorts for P.O.W.	
do	23/4/19.		Reinforcements:- NIL.	
do	24/4/19		Reinforcements:- 1 O.R. From 63rd. Bn .M.G.C. On expiration of leave to U.K. Capt. R.W.Goldsborough, Lieut.G.Wilkie, 2/Lieut. W.D.M.Davis & 100 O.Rs. proceeded to No.24 Ordnance Depot, DOMLEGER, for duty as ammunition guard.	

D.D.&L., London, E.C.
Wt W17771/M2931 750,000 5/17 Sch.52 Forms/C2118/14
(A2-04)

Army Form C. 2118.

WAR DIARY
or
INTELLIGENCE SUMMARY.
(Erase heading not required.)

Instructions regarding War Diaries and Intelligence Summaries are contained in F. S. Regs., Part II. and the Staff Manual respectively. Title pages will be prepared in manuscript.

Place	Date	Hour	Summary of Events and Information	Remarks and references to Appendices
ABBEVILLE.	25/4/19		Reinforcements:- 2/Lieut. T.F.RYAN From 38th. Bn. M.G.C. 66 O.Rs. From 38th.Bn. M.G.C.	Ref. Map ABBEVILLE 14 1/100,000
do	26/4/19		Reinforcements:- 2 O.Rs. From 31st. Bn. M.G.C. & ETAPLES G.B.D.	
do	27/4/19		Reinforcements:- 1 O.R. From 63rd Bn. M.G.C. & ETAPLES G.B.D. 4 O.Rs. From 38th. Bn. M.G.C. On expiration of leave to U.K.	
do	28/4/19		Reinforcements:- NIL.	
do	29/4/19		Reinforcements:- 2 O.Rs. From 31st, Bn. M.G.C. 1 " " 63rd. " "	
do	30/4/19		Reinforcements:- 2 O.Rs, From 39th. Bn. M.G.C.	

Strength of Battalion (excluding Officers & O.Rs. who have proceeded for Dispersal, but for whom no Authority has been received to strike off strength):- 53 Officers & 816 O.Rs.

61st. Battalion Machine Gun Corps.

WAR DIARY.

1st. May 1919 to 31st. May 1919.

(Volume No. 15)

(6392) Wt. W6192/P875 1,500,000 4/18 McA & W Ltd (E 2815) Forms W3091/4.   Army Form W.3091.

Cover for Documents.

Nature of Enclosures.

Notes, or Letters written.

Army Form W.3091.

Army Form C. 2118.

WAR DIARY
or
INTELLIGENCE SUMMARY.
(Erase heading not required.)

Instructions regarding War Diaries and Intelligence Summaries are contained in F.S. Regs., Part II. and the Staff Manual respectively. Title pages will be prepared in manuscript.

Place	Date	Hour	Summary of Events and Information	Remarks and references to Appendices
ABBEVILLE.	1/5/19.		Reinforcements:- 1 O.R. from 63rd. Battalion M.G.Corps.	Ref. Map ABBEVILLE 14 1/100,000
do.	2/5/19.		Reinforcements:- NIL.	
do.	3/5/19.		Reinforcements:- 1 O.R. from Base Depot & 8th. Battalion M.G.Corps.	
do.	4/5/19.		Reinforcements:- 7 O.Rs. from 35th. Battalion M.G.Corps.	
do.	5/5/19.		Reinforcements:- 1 " " 39th. " " "	
do.	6/5/19.		Reinforcements:- NIL.	
do.	7/5/19.		Reinforcements:- Lieut. H.WILSON 2/Lieut. A.H.D.BENNETT . Lieut. P.W.DEXTER 2/Lieut. G.B.GOLDSBROUGH 2/Lieut. F.C.L.BROOKS Joined on appointment from 2/Lieut. M.FAIRBAIRN Commandant, BOULOGNE and Lieut. H.L.T.ROWELL M.G.T.C. GRANTHAM. 2/Lieut. W.CLARK 2/Lieut. A.G.ROBERTSON Lieut. F.H.POOLE. Lieut. W.T.CALDWELL 2/Lieut. H.PRAKE	
do.	8/5/19.		Reinforcements:- 2/Lieut. J.H.G.CLARK Joined on appointment from Commandant, BOULOGNE, and M.G.T.C. GRANTHAM.	
do.	9/5/19.		Reinforcements:- 1 O.R. from Base Depot and 63rd. Battalion M.G.Corps.	
do.	10/5/19.		Reinforcements:- 14 O.Rs. from 39th. Battalion Machine Gun Corps. 1 " " " Hospital.	
do.	11/5/19.		Reinforcements:- NIL.	

Army Form C. 2118.

WAR DIARY
or
INTELLIGENCE SUMMARY.
(Erase heading not required.)

Instructions regarding War Diaries and Intelligence Summaries are contained in F. S. Regs., Part II. and the Staff Manual respectively. Title pages will be prepared in manuscript.

Place	Date	Hour	Summary of Events and Information	Remarks and references to Appendices
ABBEVILLE.	12/5/19.		Reinforcements:- 3 O.Rs. from Hospital.	Ref. Map. ABBEVILLE 1/100,000
do.	13/5/19.		Reinforcements:- 3 " " " " 1 " " 31st. Battalion M.G.Corps.	
do.	14/5/19.		Reinforcements:- NIL.	
do.	15/5/19.		Reinforcements:- 1 O.R. from Hospital.	
do.	16/5/19.		Reinforcements:- 1 " " " "	
do.	17/5/19.		Reinforcements:- 1 " " 63rd. Battalion M.G.Corps.	
do.	18/5/19.		Reinforcements:- 1 " " Hospital.	
do.	19/5/19.		Reinforcements:- 7 " " 35th. Battalion M.G.Corps.	
do.	20/5/19.		Reinforcements:- 1 " " Base Depot.	
do.	21/5/19.		Reinforcements:- NIL.	
do.	22/5/19.		Reinforcements:- 1 O.R. from Hospital.	
do.	23/5/19.		Reinforcements:- 2/Lieut. O.B.TEMPERTON Joined on Appointment from 5th. Bn. South Wales Borderers. 1 O.R. from Hospital. 5 O.R. from Base Depot.	
do.	24/5/19.		Reinforcements:- NIL.	
do.	25/5/19.		Reinforcements:- NIL.	
do.	26/5/19.		Reinforcements:- NIL.	
do.	27/5/19.		Reinforcements:- 2 O.Rs. from Base Depot.	

Army Form C. 2118.

WAR DIARY
or
INTELLIGENCE SUMMARY.
(Erase heading not required.)

Instructions regarding War Diaries and Intelligence Summaries are contained in F. S. Regs., Part II. and the Staff Manual respectively. Title pages will be prepared in manuscript.

Place	Date	Hour	Summary of Events and Information	Remarks and references to Appendices
ABBEVILLE	28/5/19.		Reinforcements:- 1 O.R. from Hospital.	Ref. Map ABBEVILLE 1/100,000 ABBEVILLE 14
do.	29/5/19.		Reinforcements:- 2 O.Rs. from Base Depot.	
do.	30/5/19.		Reinforcements:- NIL.	
do.	31/5/19.		Reinforcements:- 2/Lieut. H.MAKIN from Hospital. 1 O.R. from Base Depot.	
			All detachments concentrated at No. 5 Veterinary Hospital, ABBEVILLE, on completion of reliefs by 2/16th. London Regt.	
			<u>Fighting Strength of Battalion</u>:- 48 Officers and 870 Other Ranks.	

Headquarters,
61st. Division "A"

PA 1098/1

Attached please find War Diary of this Unit for the Month of June, 1919.

30/6/19.

[signature]
Lieut-Colonel,
Commanding 61st. Battalion Machine Gun Corps.

61st. Battalion Machine Gun Corps.

WAR DIARY.

1st. JUNE 1919 to 30th. JUNE 1919.

(Volume No. 17.)

(6392) Wt. W6192/P875 1,500,000 4/18 McA & W Ltd (E 2815) Forms W3091/4.   Army Form W.3091.

Cover for Documents.

Nature of Enclosures.

Notes, or Letters written.

WAR DIARY
or
INTELLIGENCE SUMMARY.

(Erase heading not required.)

Army Form C. 2118.

Instructions regarding War Diaries and Intelligence Summaries are contained in F.S. Regs., Part II. and the Staff Manual respectively. Title pages will be prepared in manuscript.

Place	Date	Hour	Summary of Events and Information	Remarks and references to Appendices
ABBEVILLE.	1/6/19.		Reinforcements:- NIL. Battalion Transport proceeded by road from ABBEVILLE to ROUEN.	Ref.Map, ABBEVILLE 14 1/100,000
do.	2/6/19.		Reinforcements:- NIL. "A" & "C" Companies moved from ABBEVILLE to ROUEN by rail as per 61st. Div. Instructions.	Entraining Table attached.
do.	3/6/19.		Reinforcements:- NIL. "Headquarters", "B" & "D" Companies moved from ABBEVILLE to ROUEN by rail as per 61st. Div. Instructions.	
ROUEN.	4/6/19.		Reinforcements:- NIL. Battalion Headquarters and All Companies concentrated in General Reinforcements Base Depot, ROUEN. Battalion Transport arrived in ROUEN and quartered in No.15 Vet.Hospital, ROUEN.	
do.	5/6/19.		Reinforcements:- NIL.	
do.	6/6/19.		Reinforcements:- NIL.	
do.	7/6/19.		Reinforcements:- NIL. Guards provided by 6th. Queen's R.W.S.Regt. and 10th.Bn.Scottish Rifles taken over by this Battalion.	
do.	8/6/19.		Reinforcements:- 1 O.R. from 83rd.Bn. M.G.Corps. 1 " : Hospital & Base Depot. 1 " : 39th.Bn.M.G.Corps. The Battalion moved from General Reinforcements Base Depot, ROUEN to Medical Board Base Depot, ROUEN.	
do.	9/6/19.		Reinforcements:- NIL. Major W.H.BROOKS Assumed Command during the temporary absence of Lieut-Colonel N.G.BURNAND D.S.O. on leave to U.K.	
do.	10/6/19.		Reinforcements:- 1 O.R. from Hospital.	

Army Form C. 2118.

WAR DIARY
or
INTELLIGENCE SUMMARY.
(Erase heading not required.)

Instructions regarding War Diaries and Intelligence Summaries are contained in F. S. Regs., Part II. and the Staff Manual respectively. Title pages will be prepared in manuscript.

Place	Date	Hour	Summary of Events and Information	Remarks and references to Appendices
ROUEN	11/6/19		Reinforcements:- NIL.	A188
do.	12/6/19		Reinforcements:- NIL.	A188
do.	13/6/19		Reinforcements:- NIL.	A188
do.	14/6/19		Reinforcements:- NIL.	A188
do.	15/6/19		Reinforcements:- NIL.	A188
do.	16/6/19		Reinforcements:- NIL.	A188
do.	17/6/19		Reinforcements:- NIL.	A188
do.	18/6/19		Reinforcements:- NIL.	A188
do.	19/6/19		Reinforcements:- 2 O.Rs. from Hospital.	A188
do.	20/6/19		Reinforcements:- 2 " " "	A188
do.	21/6/19		Reinforcements:- NIL.	A188
do.	22/6/19		Reinforcements:- NIL.	A188
do.	23/6/19		Reinforcements:- 3 O.Rs. from Hospital.	A188
do.	24/6/19		Reinforcements:- 1 " " "	A188
do.	25/6/19		Reinforcements:- NIL. Lieut-Colonel N.G.BURNAND D.S.O. Re-assumes Command on return from leave to U.K.	A188
do.	26/6/19		Reinforcements:- NIL.	

Army Form C. 2118.

WAR DIARY
or
INTELLIGENCE SUMMARY.
(Erase heading not required.)

Instructions regarding War Diaries and Intelligence Summaries are contained in F. S. Regs., Part II. and the Staff Manual respectively. Title pages will be prepared in manuscript.

Place	Date	Hour	Summary of Events and Information	Remarks and references to Appendices
ROUEN	27/6/19.		Reinforcements:- NIL.	AA&B
do.	28/6/19.		Reinforcements:- NIL.	AA&B
do.	29/6/19.		Reinforcements:- NIL.	AA&B
do.	30/6/19.		Reinforcements:- NIL.	AA&B
			Strength of Battalion:- (Excluding Officers and O.Rs. who have proceeded for Dispersal, but for whom no authority has been received to strike off strength)	
			46 Officers & 851 O.Rs.	

M. Drummond Lt.
Comdg. 61st Bn. R.F.C.

61st Battalion Machine Gun Corps.

ADMINISTRATIVE INSTRUCTIONS No. 1.

1.   (a) The 2/16th London Regt., will take over the duties on attached table now performed by this Battalion on the 31st May, 1919.

     (b) On relief, the Battalion will concentrate as follows:-

        "A" & "C" Coys. - at School of Farriery No.14 Vet. Hospital.

        "B" & "D"   :   : No.5 Vet. Hospital.

   Coy. offices, stores, transport, (both vehicles and animals) of all Companies will remain at Battalion Headquarters.

2.   The Lorries which convey the detachments of the 2/16th London Regt., to DOMLEGER & NOYELLES, will bring back the detachments of the 61st Bn. M.G.Corps to No.5 Vet. Hospital.

3.   The following guides will be detailed to report to O.C.2/16th London Regt., at the Signal Depot, ABBEVILLE, at 09.00 hours on the 31st May, 1919, to accompany all detachments of relieving Units to their destination.
   The guides will return with the incoming detachments.

No.2 P.O.W.Coy,Main Cage.	1 Officer of "C" Coy.
DOMLEGER, Ammuntion Guard.	1 N.C.O. to be detailed by O.i/c. Domleger Detachment.
NOYELLES, Detachment.	1 N.C.O. to be detailed by O.i/c. Noyelles Detachment.
A.P.M. Detention Compound.	1 N.C.O. to be detailed by O.C."B"Coy.
FOCH'S CAMP.	1 N.C.O. to be detailed by O.i/c. Foch's Camp Detachment.

4.   The incoming detachments of this Battalion will be rationed by Battalion Headquarters from the day following that on which they concentrate.

5.   ACKNOWLEDGE.

                                                  Capt. & Adjt.

No.5 Vet.Hospital   61st Battalion Machine Gun Corps.
30/5/19.

Distribution.

Copy No.	
1	Commanding Officer.
2	2nd-in-Command.
3	O.C."A"Coy (Details)
4	: "B" : :
5	: "C" : :
6	: "D" : :
7	O.C.Ammuntion Guard,DOMLEGER.
8	: "A" Coy Detachment, Main Cage.
9	: "C" : do. do.
10	O.i/c. Detachment, NOYELLES.
11	do. do. FOCH'S CAMP.
12	Quartermaster.
13	61st Division "A".
14	O.i/c.Advance Party,2/16th London Regt.,
15	H.Q's. 90th Inf. Bde.
16	Headquarters, ABBEVILLE AREA.
17 & 18	War Diary.
19 & 20	File.

61st Battalion Machine Gun Corps.

UNIT.	FROM.	TO	RELIEVED BY.	MARCH OR LORRY.	NUMBER OF LORRIES.	REMARKS.
61st Bn. M.G.Corps.	Main Cage, No.2 P.O.W.Coy. ABBEVILLE.	No.5 Vet. Hospital.	2/16th London Regt.,	March.		Kit by Horse Transport to be supplied by Coys. concerned.
-do-	No.24 Ordnance Depot, DOMLEGER.	-do-	-do-	Lorry	7	For Personnel & Kit.
-do-	Detention Compound, ABBEVILLE.	-do-	-do-	March		Kit by Horse Transport to be supplied by "B" Coy.
-do-	FOCH'S Camp.	-do-	-do-	March		Kit by Horse Transport to be supplied by Coys. concerned.
-do-	E.F.C., NOYELLES.	-do-	-do-	Lorry	1	For personnel & Kit.

No.5 Vet. Hospital.
30/5/19.

[signature]
Capt. & Adjt.
61st Battalion Machine Gun Corps.

Copy No.------

61st Battalion Machine Gun Corps.

ADMINISTRATIVE INSTRUCTIONS No.2

1. The Battalion, less Transport, will move by rail from ABBEVILLE to ROUEN, in accordance with Entraining Table issued with these instructions. - (Table "A").

    The whole of the Battalion Transport will move by march route under instructions already issued, leaving No.5 Vet. Hospital at 05.30 hours on Monday next 2nd June, 1919, and arriving at ROUEN on the morning of the 5th June, 1919.

2. Companies will pass the starting point (No.5 Vet. Hospital) at 19.45 hours on their day of departure. DRESS:- Full Marching Order.

3. STORES & BAGGAGE.

    All Companies and H.Q's will dump the Stores and Baggage proceeding by train in the square, No.5 Vet. Hospital, on the morning of the day of departure.

    It must be clearly marked with Company letters and destination. A Guard will be detailed from each Company to look after the Company dump, and they will be responsible for it until its arrival at ROUEN.

    All Stores and Baggage will be conveyed by Lorry to the MAIN STATION, ABBEVILLE, one hour before time of entraining.

    Sections dixies will be carried in the train.

    Blankets will be rolled in bundles of Ten.

4. RATIONS.

    Rations will be carried as follows:-

    Transport up to and including Thursday 5th June, 1919.
    "A" & "C" Coys.   do.   do. Wednesday 4th   :   :
    "B","D" & "HQ" Coys.   do.   Thursday 5th   :   :

5. WATER.

    All personnel will travel with water bottles filled.

6. LOADING & UNLOADING PARTIES.

    Each Company will detail a suitable loading and unloading party for stores and baggage.

7. (a) One Officer from "A" and one from "B" Coys. will be detailed to act as entraining and detraining officers for "A" & "C" Coys. and "B","D" & "HQ" Coys. respectively, and they will make full arrangements for the entrainment of the Coys. concerned.

   (b) Each Company will detail an N.C.O. for entraining duty, who will report to the entraining officer one hour before their company is due to commence entraining.

8. Capt. A.V.COULTER will act as O.C.Train conveying "A" & "C" Coys.

    Major W.H.BROOKS will act as O.C.Train conveying "B","D" & "HQ" Coys.

9. Os.C.Companies will ensure that all Barrack Rooms and Hutments are thoroughly clean before departure.

/10.........

-2-

10. On arrival at ROUEN, guides will meet Companies at the Station and guide them to the GENERAL REINFORCEMENTS BASE DEPOT.

11. On arrival of the Transport at ROUEN the accompanying Lorries will return to the 61st Divisional M.T.Coy. at LE TREPORT.

12. ACKNOWLEDGE.

[signature]

No.5 Vet.
1/6/19.
                    Capt. & Adjt.
        61st Battalion Machine Gun Corps.

Distribution.

Copy No.

1	Commanding Officer.
2	2nd-in-Command.
3	Quartermaster.
4 & 5	File.
6 & 7	War Diary.
8	61st Division "A"
9	H.Q.Abbeville Area.
10	O.C."A" Coy.
11	: "B" :
12	: "C" :
13	: "D" :
14	Entraining Officer "AC" Coys.
15	do. do. "BD" :
16	O.C.2/16th London Regt.,
17	90th Inf. Bde.
18	D.A.D.R.T.
19	Commandant, ROUEN.
20	O.i/c., Advance Party 61st.Bn.M.G.C.
21	R.T.O.,ABBEVILLE.

61st Battalion Machine Gun Corps.

ENTRAINING TABLE "A" issued with ADMINISTRATIVE INSTRUCTIONS No.2.

1	2	3	4	5	6	7
DATE	UNIT	FROM	TO	NUMBER OF TRAIN.	TIME OF DEPARTURE	REMARKS.
2nd. June,19.	"A" & "C" Coys.	ABBEVILLE (Main Station)	ROUEN	1	21.50 hours.	Stores & Baggage to load at 19.30 hours 2nd June,1919. Personnel to ontrain at 20.30 hrs.
3rd June,19.	"B","D" & "HQ" Coys.	ABBEVILLE (Main Station)	ROUEN	2	21.50 hours.	Stores & Baggage to load at 19.30 hours 3rd June,1919. Personnel to ontrain at 20.30 hrs.

Capt. & Adjt.
61st Battalion Machine Gun Corps.

No.5 Vet.
1/6/19.

61st Battalion Machine Gun Corps.

COMPOSITION OF TRAINS - MOVE OF BATTALION TO ROUEN - TABLE "B".

1	2	3		4
	Unit	Personnel.		REMARKS.
No. of Train.	61st Bn. M.G.C.	Offrs.	O.Rs.	
1	"A" & "C" Coys.	12	255	3 Trucks on Train for Baggage & Stores.
2	"B","D" & "HQ"Coys.	16	283	3 Trucks on Train for Baggage & Stores.

61st Battalion Machine Gun Corps.

Capt. & Adjt.

No.5 Vet.
1/6/19.

61st.Bn.M.G.C.No.GR.24/187.

1. The 61st Bn. M.G.Corps will take over the Guards now provided by 6th Queens R.W.S. Regt., and 10th Bn. Scottish Rifles, as per attached Table, tomorrow, 7th June, 1919.

2. "A" & "C" Coys. will take over the Guards at present found by the 6th Queens R.W.S. Regt., commencing with "A" Coy tomorrow, 7th instant.
   "B" & "D" Coys. will relieve Guards at present found by the Scottish Rifles, commencing with "B" Coy. tomorrow, 7th instant.

3. Guards will parade at the following hours tomorrow:-

   All except Night Guards at 09.00 hours.
   Night Guards.   ..   : 18.30 :

   Dress:- Full Marching Order, with blankets.

4. GUIDES.

   A guide from each Guard will report to Headquarters, 61st Bn. M.G.Corps at 09.00 hours tomorrow, with the exception of the Night Guards, who will report at 18.30 hours, together with Lorries for Guards that are conveyed by Lorry, and conduct relieving Guards to their respective destinations.

5. RATIONS.
              guards
   All   will carry 24 hours rations with the exception of Night Guards, who will take Tea for the night and Breakfast for the following morning.
   Night Guards dismount at 08.00 hours.

6. The Guard at LAUNAY PETROL DEPOT, should have a Cook and Cooking Utensils.

7. Completion of reliefs will be reported to these Headquarters as soon as possible.

8. ACKNOWLEDGE.

                                            Capt. & Adjt.
G.R.B.D.ROUEN.   61st Battalion Machine Gun Corps.

   6/6/19.

                        DISTRIBUTION.

   Copy No.   Copy No.

      1   Commanding Officer   2   2nd-in-Command.
      3   Quartermaster.   4   O.C."A" Coy.
      5   O.C."B"Coy.   6   O.C."C" :
      7   O.C."D" :   8   Staff Captain,
      9   6th Bn.Queens R.W.S.Regt.,   Reinforcements.
     10   10th Bn.Scottish Rifles.   11   19th Inf.Bde.
     12   O.i/c.,Bn.Transport.   13&14 File.
     15 & 16 War Diary.

GUARDS to be taken over by 61st Battalion Machine Gun Corps.

LOCATION.	STRENGTH.					In relief of.	Proceeding by.	REMARKS.
	Offrs.	Sgts.	Cpls.	L/Cpls.	Ptes.	TOTAL			
No.1 Military Prisoners Ordnance Depot	1	1	1	1	33	37		March Route.	Horse Transport for Rations and kit to be supplied by Company concerned.
Main Triage.		1	1	1	9	11	6th. Bn.	Lorry	
No.8 Labour Camp		1		1	12	14	Queens R.W.S.	Lorry	
Ammuntion Jetty *		1	1		18	19	Regiment.	Lorry	
			1		6	8		Lorry	
Vehicle Park – Reve Gauoh Stn. * F.P.Compound.		1		1	9	11	March Route.		Horse Transport for Rations and kit to be supplied by Company concerned.
No.5 Q.M.A.A.G. *		1	1	1	18	20		do. do.	
No.6 General Hospital.		1		1	5	4	Scottish	do. do.	
Launay Petrol Depot.		1	1	1	12	14	Rifles.	Lorry	
Bedford Petrol Guard.		1		1	12	14		Lorry	
Asiatic Petrol Guard.					4	5		Lorry	

N.B.- Duration of Guards:- All Guards are 24 hours, with the exception of those marked with an asterisk, which are Night Guards only.

Capt. & Adjt.
61st Battalion Machine Gun Corps.

8/6/19.

61st Bn. M.G.C. BA/149/892.

1. The Battalion will move to the MEDICAL BOARD BASE DEPOT, tomorrow, 8th June, 1919.

2. Companies and Bn. H.Q's will parade on the square, opposite their Company lines at 14.30 hours.
   DRESS:- Drill Order.

3. STORES.

   All Stores will be moved before 12.00 hours tomorrow. For this purpose G.S.Waggons are allotted as follows:-

   Battalion Headquarters. .. 1
   Each Company. 1

   O.i/c., of Transport will arrange for above to report to G.R.B.D. as allotted at 09.00 hours, with feeds for animals.
   When Stores & Baggage have been conveyed to destination, the G.S.Waggons will report as detailed above, at 12.00 hours and load up Officers Valises and mens packs, marching with the Battalion at 14.30 hours.

4. TRANSPORT.

   Transport Officers will arrange for one pair of horses for each fighting limber to be at Battn. H.Q's at 14.00 hours tomorrow, together with all officers chargers.

5. Os.C.Coys. will ensure that all Hutments and lines are thoroughly clean before departure.

6. Battalion Headquarters will close at the G.R.B.D. at 14.30 hours tomorrow, and re-open at the same hour at MEDICAL BOARD BASE DEPOT.

7. ACKNOWLEDGE.

                                          Capt. & Adjt.
GRBD. ROUEN.   61st Battalion Machine Gun Corps.
   7/6/19.

Copy No.	DISTRIBUTION.	Copy No.	
1	Commanding Officer.	8	O.i/c.Bn.Transport.
2	2nd-In-Command.	9	19th Inf. Bde.
3	Quartermaster.	10	61st Division "A"
4	O.C. "A" Coy.	11	C.O.10thBn.Scottish Rifles.
5	: "B" :		
6	: "C" :	12	Staff Captn.
7	: "D" :		Reinforcements.
13.	Commandant, ROUEN.	14	O.C.

Army Form C. 2118.

61 Bn M.G Corps
Jul 18

WAR DIARY
—or—
INTELLIGENCE SUMMARY
(Erase heading not required.)

Place	Date	Hour	Summary of Events and Information	Remarks and references to Appendices
ROUEN.	1/7/19.		Reinforcements:— 2 O.R. from Hospital.	Ref. Map,
do	2/7/19.		Reinforcements:— NIL.	
do	3/7/19.		Reinforcements:— NIL.	
do	4/7/19.		Reinforcements:— NIL.	
do	5/7/19.		Reinforcements:— 1 O.R. from Hospital.	
do	6/7/19.		Reinforcements:— 1 O.R. from 4th Battalion, Machine Gun Corps.	
do	7/7/19.		Reinforcements:— 1 O.R. from Hospital.	
do	8/7/19.		Reinforcements:— NIL.	
do	9/7/19.		Reinforcements:— NIL.	
do	10/7/19.		Reinforcements:— NIL.	
do	11/7/19.		Reinforcements:— NIL.	
do	12/7/19.		Reinforcements:— NIL.	
do	13/7/19.		Reinforcements:— NIL.	
do	14/7/19.		Reinforcements:— NIL.	
do	15/7/19.		Reinforcements:— NIL.	
do	16/7/19.		Reinforcements:— NIL.	
do	17/7/19.		Reinforcements:— NIL.	

Army Form C. 2118.

WAR DIARY
INTELLIGENCE SUMMARY
(Erase heading not required).

Instructions regarding War Diaries and Intelligence Summaries are contained in F.S. Regs., Part II. and the Staff Manual respectively. Title pages will be prepared in manuscript.

Place	Date	Hour	Summary of Events and Information	Remarks and references to Appendices
ROUEN.	18/7/19.		Reinforcements:- NIL.	
do	19/7/19.		Reinforcements:- NIL.	
do	20/7/19.		Reinforcements:- NIL.	
do	21/7/19.		Reinforcements:- 1 O.R. from Hospital.	
do	22/7/19.		Reinforcements:- NIL.	
do	23/7/19.		Reinforcements:- NIL.	
do	24/7/19.		Reinforcements:- NIL.	
do	25/7/19.		Reinforcements:- 1 O.R. (R.S.M.) from 11th Battalion, M.G.C. and Base Depot.	
do	26/7/19.		Reinforcements:- NIL.	
do	27/7/19.		Reinforcements:- NIL.	
do	28/7/19.		Reinforcements:- NIL.	
do	29/7/19.		Strength Decrease:- 124 O.Rs Transferred to 33rd Battalion, M.G.Corps.	
do	30/7/19.		Strength Decrease:- 5 O.Rs Transferred to 33rd Battalion, M.G.Corps.	
do	31/7/19.		Strength Decrease:- Major C.M.HOWARD, M.C., Transferred to 33rd Bn. M.G.Corps.	
			Strength of Battalion:- (Including Officers & O.Rs who have proceeded for Dispersal, but for whom no authority has been received to strike off strength).	
			44 Officers and 699 Other Ranks.	

61st. BATTALION MACHINE GUN CORPS.

WAR DIARY.

1st. AUGUST 1919 to 31st. AUGUST 1919.

(Volume No. 18)

CONFIDENTIAL

(6392) Wt. W6192/P875 1,500,000 4/18 McA & W Ltd (E 2815) Forms W3091/4.   Army Form W.3091.

Cover for Documents.

Nature of Enclosures.

Notes, or Letters written.

Army Form C. 2118.

WAR DIARY
or
INTELLIGENCE SUMMARY.
(Erase heading not required.)

Instructions regarding War Diaries and Intelligence Summaries are contained in F. S. Regs., Part II. and the Staff Manual respectively. Title pages will be prepared in manuscript.

Place	Date	Hour	Summary of Events and Information	Remarks and references to Appendices
ROUEN	1/8/19.		Battalion Training. Reinforcements:- NIL.	
"	2/8/19.		Battalion Training. Reinforcements:- 1 O.R. From Hospital.	
"	3/8/19.		Battalion Training. Reinforcements:- NIL.	
"	4/8/19.		Battalion Training. Reinforcements:- NIL.	
"	5/8/19.		Battalion Training. Reinforcements:- 2 O.Rs. From Hospital.	
"	6/8/19.		Battalion Training. Reinforcements:- NIL.	
"	7/8/19.		Battalion Training. Reinforcements:- NIL.	
"	8/8/19.		Battalion Training. Reinforcements:- NIL.	
"	9/8/19.		Battalion Training. Reinforcements:- 134 O.Rs. From 33rd.Battalion M.G.Corps.	
"	10/8/19.		Battalion Training. Reinforcements:- 30 " " " " "	
"	11/8/19.		Battalion Training. Reinforcements:- NIL.	
"	12/8/19.		Battalion Training. Reinforcements:- NIL.	
"	13/8/19.		Battalion Training. Reinforcements:- 2 O.Rs. From Hospital.	
"	14/8/19.		Battalion Training. Reinforcements:- NIL.	
"	15/8/19.		Battalion Training. Reinforcements:- 1 O.R. From Hospital.	
"	16/8/19.		Battalion Training. Reinforcements:- NIL.	
"	17/8/19.		Battalion Training. Reinforcements:- NIL.	
"	18/8/19.		Battalion Training. Reinforcements:- NIL.	

Army Form C. 2118.

WAR DIARY
or
INTELLIGENCE SUMMARY.

(Erase heading not required.)

Instructions regarding War Diaries and Intelligence Summaries are contained in F. S. Regs., Part II. and the Staff Manual respectively. Title pages will be prepared in manuscript.

Place	Date	Hour	Summary of Events and Information	Remarks and references to Appendices
ROUEN.	19/8/19.		Battalion Training. Reinforcements:- NIL.	
"	20/8/19.		Battalion Training. Reinforcements:- 1 O.R. From Hospital.	
"	21/8/19.		Battalion Training. Reinforcements:- 1 O.R. From Base Depot.	
"	22/8/19.		Battalion Training. Reinforcements:- 1 O.R. From Hospital.	
"	23/8/19.		Battalion Training. Reinforcements:- NIL.	
"	24/8/19.		Battalion Training. Reinforcements:- 1 O.R. From Base Depot.	
"	25/8/19.		Battalion Training. Reinforcements:- NIL.	
"	26/8/19.		Battalion Training. Reinforcements:- NIL.	
"	27/8/19.		Battalion Training. Reinforcements:- NIL..	
"	28/8/19.		Battalion Training. Reinforcements:- 1 O.R. From Base Depot.	
"	29/8/19.		Battalion Training. Reinforcements:- 2 O.Bs. From Hospital.	
"	30/8/19.		Battalion Training. Reinforcements:- NIL.	
"	31/8/19.		Battalion Training. Reinforcements:- NIL.	
			Total Strength of Battalion:- 43 Officers & 663 O.Rs.	

M. Munro,
Lieut-Colonel,
Commanding 61st. Battalion Machine Gun Corps.

CONFIDENTIAL

61st. Battalion Machine Gun Corps.

WAR DIARY.

1st. September 1919 to 30th. September 1919.

(Volume No. 19)

(6392) Wt. W6192/P875 1,500,000 4/18 McA & W Ltd (E 2815) Forms W3091/4.   Army Form W.3091.

Cover for Documents.

Nature of Enclosures.

Notes, or Letters written.

Army Form C. 2118.

WAR DIARY
or
INTELLIGENCE SUMMARY.
(Erase heading not required.)

Instructions regarding War Diaries and Intelligence Summaries are contained in F. S. Regs., Part II. and the Staff Manual respectively. Title pages will be prepared in manuscript.

Place	Date	Hour	Summary of Events and Information	Remarks and references to Appendices
ROUEN	1/9/19.		Battalion Training. Reinforcements:- NIL.	
do.	3/9/19.		Battalion Training. Reinforcements:- 1 O.R. From 33rd.Bn.M.G.Corps. 3 " " " 57th. " " "	
do.	5/9/19.		Battalion Training. Reinforcements:- 1 " " " Hospital.	
do.	6/9/19.		Battalion Training. Reinforcements:- 2 " " " " 33 " " " 33rd.Bn.M.G.Corps.	
do.	7/9/19.		Battalion Training. Reinforcements:- 1 " " " Hospital.	
do.	9/9/19.		Battalion Training. Reinforcements:- 2 " " " "	
do.	10/9/19.		Battalion Training. Reinforcements:- 2 " " " "	
do.	11/9/19.		Battalion Training. Reinforcements:- Lieut. J.R.A.PRICE From 33rd.Bn.M.G.Corps.	
do.	14/9/19.		Battalion Training. Reinforcements:- 2 O.R. From Hospital.	
do.	15/9/19.		Battalion Training. Reinforcements:- NIL. Lieut-Colonel N.G.BURNAND D.S.O. Proceeded to U.K. for duty. Major W.H.BROOKS assumed Command of Battalion.	
do.	17/9/19.		Battalion Training. Reinforcements:- 2 O.R. From Hospital.	
do.	19/9/19.		Battalion Training. Reinforcements:- 1 " " " "	
do.	21/9/19.		Battalion Training. Reinforcements:- 1 " " " "	
do.	25/9/19.		Battalion Training. Reinforcements:- 1 " " " 30th.Bn.M.G.Corps. 3 " " " Hospital.	
do.	20/9/19.		Battalion Training. Reinforcements:- 2 " " " "	

Army Form C. 2118.

WAR DIARY
or
INTELLIGENCE SUMMARY.
(Erase heading not required.)

Place	Date	Hour	Summary of Events and Information	Remarks and references to Appendices
ROUEN	26/9/19. (Contd.)		Battalion Training. All animals od Battalion, except 10 Riders, 4 L.D. and 2 H.D. proceeded by road to "Z" Horse Depot, NEUFCHATEL (Boulogne). (Copy of instructions attached.)	
			Strength of Battalion:- 29 Officers and 323 Other Ranks.	

W. H. Brooks. Major.

Comdg. 51st Battn. M.G.C.

61st Bn. M.G.Corps TM/126/1.

1. All the animals of the Battalion, less 10 Riders, 1 L.D., and 2 H.D. will be handed into the Depot at NEUFCHATEL (BOULOGNE).

2. They will proceed by march route, starting at 07.00 hours on the 26th September, 1919. The march will be done in the following stages:-

       1st Day.   NEUFCHATEL.
       2nd   :   BLANGY.
       3rd   :   ABBEVILLE.
       4th   :   MONTREUIL.
       5th   :   NEUFCHATEL (BOULOGNE)

Lieut.G.STENL,M.C. will be in charge of the column.
Personnel of the column will comprise:-

       Transport Officer   "C" Coy.
       Transport Sergeant
         :   Corporal
       1 Driver to 3 animals (approx)

3. 3 Lorries will be provided for rations, forage and blankets.
The Battalion Quartermaster will arrange to draw 3 days Rations and Forage. Supplies will again be drawn at ABBEVILLE for the remaining 2 days.
O.C.Column will arrange for a Corporal to report to the Quartermaster on the morning of the 26th September to pick up lorries and take them on to the first halting place (NEUFCHATEL), having obtained the three days supplies. Exact time will be notified later.
Great Coats and 2 Blankets per man will be taken.

4. Dress:- Belt, Water Bottle, and Haversack.

               W.Caldwell
               Lieut. & A/Adjt.
M.B.B.D.   61st Battalion Machine Gun Corps.
ROUEN.
24/9/19.

Copy No.	DISTRIBUTION.	Copy No.	
1	Commanding Officer	2	182 Inf. Bde.
3	O.C.Troops, ROUEN.	4	Transport Officer
5	O.C."A" Coy.	6	O.C."B" Coy.
7	O.C."C" Coy.	8	O.C."D" :
9	Quartermaster.	10 & 11	War Diary.
	12 & 13 File.